The Undergraduate
Research Handbook

Palgrave Study Skills

Business Degree Success
Career Skills
Cite Them Right (8th edn)
Critical Thinking Skills (2nd edn)
e-Learning Skills (2nd edn)
The Exam Skills Handbook (2nd edn)
Great Ways to Learn Anatomy and Physiology
How to Begin Studying English Literature (3rd edn)
How to Manage Your Distance and Open Learning
   Course
How to Manage Your Postgraduate Course
How to Study Foreign Languages
How to Study Linguistics (2nd edn)
How to Use Your Reading in Your Essays
How to Write Better Essays (2nd edn)
How to Write Your Undergraduate Dissertation
Information Skills
The International Student Handbook
IT Skills for Successful Study
The Mature Student's Guide to Writing (3rd edn)
The Mature Student's Handbook
The Palgrave Student Planner
Practical Criticism
Presentation Skills for Students (2nd edn)

The Principles of Writing in Psychology
Professional writing (2nd edn)
Researching Online
Skills for Success (2nd edn)
The Student's Guide to Writing (3rd edn)
Study Skills Connected
Study Skills for International Postgraduates
The Study Skills Handbook (3rd edn)
Study Skills for Speakers of English as a Second
   Language
Studying History (3rd edn)
Studying Law (3rd edn)
Studying Modern Drama (2nd edn)
Studying Psychology (2nd edn)
Teaching Study Skills and Supporting Learning
The Undergraduate Research Handbook
The Work-Based Learning Student Handbook
Work Placements – A Survival Guide for Students
Write it Right (2nd edn)
Writing for Engineers (3rd edn)
Writing for Law
Writing for Nursing and Midwifery Students
   (2nd edn)
You2Uni

Pocket Study Skills

14 Days to Exam Success
Blogs, Wikis, Podcasts and More
Brilliant Writing Tips for Students
Completing Your PhD
Doing Research
Getting Critical
Planning Your Essay
Planning Your PhD
Reading and Making Notes

Referencing and Understanding Plagiarism
Reflective Writing
Report Writing
Science Study Skills
Studying with Dyslexia
Success in Groupwork
Time Management
Writing for University

Palgrave Research Skills

Authoring a PhD
The Foundations of Research (2nd edn)
The Good Supervisor (2nd edn)
The Postgraduate Research Handbook (2nd edn)
Structuring Your Research Thesis

For a complete listing of all our titles in this area please visit www.palgrave.com/studyskills

The Undergraduate Research Handbook

Gina Wisker

First published 2009 by
PALGRAVE MACMILLAN

Palgrave Macmillan in the UK is an imprint of Macmillan Publishers Limited,
registered in England, company number 785998, of Houndmills, Basingstoke,
Hampshire RG21 6XS.

Palgrave Macmillan in the US is a division of St Martin's Press LLC,
175 Fifth Avenue, New York, NY 10010.

Palgrave Macmillan is the global academic imprint of the above companies
and has companies and representatives throughout the world.

Palgrave® and Macmillan® are registered trademarks in the United States,
the United Kingdom, Europe and other countries.

ISBN-13: 978–0–230–52097–4

This book is printed on paper suitable for recycling and made from fully
managed and sustained forest sources. Logging, pulping and manufacturing
processes are expected to conform to the environmental regulations of the
country of origin.

A catalogue record for this book is available from the British Library.

A catalog record for this book is available from the Library of Congress.

Printed in China

Contents

Glossary

Abstract

This is more than a summary of the content of a dissertation, thesis, journal article, or other text; it lets a reader see what important contribution is being made by the research and written piece. The abstract is what is read first by a reader and so must be written clearly and in a straightforward and interesting manner so that they wish to read on. It should state the aims, outcomes and achievements of the dissertation or thesis (article or other), the theories used, the arguments, and the importance of its contribution to knowledge. Usually 300 words in length, it outlines the aim and focus of the study and it should identify, and answer, your main research question and sub-questions: 'What is this dissertation/thesis/research/essay about? What does it argue, prove, suggest?' 'What has it achieved of importance?' It should be written in the third person and in passive tone, for example, 'It is argued that . . .' 'In discussing . . .' 'Using . . .' 'Evidence is presented which suggests that . . .'. You will probably write the abstract right at the end of your work and after you have written everything else, when you can stand back and get a clear picture of your achievement. If published, the abstract along with complete reference details and key words are stored in abstracting and indexing services in libraries and archives so that they can be searched electronically.

Action research

This is a form of applied research and practitioner research in which researchers incorporate the participants in the design of the study, the process of investigation and the implementation of the findings (as collaborators). It feeds back to the participants and it engages the management and the whole organisation in the study (in a partnership) in the reflection and the changes related to the research process and outcomes. It is a way of modelling the next stage of the research. It involves reflective practice, reflection and innovation. Action research seeks to implement change, for example in policy, through the research itself. It also encourages the development of those involved.

Bias

Any influence that systematically distorts the results of a research study produces bias. It will obscure the true nature of what is being studied, and may be caused by the researcher or by the procedures for collecting data, including sampling. A reflexive account of the research can address the issues of trust that the existence of bias highlights. Subjectivity exists in both social science and 'pure' science research, although we should always try to acknowledge and reduce it. It is clearly present in research methodology that relies on the construction of knowledge, where it is acknowledged that the sample, methods and design are all in variation and affected by time, place, the researcher, the sample, research practices and interpretative processes, among other things. Attempts at the removal of bias and opinion are enabled by a robust research design and triangulation of methods. Even in 'pure' scientific research, where scientists carry out well managed and well documented experiments, their choice of experiments and, to some extent, the questions they ask of the data produced in order to interpret it are based on essentially subjective research questions and a need to know some things rather than others. This can be determined by different times and places, different needs and abilities, the opportunities for different kinds of study, and different subjects.

Boundary

In research, a boundary is drawn to enable the researcher to focus on what is relevant to the study. The ways in which you critically review information and data used, choose theory to underpin the research questions you are asking, and select which elements of what you are discovering to focus on in your writing, are all guided by their relevance. This relevance is to your research question, its contribution to knowledge in the field, the need for this piece of research, and your own interests at this point.

Chapter 7 on the literature review and Chapter 14 on analysing your findings focus further on these issues of relevance when considering stages of the development of your research design. We look there at the analogy of a piece of cake. Think of the whole field of reading or influences as the whole piece of cake, and what you are going to focus on and use, then think of your research as part of your slice of the cake so that you have a manageable, 'boundaried' and do-able piece of research which you can explain and defend, and which does not try to look at everything – however interesting everything is (because you will never be able to say anything in a focused fashion if you try and look at too much).

The same kind of selection process of what is relevant to your research question and your argument takes place when you look at all the reading you have done, all the data you have collected, all the sketchbooks you have kept, all the statistics you have gathered, and wonder 'what on earth do I do with all this data?' At this point, you also need to focus on what is relevant to your research question, your intended outcome, and to be ruthless with what you cut out – that which doesn't clearly fit the research agenda and format (however, you can save them 'for later research' in another file . . .).

Conceptual framework

The framework of ideas that underpins the research you propose to carry out is called the conceptual framework. It need not be excessively complex, but remember you are not merely asking research questions, you are problematising – unpicking, questioning – the ideas, values and terms you are using which underpin your question. You are using theories to help you approach, explore, interpret and understand the question, the whole area of thinking in which it fits, and the ways of understanding the information that is produced, by asking the question using your methodology and methods (questionnaire, observation, narrative etc.) and the vehicles (interview schedules, observation schedules, diaries etc.).

Constructivism

A school of thought based on Piaget's theoretical view that infants are not born with knowledge about the world, but instead gradually construct knowledge and the ability to represent reality mentally. The constructivist approach to research focuses centrally on qualitative analysis of how social concepts, and also 'things', are socially constructed. It is the epistemological view that the phenomena of the social and cultural world and their meanings are not objective but are created in human social interaction – that is, they are socially constructed.

Data

Data are the product of the research itself; determined by the research process, they are the units of information (singular 'datum', plural 'data') that are generated and recorded. In quantitative research, data is numerical, and in qualitative research, data consists of words, images or objects. Once you have gathered your data you will need to manage it, carefully sort and label it, analyse it, look for patterns and themes within it, then interpret it in a dialogue with the theories underpinning your work, and subsequently develop findings. You select from your data and present it as evidence to back up your research claims.

Deductive reasoning

This involves drawing specific, logical and concrete conclusions from general and abstract principles or statements through a process of deduction (the opposite of induction).

Discourse analysis

This is the study, using linguistic analysis techniques, of the use of language (naturally occurring connected speech) and written discourse in social contexts, and in particular the interaction or dialogue between speakers. The researcher employs discourse analysis to understand the way versions or the world, society, events and psyche are produced or constructed through language. Foucault's theory of discourse analysis relates the construction of subjects with various forms of knowledge and power. Semiotics, deconstruction and narrative analysis are forms of discourse analysis.

Emancipatory research

In this type of research the researcher's main aim is to empower the participants of the study, who are usually marginalised groups or communities in society. One outcome of the research could be improved services for the community. It engages members of the community as co-constructors or validators of knowledge, and the researcher is an insider.

Empirical

The notion that knowledge comes through factual research based on direct experience gathered through the senses, such as visual observation, through experience or experiments. More loosely, it has been used to describe research that is based on experience rather than theorising and so contains little in the way of reflection or theory, preferring to report 'facts' as they appear to be. Philosophically this assumes that the world is knowable through sense-data, although in practical use, 'empirical' is usually coupled with words such as 'evidence', and 'data', which can be seen as describing the hard facts gathered during experiments or fieldwork (and researchers often then proceed to use these facts as data and start to interpret them – using theory).

Epistemology

The philosophical theory of knowledge, that addresses questions about what can be known, how we can know what we know, and whether this knowledge is reliable or not. It explains the construction of knowledge, and beliefs about the ways in which knowledge is defined, constructed or discovered.

Ethics

A branch of moral philosophy and a field of everyday thinking that deals with questions of what is morally right and wrong. It is applied philosophy and asks questions such as what 'should' happen or what 'should' be done about everyday moral dilemmas. Research ethics relate to the standards that should be upheld to ensure that research is not undertaken for harmful or evil purposes and that no harm or risk comes to anyone or any living thing while research is carried out. Ethical considerations should be taken into account at each stage of the research design and include informed consent, voluntary participation and respect for confidentiality. Taking ethics into consideration also involves issues of safety, protection, rights (such as intellectual property) and privacy.

Ethnography

A qualitative research methodology that enables a detailed description and interpretation of a cultural or social group to be generated. The researcher examines specific social settings and systematically describes the culture of a group of people of which the researcher is a member at least for the research purposes (they do not have to be participants but do conduct the research with the people involved directly). Data collection is primarily through participant observation or through one-to-one interviews. The importance of context when gathering data is stressed, as only in this way can an understanding of social processes and the behaviours that come from them be developed. The goal of ethnographic research is to understand the natives'/insiders' view of their own world. Originally it was associated with anthropology and still favours naturalistic forms of data collection such as fieldwork – that is, time spent 'living' within a community.

Ethnography is concerned with experience as it is lived, felt or undergone, and so it involves a concern with your consciousness and that of the participants or subjects. To research perceptions of consciousness, the ethnographer participates in people's daily lives for a period of time, watching what happens, listening to what is said, asking questions, studying documents, and collecting whatever data is available to throw light on the issue with which the research is concerned.

Focus group

Focus groups are small groups of usually around 6–10 individuals who have common experiences or interests and who are brought together by the researcher specifically to focus on and discuss certain issues, under the guidance of a facilitator.

The focus group may be used to assess group dynamics, but is more often used to generate a range of opinions. Focus groups enable close scrutiny and lengthy discussion. They can be repeated over time and be used to test out ideas. Like any other research samples, if studied over time, they will actually change in responses and attitudes and so this will affect any random sample quality they initially had. The focus group is also constantly affected by the presence of the researcher, and this will need to be taken into consideration.

Generalisability

The degree to which it is justifiable to apply to a wider population explanations and descriptions that research has found to apply in a particular sample or example.

If research is generalisable it can be put towards use in other research, because others can use this same research method with similar subjects in similar circumstances and gain similar enough results.

Grounded theory

Grounded theory literally grows from the research experience and context. It is the converse of using a theory to explore a situation, as with grounded theory the theory grows from the grounding in real experiences. It is a qualitative research methodology with systematic guides for the collection and analysis of data, which aims to generate a theory that is 'grounded in' or formed from the data and is based on inductive reasoning. It also contrasts with other approaches that stop at the point of describing the participants' experiences.

Hypothesis

Hypotheses tend to be used in research based in beliefs about the world being discoverable, fact based, and that exploration and experimentation will yield truths and facts. A hypothesis is an assumption, a hunch or an educated guess and a testable proposition that captures the researcher's understanding of the situation being studied. Research begins with an idea based on a belief or assumption presented as a statement to be tested. This belief or assumption will then be verified (and proved or disproved) through tests and experiments, to reach a conclusion.

Inductive reasoning and research design

This involves drawing a general principle or conclusion from specific principles or examples through a logical process of induction (the opposite of deduction, which starts with the principles and tests them). It is carried out by developing and growing a theory from data collected on people's views and feelings that have been produced from the results of questioning or interviewing. A research project can have a mixture of inductive (developing theory, growing it from research data) and deductive (testing established theories) stages but if this is the case then it is important to explain how the research design enables you to explore and build at one stage (inductive), and test out at another (deductive).

Interpretivism

Researchers use this approach to gain a better understanding of the underlying processes that may influence behaviour. Interpretivism grows from the belief that we interpret evidence, data, rather than there being fixed values and meanings. It emphasises the meaningful nature of people's participation in social and cultural life. Researchers analyse the meanings people confer upon their own and others' actions, words, settings and contexts, and make meaning themselves out of research information.

Limitation

In social science research, your sample, research process or findings will never be exactly the same as the sample, research process or findings of another researcher because a limitation exists when dealing with the complex differences in human behaviour such that no precise replication of sample, research or findings is possible. Some research is therefore not generalisable to other research but it may still be used to inform other research; generalisability depends on the limitations within that piece of research.

In social science research, this would mean identifying that, for example, the people whose practices you are researching will differ from any other sample anyone else might use. A limitation would be that you cannot generalise from what you have discovered, so that while the results and findings could be used to inform someone else's research, they cannot be seen as identical because no other research would exactly replicate your own, as human actions are never identical, neither are people.

Another limitation might be the time available, so you could say, to be perfectly accurate, that you could have gathered more data on museums, found more creative sketchbooks or analysed episodes of *Friends* more deeply, investigated the circumstances around which audience figures were produced or propaganda delivered – depending on what you were researching at that time and what prevented you from carrying out any more research than you did.

Whatever the limitations, as a researcher you still have to be sure that you've taken all the precautions you can so that what you are reporting and the basis upon which you are interpreting the findings from your research are as accurate as you can make them. You need to be able to show that you have taken every care to check your sources and recordings and set up robust analysis practices where appropriate. You have to be certain that carrying out the process of the research hasn't distorted or damaged the data and therefore what you can say about it.

Literature review

This is the process of evaluating the output from a literature search by producing an annotated bibliography, which is a collection of carefully and meaningfully selected literature sources that informs the research theory and research design. It is not a dead list of books or journal articles, but rather an engagement with the ideas and arguments in those books or articles, showing how themes and ideas develop and starting to suggest where your own work might begin to make a contribution. Some literature reviews stand alone from new research, however, so would not involve your discussing your own research and its contribution.

Literature search

The process of identifying and locating existing published research and theory on the subject the researcher is interested in researching that forms the basis for further exploration by the researcher in the aim of filling any gap in knowledge in this field of literature. This is usefully done with the help of the librarians, and online search engines such as Google Scholar, using key words and similar words.

Methodology

Some people tend to confuse methodology and methods. One is the overall system based on beliefs, building the research design; the other, methods, are the tools actioning the research design. Your research methodology is based on the way you see the world, your beliefs about existence and being in the world and your relationship to that (ontology), and the way you believe knowledge is produced and constructed or discovered and fixed (epistemology).

Methodology is the ideas-based system that can enable you to address your research question/problem/hypothesis. It underpins the research design, i.e., the plan for the research, defining, among other things, the methods and the actual research tools or vehicles used to collect the data. 'Research methodologies', therefore, comprise the theoretical frameworks and concepts in which approaches and methods are situated; they provide the rationale and justification (intellectual, epistemological and ethical) for the methods that are selected and the ways in which they are used.

Methods

While *methodology* is a system, an overall approach based on a view of the world, *methods* are the ways of actioning, putting into practice, the underpinning beliefs, ideas and questions generated by methodology in order to question or test the world and gather data. Methods are the researchers' toolkit, broadly divided into quantitative and qualitative method types; the researcher selects the most appropriate 'tool' or method for their field of research. Social science research generally employs qualitative research methods, and 'pure' science employs quantitative research methods. Some fields use a combination of the two methods and in some studies researchers employ mixed research methods depending on the nature of their study and the tools available to them.

Narrative enquiry

Narrative enquiry is the process of gathering information for the purpose of research through storytelling. The researcher then writes a narrative of the experience. The study of narrative is the study of the ways humans experience the world; it suggests people's lives consist of stories.

Field notes, interviews, journals, letters, autobiographies, and orally told stories are all methods of narrative enquiry. A researcher might look at such things as notes and journal entries, and might also interview subjects and spend time observing them. After this, the researcher would construct her own narrative of the study. Narrative enquiry is appropriate to many social science fields.

Ontology

A branch of philosophy concerned with the theory of being and existence, worldview and a sense of self in the world and of how other living things exist. This can be distinguished from epistemology, which is concerned with what and how we can know about what exists.

Operationalise

This literally means to put an idea into action, into operation. Usually used in quantitative research to describe the 'translation', actioning or putting into operation of theoretical concepts within measurable categories and variables. However, it is also used in qualitative research to refer to the links between a theoretical idea and the kinds of examples of it (events, actions, discourses, descriptions etc.) that could occur in the data collected for a project.

Paradigm

Research paradigms are, like theory, based on ways in which we view the world, and believe that it is understandable, can be explored, fixed, or interpreted. Your research will grow from and be based in research paradigms.

The term was introduced by Thomas Kuhn to refer to the overall conception, ways of working and worldviews shared by scientists in a discipline at a particular time. In Kuhn's view, paradigm shifts occur from time to time as scientific communities experience revolutions of thought.

Phenomenography

Phenomenography grows from the philosophical area of argument and perception known as phenomenology, also a theory used in research. Both theories attempt to capture beliefs as well as reasons for actions in a social context and recognise that many of our beliefs and reasons cannot be openly expressed. Phenomenography looks at 'being in the world' and focuses on interactions between people in complex situations. It tends to be used in learning situations, while phenomenology can study interactions in many different situations.

Phenomenology

Like phenomenography, this theory or research methodology attempts to capture beliefs as well as reasons for actions in a social context and recognises that many of our beliefs and reasons cannot be openly expressed. It has its roots in philosophy and focuses on the lived experience of individuals. It grew from the work of late nineteenth- and early twentieth-century philosophers including Immanuel Kant, Edmund Husserl, Maurice Merleau-Ponty and Jean-Paul Sartre. The social world is seen as a social construction, and an achievement of people.

It is an approach that expects the feeling and the meaning of having experienced or experiencing the phenomenon under investigation to be described, as opposed to a more external description of what the experience was. This approach allows the reader to have a better understanding of what it was like to have experienced a particular phenomenon.

Positivism

A philosophical position that assumes that human behaviour is determined by external stimuli and that it is possible to use the principles and methods traditionally employed by the natural scientist, particularly deductive logic and quantitative research, to observe and measure social phenomena. Positivism assumes that life is regulated through natural laws, which social sciences have to uncover and document.

It is a fixed and knowable view of the world which can be discovered and explained and exists independently of our experience of it. It is most related to the scientific method approach to research in 'pure' science and less related to approaches in social science.

Primary sources

A primary source is an original source of information such as newspapers, newsreel footage, letters, diaries, government documents, witness statements, and questionnaire data which has been produced at the time and place studied. Seeking out and locating primary sources provides the researcher with ideas and evidence and is a rich part of the research journey. They are unanalysed records of events as they are first described, or original data about cases, settings or people. Such sources may be raw data collected as part of a research project or may be textual, visual and sometimes numerical sources that were not produced originally for research purposes, e.g. letters, movies, organisational documents, poems, raw tabulations of census data, video recordings and diaries.

Reliability

The degree to which different observers, researchers etc. (or the same observers on different occasions) make the same observations or collect the same data about the same object of study. The concept is highly contentious in qualitative research where it is often not clear what the same object of study is because contexts and people change.

It also means the degree of consistency with which data are categorised or coded by different researchers, or the same researcher on different occasions. Reliability is a key term in testing the accuracy of research. It relies on the rigour and consistency of the methods of data collection. Reliability entails being very specific in methods, often using large-scale surveys which have been carefully designed, tested and piloted and which will produce statistically significant results.

Sample

A sample is the total selected set of subjects or items of whom research questions are asked or on whom hypotheses are tested, taken from the whole available population. A sample must first be defined and chosen for a reason. It may be representative, stratified, opportunistic or random. This process of selecting a subgroup of a population to represent the entire population is called sampling.

Scientific method

A process of forming a hypothesis, testing and drawing conclusions that is the basis for scientific enquiry. It follows a series of steps: (1) identify a problem that needs solving; (2) formulate a hypothesis; (3) test the hypothesis; (4) collect and analyse the data; (5) make conclusions.

Secondary sources

Secondary sources are narrative-based or evaluative information sources collected from other authors or researchers, usually in the form of a discussion or a critical response – an analysis or re-statement of primary sources – or comment on sources or events providing information, data and the basis of evidence for arguments. These sources usually comment on, reflect on or critique events, data and primary sources. Secondary sources would be critical comments and articles, reports or books, research reports, news articles, biographies, documentaries or history books which reflect on the time and the events. Secondary sources are used to gain an understanding of a topic.

Theory

Theories help us to understand the world, make meaning from it. Researchers begin the research process by basing their study on an appropriate theory that will help them to identify, manage, structure and carry out research to test a hypothesis or ask research questions. Theory springs from a mixture of the researcher's worldview, a sense of self in the world, the ways in which the researcher believes that knowledge is constructed or discovered, and the discipline within which the research is being undertaken. Others will have researched and thought about the world and developed theories, or systems of understanding it, interpreting it, and researchers use these theories to underpin and inform the research design, and the understanding and meaning-making resulting from analysing and interpreting data from sources. With grounded theory you grow your own theory form the experience and the data, and indeed all forms of research test or develop theory. The researcher develops a theoretical framework from the theory in order to proceed with their investigation.

Triangulation

This is a process which is used in qualitative research in order to establish the interpretations and arguments which grow from analysing the data, theorising and interpreting the area under research. The area under investigation in the research is looked at from different (two or more) perspectives either simultaneously or sequentially. This is done using two or more research methods, sample groups or investigators. It is used to ensure a fuller or more accurate account of the phenomenon under investigation or to confirm interpretation through the comparison of different data sources, or ways of acquiring information about data sources.

Validity

In research, 'validity' refers to the degree to which the research provides a true picture of the situation and/or people being studied and is often referred to as 'internal validity'. You develop a research design which you trust can help you ask your research questions, and you need to believe that it is as robust and likely to ask those questions as possible. 'External validity' refers to the extent to which the data collected from the group or situation studied can be generalised to a wider population. Postmodernists, who contest that research can ever provide a single true picture of the world, contest the very possibility of validity.

Validity considers internal coherence and whether the right research questions are being asked of the data and then rigorously theorised. Research data should underpin the theories of the work and highlight any patterns and variations in the results that can then be interpreted in relation to the questions. All conclusions drawn must be appropriate to the research.

Acknowledgements

This book has developed from 30 years of working with students using research as part of their learning, whether for essays, presentations, projects, reports, dissertations or theses. I would like to thank all the students with whom I have worked and from whom I have learned, from the University of Brighton, Anglia Ruskin University, the Open University, and Cambridge University, particularly the undergraduates, Master's, PhD, EdD, continuing education and A level students. Tackling problems together and trying out ways of asking research questions, developing and actioning research designs and practices through to completion, writing and presenting have all been rich, energising, intellectually demanding and mostly good-humoured moments. Their enthusiasm and willingness to try out new ideas, deal with my strange diagrams and get on with the work with excitement and dedication have helped produce insights into the issues, ways to tackle them, and ultimately both research-informed work which makes a contribution to knowledge, and good research skills which should be useful in work and lifelong learning. I hope readers find the book helpful to their own research development.

I should like to thank Mick Healey and Alan Jenkins, whose ideas set off and underpin my own with regard to the development of students as researchers; friends and co-researchers Erik Meyer, Vernon Trafford, Gillian Robinson, Mark Warnes, Charlotte Morris, Jaki Lilly, Shosh Leshem, Miri Shacham, Yehudit od-Cohen, Meirav Tal, Margaret Kiley, and colleagues and students at the universities of Griffith, Auckland, Auckland University of Technology, Trinity Dublin, Limerick, Stellenbosch, Nottingham, and Brighton, where I have had an opportunity to develop the ideas and share the practices. The production of the book has been enormously helped by the work of my friends and colleagues, particularly Michelle Bernard, also Emily Thompson, Zoe Lee, and latterly Tracy Kellock. I should also like to thank colleagues at the University of Brighton who have supported the time my efforts have taken, the Dean of Education and Sport, Paul Griffiths, and Pro Vice Chancellor Stuart Laing.

Suzannah Burywood and Karen Griffiths at Palgrave Macmillan have been amazingly patient while the idea turned into a solid reality, and they and the unknown reviewers, and Jocelyn Stockley have helped make it what I hope is a readable, useful, essential book for students undertaking research.

Final thanks go to Roxy for keeping me company all through this journey (mostly without complaint).

Cambridge and Brighton, 2009

Introduction: How to Use This Book

This book seeks to enthuse and to equip you in the art and craft of research, from ideas to research design, carrying out the research and writing, and speaking about your research. Research is a developmental journey. It is *the* key learning activity, involving as it does enquiry, theorising and conceptualising, the excitement of searching after and shaping new knowledge, problem solving, seeking after, analysing, managing, interpreting and presenting ideas, information, findings and knowledge, developing creativity and originality, leading towards the production of research evidence-based work. For undergraduates, research begins as you start to work toward your first assignment, planning and undertaking fieldwork or experiments; reading towards an assessed task or essay; making problematic and opening up seemingly fixed issues and ideas; asking and beginning to answer questions about topics, fields or areas, on your specific, focused research project. Research skills are initially developed to enable, underpin and feed into the writing of essays, reports and independent learning projects of all kinds.

The emphasis on research for undergraduates goes on to develop mainly in your work towards dissertations or larger-scale projects, which require much longer, more extensive, planned, managed, sustained and completed research and work processes than anything else undertaken for a first degree.

Identifying questions and research methods or strategies, and organising a research project through to completion, is an exciting challenge involving commitment, individual development, interactions and hard work. Writing a research project or dissertation involves you in an intellectual exercise, theorising ideas and actions, behaviours, expressions and values which are often taken for granted; questioning what is given; being creative and original. It involves you in learning how to clearly argue your case, and to articulate your ideas and the kinds of new knowledge, new views you are developing from your research. It helps develop techniques and approaches essential for future research, for future learning, for self-development and for work-oriented development more generally.

Most undergraduates are involved in dissertations and projects. Some also become involved in other research-based activities including: work for independent learning modules/courses; showing evidence of research skills and reflection towards portfolios, including the personal development portfolio/progress file; research aimed towards the successful completion of a variety of work-orientated or work-based modules.

All of the excitement, planning, managing, exploring, care taking and completion necessary in undertaking research to fruition are equally as true for postgraduates and professionals involved in research as they are for undergraduates.

This book focuses on the development of sound research approaches and techniques for a number of differing learners, disciplines, projects and outcomes. It explores and supports the excitement of research in practice, through engagement with research, and the successful production of research-based outcomes and outputs. Although aimed primarily to support undergraduates in their research in both social science and humanities/arts subjects in the main, it is also useful for anyone beginning to undertake research, research-based projects and dissertations more generally, for postgraduates, and for those supervising small-scale research work. This book considers the needs of different kinds of learners in relation to learning styles, gender, culture, origin, ability and the management of disability. All of the book is useful for everyone undertaking any research in their learning, and a chapter is devoted to some of the needs and issues which might arise for international students in particular.

Aims

The Undergraduate Research Handbook aims to enable, support, empower and equip you to:

- develop your sense of enquiry, generation of ideas and creative thinking and at the same time develop the systemic, rigorous research practices you will need to work your way, stage by stage, through the use of research in a variety of learning experiences at undergraduate level;
- carry out appropriate research in a range of undergraduate work contexts for a range of outcomes, including research for class tasks, assessments, essays and major research projects or a dissertation;
- work your way, stage by stage, through a major research project or dissertation, accompanied, informed, directed and enabled to work through and consider a variety of models;
- link and underpin theory (of research) to your practice;
- practise exercises at each stage of the research and writing process, from drafting questions and a conceptual framework, to trying out aspects of methods in action, to handling any differences and difficulties with supervisors, to data analysis, interpretation, selection and the drawing of evidence-based claims, to breaking writing blocks and writing well in your own voice, to producing conceptual conclusions, and well rounded significant pieces of research expressed in a well written, well presented project, dissertation or other appropriate format;
- ensure that you have a sense of how to put *your own* research into practice while equally ensuring that you are aware of the stages of research and the techniques used in it more generally, so that you are developing strategies and approaches for future research in the variety of your study and latterly for paid work.

In its focus on the practices and processes of research, the book draws on my own experience as a researcher and supervisor in both arts/humanities and social sciences areas, including business and health (as these latter are generic social science approaches).

Layout

There are three sections and 23 chapters.

The first section, 'Getting started', includes chapters on the enquiring mind in action, and the principles and practices of getting started with your research, including carrying out research for a project or dissertation, theorising and conceptual frameworks, writing a research proposal, carrying out a literature review, and selecting and developing your research methodology and methods. It looks at sources, then at a range of quantitative and qualitative methods in action.

The second section, 'Managing people and processes', starts by considering the collecting, selecting, organising, and interpreting of data, looks at managing your tutor or supervisor, your time, life, paid work and research, and considers putting ethics into practice. The final section, Difference, writing and moving on', considers some of the differing needs of those of you who are international students, and those researching and writing in different disciplines. It supports the development of good writing, considers ways of overcoming difficulties with the project and the research processes and finally focuses on what examiners and employers look for and how to ensure your work matches their expectations.

Each chapter includes:

- A clear indication of the issues and practices to be covered.
- A lively, relevant, research- and experience-based introduction to and focused discussion of research techniques, and research project stages in terms of issues, needs and realistic, realisable strategies, techniques and practices.
- Underpinning of a sense of the excitement, enthusiasm and energy generated by and harnessed in research.
- Models of, for example, information searching and project development, data analysis, questionnaires and other research formats, good writing, project layouts.
- Task and activity boxes to enable readers to think, try out and reflect.
- A summary of issues covered and key points identified.
- Further reading.

How to use this book

It is hoped that you will find this book's logical progression through the stages of research, working with others, writing and completing, a useful guide for you in your own research. You might like to read the book from end to end, or to consult particular parts of it as you undertake parts of your own research. Some of the methods might not be of interest to you for the research you are currently engaged with, but reading about them could give you some ideas and arguments about why you have chosen the methods you have, and what alternatives there are. The chapter for international students is actually useful for everyone.

You are advised to access the chapters on working with others and on writing, as early as you can – just because they appear later on in the book it does not mean you would be expected to complete most of the research before you start working with your supervisor or tutor, or start to write. Quite the contrary! Researching, working with your tutor or supervisor and writing are all going on at the same time.

In each chapter, there are prompt questions, bullet-pointed lists of suggestions and issues, and there are 'Activities' for you to undertake. You should also find the 'Further reading' useful to develop your interest in certain areas a little further.

Accessible in tone, this book is both theorised and practical. It offers experience, research and evidence-based ideas, explorations, guidance, stimulus, advice, and information based on the many years I have worked with undergraduates, international students, mature returners, and postgraduates, as well as on my own research. It takes you through models, tasks and activities to enable you to think through, plan, action, write up and present your research for the variety of research-oriented undertakings in which you are involved. I do hope you both enjoy it and find it useful. Good luck in your research!

Part 1

Getting Started

1 The Enquiring Mind in Action

This chapter considers:

- the enquiring mind in action;
- research underpinning all learning – enthusiasm, motivation, theories, usefulness;
- different kinds of research;
- how you have always been a researcher of sorts;
- when you could use different kinds of enquiry and research in all your learning – research skills audit;
- your work for assessments, including essays, presentations and group work;
- research for larger projects;
- research approaches, strategies and techniques;
- skills for research.

One of the most interesting developments in higher education and further education in the UK and internationally over the last few years has been a move to encourage students to become involved with research as early as possible in their study. This recognises that research is not an exclusive activity for the dons of ancient universities or the scientists who are pushing the boundaries of our knowledge concerning, for example, medical practice, but that it can also be seen as a natural part of the way in which we go about learning. Most universities have focused provision for learner development and there is an organisation in the UK called the Association for Learning Development in Higher Education (ALDINHE) with this focus. Two major centres for developing students as researchers are at the University of Gloucester, led by Professor Mick Healey, and Oxford Brookes University, led by Professor Alan Jenkins, while the University of Brighton, for example, has developing students as researchers at the heart of its learning and teaching strategy.

These are all ways of recognising how important it is for you as a student to develop your enquiring mind, and your research approaches and skills. Research approaches and skills will be useful not only in your studies at university but in employment and life, because they are ways of thinking about the world and knowledge construction as well as ways of going about your own work.

As a student, you make a contribution to knowledge. You do not just digest it and repeat it, you make it. Making knowledge is based on asking questions, rather than taking things for granted. Instead, you wonder why? How? When? What does this mean? How might that be done? What if this were different? How does it work in that context? What do we really mean by whatever facts we are given, views we are meant to adopt, or beliefs we are told about? Why does it matter?

These and others are the most common questions that underlie our research.

By research, I am suggesting a continuum of approaches and activities (see Figure 1.1), which can be defined at one end of the continuum as the 'blue skies', groundbreaking, highly complex, intellectual, world-shattering, erudite research, which is the traditional view of research carried out full time by the highly intellectual few, and leading to substantial change and knowledge. This has to begin somewhere though, and at the other end of the continuum, we are defining research as a relatively everyday enquiry approach which has a robust research design, involves much careful work and is:

- questioning what seems taken for granted;
- problematising or asking thoughtful questions about issues, practice, events, fields;
- following up hunches and identifying problems;
- making suggestions, testing out assumptions or hypothesising;
- working to find out what is the case;
- not taking ideas and information, arguments and assertions for granted but checking them;
- wondering;
- setting out with a high level of organisation, focus and rigour to try and find out;
- then analysing the data, writing well and presenting the research and its findings and contribution in an appropriate shape – project report, assignment, dissertation. . . .

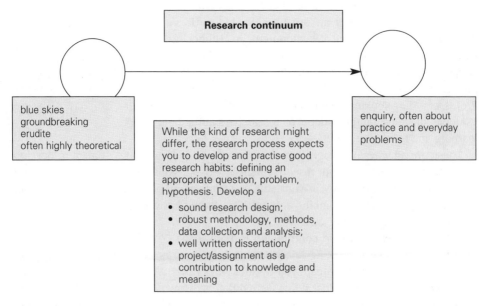

Figure 1.1

Activity

Can you identify where any of your own current or recent pieces of research might lie on this continuum?

With the first few steps of enquiry and well-planned, systematic, exploratory work, with the thinking and problematising and then the managing of information and thoughts which emerge from this process, you will have started on the first stage of your research career. This can help you to develop good research habits for the future, whether you undertake world-shattering research, or continue to use research practices as a matter of everyday enquiry and robust hard work, for example, in your employment. Those who develop such an effective approach to research and enquiry, with a problematising outlook on the world and sound research practices, have begun to be effective researchers. Enquiry and research become second nature, and the rigorous questioning, exploring, management and thinking, working out and talking about this new meaning, this new knowledge, will soon start to become a skill of your own, useful on an everyday basis in life and work, as well as during your formal study.

You have always been a researcher of sorts

Of course, you will have been carrying out some elements of research for projects and to answer questions at school, college or in the workplace since your first few days there. You will have been asking questions which led to the need to carry out some investigation, some research, since you first became interested in studying at all. You will also have been developing research and enquiry approaches and skills even in more everyday contexts, such as exploring where to go on holiday, how to grow seeds successfully, how to fix things around the house, how to train your dog, how to find the right kind of music system, and how to buy the right kind of items for your needs from the products on eBay.

Activity

Please consider:

What kind of enquiry or research have you been involved with already?

- for assignments
- in the workplace
- in everyday life

There is a range of everyday research practice. Usually, this starts with spotting an issue, need or problem, developing a hunch or a strong sense that something is or is not working in practice. This is followed by developing a question, or a hypothesis, i.e. a statement about a situation that you want to test. Then you decide how to go about the enquiry, begin the enquiry through information searching and finding out, contradictions, perhaps, and patterns. When you look closely at the information, you begin to identify continuities, themes, patterns and contradictions, critical responses, differences and variations. You weigh these up, consider the evidence and then make a decision, decide on ways forward based on weighing up these different views, arguments and evidence.

How am I using the term 'research' in this continuum? Let's look at different uses of the word in practice. Some research is experimental, some exploratory. Some sets out to explain phenomena, some to answer questions or to test a hypothesis, a belief or assumption presented as a statement to be tested.

● Some explanations of terms: hypothesis and research question

A hypothesis is an assumption or belief which you are going to test, by performing an experiment to explore how, and if, it is or is not true. You would develop a hypothesis if you were undertaking scientific research or the sort of social science research which depends on testing an assumption – for example, that most people who steal come from deprived backgrounds (not true, as it happens) or that children who are lone or first born are more likely to succeed in education than those who are in the middle of large family groups (true it seems), or to underpin an experiment, for example, testing with a control group and a research group how the research group responds to some stimulus such as three healthy meals a day. Verma and Beard (1981, p. 184) are quoted in Judith Bell's (1999) *Doing Your Research Project* for their definition of a hypothesis:

> A tentative proposition which is subject to verification through subsequent investigation. It may also be seen as the guide to the researcher in that it depicts and describes the method to be followed. In many cases hypotheses are hunches that the researcher has about the existence of relationship between variables.

A hypothesis informs or drives research which enables you to *experiment* with something, *test* whether something is the case. You are likely to be using a hypothesis if you believe that the world is fixable, facts can be discovered and known and that there are rules and laws governing what happens which can be identified and proven. This is research based on a positivistic paradigm (see Chapter 5).

A research question is a way of exploring the world and finding out about how and why something takes place and people respond, in context. Research based in a post-positivistic or interpretivist research paradigm (see Chapter 5) is likely to use a research question.

Please continue to think what kind of research you have been involved in, what your views are of what the word means, and what kinds of research you are involved with in your courses now.

Kinds of research in practice: Examples

1   He spent years in his laboratory researching the ways of turning base metals into gold.
    This kind of research involves scientific apparatus and lengthy endeavour. In the case of alchemy, which is based on a belief, it required lots of very thorough practical experimentation, and a lot of faith – unfounded as it happens, as gold was not created.

2   She spent her time in the library researching – looking through the archives of her favourite author to write a book.
    This is historical or archival document research and it involves setting about selective reading and note taking from a source or series of sources. The notes are then used as data or evidence of whatever it is the researcher is looking for in the archives – information about a life, times, critical responses – and form part of her line of argument in her own writing.

3   He was determined to research the origin of the species and set off on a long voyage to a distant island in the Galapagos, where he found some species that had not yet been seen by others, and by years of careful scrutiny and comparisons with other species he was able to determine some important new ideas and information about evolution.
    This is a long-term study based initially perhaps on some experience, or on a hunch? Some lucky accidents? Perhaps he thought there might be some unproven theories about how animals and people developed, and finding some strange creatures set him off to discover whether this hunch was true, or perhaps he discovered them almost accidentally and then developed the theory. In one version, he is testing and proving (or disproving) theories and hunches; in another, discovering, developing theories, then testing and proving (or disproving).

4   He wanted the job badly and so carried out research into it.
    This is a quicker and more practical activity with a single goal, but has some of the same characteristics as other research. He probably looks into the company he wants to work for on the Internet, then asks around, finds out some specific things about their practices and how they are thought of by others. This is some background information – it produces a sense of the company for him, so he can decide whether he wants to work for them and what to emphasise in his own application and then interview, should he get one. This kind of research probably does not take long and, indeed, it is short term, to answer just a few fast questions, but it is underpinned by several important questions about the company, such as – their practices? their identity? what people think about them? what they do? This is a fact-finding activity, but it helps him to put an application then a good interview together.

5   I was asked to produce a report and give a presentation on the environmental effects of housing for a development on the outskirts of town. I gathered information about numbers of houses, pollution, parking, effects on the

countryside, and infrastructure and presented this to those who had commissioned the report.

This is commissioned, probably quickly executed, project-based research that addresses specific questions set by others, and gathers a variety of appropriate information in order to present one or more cases and make recommendations, so that those who commissioned it, and others, can make up their minds about future actions.

6   She wanted to develop a course for mature women returners to education, but she did not know very much about what subjects they would be interested in, how they might study, their learning backgrounds, when they might study and how successful such students were so far. She looked through the registration information and the qualifications information of her own university and contacted the national statistical bodies who compile national statistics (Higher Education Statistics Agency (HESA) in the UK). She matched information about entry qualifications to the quality of the degrees gained by mature women returners without standard qualifications (A levels) and discovered patterns of high attainment which suggested that this group, if it was a group, could be successful in higher education. In order to find out what the students perceived as enabling them to be successful, she developed an interview schedule and interviewed a number of mature women student returners at her own university.

This is social science, educational research within a post-positivistic mixed methodology – both quantitative statistics and qualitative data based on perceptions using mixed methods, i.e. quantitative data collected in surveys and analysed locally or nationally, and qualitative interviews asking for interpretations and perceptions.

Some of this research starts with an idea, a hunch, an interest, a problem. Some of it stops with just gathering facts, and might well be based on the belief that all research is facts that can be gathered. These facts, however, need to be within a framework – of a question or an agreement. The facts need interpreting, and the facts you gather are all dependent on what you are asking, where and how you are asking, and even the reason for asking, because that helps interpret and shape them. Just gathering facts and information in itself is an early, necessary stage of research but not enough.

Research is fundamental to how we learn

Research is a fundamental way of asking questions and finding out answers (and discovering debates about these answers and how to interpret them). It is a fundamental element in how we learn. So, how does it work?

- Experience, some ideas and thoughts, some questions, an interest in finding out how, why, when, what if, what if not, or what does it mean?
- You will always need a question, problem, hunch, or hypothesis. These are beliefs or questions, based on evidence or assumptions which need to be tested (hypothesis) or explored and addressed (question). They are enabled by developing a research design of manageable and realisable methods, to test your hypothesis or to ask your question about your object of enquiry.
- Then, a systematic exploration of a focused question, problem or hypothesis, using underpinning theories and concepts (broadly speaking – ideas), methodology and methods (beliefs about how knowledge is created, how information is gathered and interpreted, and the ways to gather that information).
- Foraging for sources of information and gathering information which relates to that questi~~on or idea, and analysing and interpreting it.~~
- Building a ~~n argument, and... forma-~~ tion, your ~~...~~ e found and ~~...~~ uting to our incr ~~...~~ r further un ~~... conclusions).~~

  Bullet point 2 and 6 are good tips to remember.

- You might ~~...might~~ *not* prove your point, answer your question, prove or disprove y~~o~~ur hypothesis, or solve your problem. Research is fickle, what you find might not be what you were looking for, and a negative result or more questions are just as important to the research endeavour as proving your point! But you will contribute to knowledge and meaning in finding out, and you will develop your research skills further if your work has been using rigorous, well-organised, well-managed research methods. From the data and information you find, you will have forms of evidence to back your ideas, arguments and claims, and you will have been practising your writing in a variety of forms, including notes, categorising and summarising, analysing and explaining, reflecting, arguing, referencing and evidencing whatever you say.

As you come to the end of your piece of research, however long or short, it is important to remember you cannot make a claim without having some selected, focused evidence – facts, experimental data, quotations from interviews or from books, some discussion and interpretation of this, and a claim.

One of my mottos is:

No evidence without a claim, and no claim without evidence.

You could outline everything you have found out, but that is not really contributing to research, knowledge and meaning, it is just collecting for the sake of it. You can't claim to have solved a problem, found a solution or expanded our understanding unless you can show you have read, asked questions about, managed the data and interpreted it and that it can start to illustrate or prove what you are claiming.

There is another popular motto: Research is both inspiration – the ideas, the problems, the definitions of the issues, a creative set of movements when you interpret what you have found with theories, and the words of others helping you to theorise and to focus, and lots of perspiration – it is rigorous, you read, you collect information and data, you select, interpret, write and present in a range of ways. It is imaginative, thoughtful, full of ideas and well organised. It needs to be:

- critical – of ideas and information, to question them;
- conceptual – work at the level of theorising, of ideas not just facts, presenting information in a theorised, argued form;
- and creative – adding something new to our understanding and knowledge.

Being good at this broad range of skills is an excellent basis for all forms of learning and work in the future.

You will be asked to carry out relatively small research activities in your everyday study as a student, even if no one actually defines this as research. Remember, you are not being called upon to invent something from scratch, split the atom or find a new species. Effective research practices are good learning and enquiry habits. They will be useful in your everyday life and your study. Get into good habits early on.

Larger research projects

Much of your research will be for the major project or dissertation in the third year. Most universities expect students to be involved in such projects to develop dissertations or similar lengthy pieces of work. As with smaller activities, it is a good idea to think ahead and beyond the research itself and consider:

- How might this help me focus on something which could lead to a job in the future?
- How might this be useful?
- How might it be sufficiently unusual and original?

Some students find that if they take a world-, experience- and life-related research project, this might be of direct interest to future employers looking for exactly this kind of focus, and the skills that go with it to produce both the research, and its presentation in a written or/and spoken form.

Some such topics might include research into:

- the micro-financing of market stalls in your home town;
- the advertising and marketing image of short haul flights on a low cost airline;
- provision of day-care centres for the elderly;

- how schools have tackled truancy;
- reasons behind and effects of contradictory policies about drug use in night shelters for the homeless;
- the relationship between historical context and the imaginative representation of it in poetry by First World War poets;
- how students of weaving use fashion collections as an influence on their work.

And any number of other topical, interesting, focused areas that relate to the 'real world'. It is possible not only that you can pursue your own interest, but that the topics themselves might be of interest to future employers, could be developed further and feed into your portfolio or CV ready for applications for courses or jobs.

Skills and practices for Research

It is useful to consider some of the skills and practices which you will use in research. Some of these you may be familiar with, and if you think about it, you have already developed some of the skills in work at school, college or paid employment. The development of other skills should be possible through engaging with this book and its activities, while some others will need you to plan and find opportunities to develop.

Activity

Look at the skills audit below and note where you can rate your own skills and skills needs.

Research-related practices & skills	A strength	Quite good	Needs development	Some experience
Identifying research needs and topics				
Framing and asking research questions				
Developing				
Literature reviewing				
Theorising topics and underpinning questions with theories				
Developing a workable conceptual framework				
Developing research designs				
Time management				
Good numeracy				
Writing skills				
Problem identification and problem solving				
Self-motivation				
Working to an agreed research brief				

© Gina Wisker (2009) *The Undergratuate Research Handbook*, Palgrave Macmillan Ltd

Research-related practices & skills	A strength	Quite good	Needs development	Some experience
Communication with other people				
Selecting and using methodology				
Using quantitative research methods				
Using qualitative research methods				
Seeking out and acquiring primary sources				
Finding and using secondary sources				
Carrying out fieldwork effectively				
Gathering data effectively				
Taking notes				
Selecting, summarising, synthesising, analysing, reflecting on notes				
Managing data – cataloguing, categorising, labelling, documenting				
Analysing statistical data				
Analysing text and other data, noting patterns, themes, discussion				
Developing an argument				
Writing in a coherent, readable manner				
Referencing				
Presenting an argued research case				
Finishing work off in time and to a good standard				

Once you have audited your skills so far, you might talk with your tutor or supervisor about skills you need to develop, seek out helpful books (some of those referenced at the end of the chapters here, in the 'Further reading' sections, for example) and plan how you might work to develop these skills further. The same audit appears at the end of this book for you to consider how far you have developed your skills, and how you might offer evidence of them to a future employer.

Research for small-scale assessments

Essay

The most common form of assessment during term time is an essay. Research to be carried out for an essay is a small-scale version of the kind of research you would do for a project or dissertation.

Below is a short email exchange between a tutor and a student which helps the student to plan research for an essay. Please read it and consider how the dialogue helps the student to shape the work they need to do in order to ensure that this is a manageable and also a conceptual and critical piece of work, achievable in the time available.

Kat: After our lecture on fairytales and Angela Carter and the feminists, the other day, I want to write my essay about fairytales.

T: That sounds interesting – what is it about fairytales that interests you? Do you have:

A theme
A question
Some particular fairytales and what they might represent, in mind?

Kat: I thought I would look at the history of fairytales and then take several of them and write about them and what they are teaching (they are teaching something – right? not just entertaining us??), and then look at Carter, Namjoshi, Winterson, and the Virago books of fairytales and see what they are doing and if they are changing them and if so why and what effects this has. Or maybe I'll look at different fairytales in different cultures and see what the differences are and why.

Or I could just do an in-depth study of one author and how she has rewritten fairytales and why?

T: Great – you are getting closer to a question here –

There are three possibilities – why don't you get a side of A4 and write a bullet-pointed list – a bit on each about what your question or the issue is about the tales that interest you, whose fairytales you'll use, which tales you'll use, and see which of these three questions really interests you and looks possible.

Kat: I just did that and I'd like to do the first one – the others felt more difficult – I'm not sure how I would find out about the cultural differences, and just looking at the one author won't give me the space to develop an argument about fairytales and their changes when written by feminists.

T: Good – now you've chosen one you want which is do-able – but I think you might be doing too much for a 2,000-word essay!

A few more thoughts –

- Can you narrow this down a bit?
- How much history do you think you need? What is it in there for? – to tell us all about where they come from? How they developed? Who collected them? How they changed? How they are affected by cultural difference and over time?
- How many stories do you think you can write about so that you don't end up just briefly telling us the story? Can you narrow it down maybe to one or two fairytales? One or two authors? And then work out what it is you think is happening, the change, why, how?

●   If you want to look at the effect – how would you go about that? Are you going to ask a group of people, your friends maybe, in an interview or a questionnaire? Or do you want to stick to exploring the tales set in the context of the critical discussion about how they were developed and used, and how or if the feminist authors, particularly the one(s) you choose, have rewritten them? With this you would not be asking people about their responses but dealing with the debate between the critics and using your own critical response about the ways in which they have changed the tales and to what effect. What do you think?

Kat: Well, it was more that Carter seems to rewrite them – Little Red Riding Hood was the one I was interested in – and I wondered how and why she was rewriting them.

T: Why do you think? See what Marina Warner says in *From the Beast to the Blonde* on the ways fairytales would teach children how to behave socially, what to expect – and that this tended to develop stereotypes of women as either delicate victims in need of protection (by men, from men) or wicked stepmothers/fairies/hags attacking other women (as in 'Snow White'). Have you looked at Patricia Duncker's article in *Literature and History* on 'rewriting the fairytales'? (they are both on the reading list). She thinks Carter rewrites but doesn't fundamentally change the social instructions underlying the tales, because those are embedded socially – what do you think? And what do you think Carter's rewrite of Little Red Riding Hood, i.e. 'The Company of Wolves', is arguing? How? Where?

Kat: OK I think I'll give a brief outline of the history – about a paragraph, mentioning that the old women would retell the tales but the collectors and publishers were men – Perrault, the Brothers Grimm.

Then I'll research the Little Red Riding Hood story, work out what it is telling young people, read Warner and Duncker, and a few others, and use their theories about gender stereotypes and myths and then see what I think is happening in 'The Company of Wolves' – how does that sound?

T: Great! It is focused and you have some useful background research (try Zipes and Bettelheim on the history and use of fairytales) and critical research in there (Warner, Duncker) – now what we need is a title, a short plan, an idea of how long it is going to take you – and I look forward to seeing it in draft. If you have any questions just get in touch and we'll meet when you have got some way into it.

What has this exchange helped to develop? My thoughts about it are that it helps focus on:

●   A topic area, and the start of a research question.
●   A narrower set of questions and sources to work with so that it is possible to focus down and not get swamped with too many examples and details.
●   Some historical background – but not too much because the focus of the essay is not history.

- Some respon̶̶   ̶̶ ̶ut not too much be̶   ̶ ̶ ̶ le essay is not people's r̶e̶s̶p̶o̶ ̶ ̶s̶.
- A developing line of argument about women writers, particularly Carter, rewriting the tales to effectively critique the stereotypes.

Kat's **research action points** might look like this:

1   Find out about the history of fairytales.
2   Read selected bits of Marina Warner and all of Duncker's essay.
3   Reread both Little Red Riding Hood in a couple of examples and Carter's tale and work out what stereotypes she is challenging and how effectively I and the critics think she is challenging them.
4   Get writing!

Research for presentations

If you are preparing a presentation, you will need to go through the same kind of planning of the research area, narrowing to a question, deciding on where to carry out your research and what kind of research, and then developing a timeline to get the work done. Consider the length of the presentation. You will need to carry out more research than you can share with the audience in order to cut it back to the key points to show and talk through. Knowing more about the field ensures you present a sense of confidence, and can answer questions which might go beyond the information and arguments you present.

With a presentation you would need to allow further time to prepare handouts and probably PowerPoint® slides to deliver the presentation.

You would need to identify and determine:

- Key points to put in bullets on the PowerPoint slides.
- Illustrations to keep your audience interested.
- A handout with the outline of the talk and the PowerPoint slides (six to a page, pure black and white and framed, or fewer to a page and space for notes).
- A handout with quotations or graphs (as appropriate to your topic) for deeper exploration, perhaps beyond the presentation itself.
- Some questions for the audience to consider, to get them involved in the talk.

Sometimes it is really helpful to have to present your research before you write it up in an essay, project or dissertation because by having to cut it right down to the question, research area, findings and argument, with some illustration/evidence and a conclusion, you have the perfect skeleton on which to hang all the information, examples and argument you have been developing in your research and work. It helps narrow the focus and clarify the argument.

Research in groups

You might well be asked to carry out a research project with a few of your colleagues or friends. This has all the benefits and all of the potential problems of group work with the process of research as the focus. Researching with friends or colleagues in a small group:

- Probably cuts down the amount of work you have to do yourself.
- Forces you all to brainstorm, then narrow down a topic to a manageable question and research design.
- Ensures you identify different elements of the work to be done to gather the primary and secondary sources.
- Ensures you produce good notes and have a clear understanding of the material and your argument – because you have to share it with your colleagues even before anyone else sees it and you must make sense of it for that purpose in the first instance.
- Forces you to manage the time – if you plan the work, time the carrying out of elements of the research, plan when you will meet to share and explain what you have done and put it together;
- start to write up parts of the group work;
- then shape and refine it so it is a whole without excess overlapping or repetition, and with a coherent argument running through it. If it is a group presentation ensure that you have time to rehearse so it runs smoothly and the research, the question, argument, evidence and quality of the presentation are all properly developed.

Beware! Don't:

- Allow one person to do all of the work. There are team roles you can take into consideration and develop but you still all need to be carrying out the research in your own sections. One person might be a better planner, so that can be his/her role (and perhaps you can learn from this and be the planner next time), but if he or she does all of the work you won't be learning how to research and it won't really be your work or your mark.
- Let anyone get away with doing little or nothing. Share the work out evenly and come together to explain what you are finding out and what it means, where the gaps are and what to do to pull the whole into a group effort to present and/or write up.
- Leave yourselves too little time.
- Underestimate how long it takes to share, understand and get a sense that this is a group effort in a coherent piece.

The skills you learn in a group research activity are all those of research more generally but with the added skills of team-working, communication, better planning and management. These will all be very useful as you move through and beyond your degree and use your research skills, because we are often asked to develop projects with others and to find ways of co-presenting.

**Activity:
Think ahead – what research might you be
interested in carrying out?**

Answering these questions will help you to identify research areas in which you might be interested and to plan for future work.

- What fascinates you?
- What could be useful for a future job?
- What addresses a gap in knowledge so that you have something to contribute?
- What can realistically be researched in the time available in your context?
- Who can help you with this? Provide IT support, supervision, peer support?
- Will you be able to access primary sources (original material) and secondary sources (critical and commentary material about your areas)?
- Is this piece of research 'do-able' in the time available?
- Can you create a manageable action plan to carry it out?
- What has an initial literature search suggested about the field, what work is in it, what's been found out already, what is topical, and what are the main issues and arguments in the field?
- How might your work fit in with this? And develop some areas further?

Summary

In this chapter we have considered:

- Enquiry and research as everyday and useful approaches and skills.
- Developing aspects of research activities from questions to completion.
- Research leading to useful skills for employment.

Further reading

Bell, J. (1999) *Doing Your Research Project* (Buckingham: Open University Press).
Davies, M. B. (2007) *Doing a Research Project* (Basingstoke: Palgrave Macmillan).

2 Starting Research

This chapter considers:

- ► when to use research;
- ► your research and learning background;
- ► different conceptions of and approaches to research for different outcomes;
- ► learning leaps;
- ► assessing and planning the research for learning, assessments, essays, presentations and larger-scale projects;
- ► planning to carry out research for an assessment, an essay or a presentation;
- ► information and data-gathering;
- ► library activities;
- ► fieldwork;
- ► useful ways of thinking and working;
- ► other people's arguments;
- ► critical thinking;
- ► reflection.

● Getting started

This chapter focuses you on why, when and how you might need to be involved in research and enquiry while at university; it introduces you to ways of defining the research areas and forms of research, and it considers what can be thought of as sources of information and data gathering.

● When will I use research? Your research and learning background. Different conceptions of and approaches to research for different outcomes

In higher education, having an enquiring mind, identifying problems and questions, critically exploring and evaluating information and ideas that you read about or hear about, and constructing your own responses and your own knowledge to add to the debates are all learning activities which are expected of you. Many students have come straight from school into higher education, or have been in employment and are used to practical work activities. You might have been used to more teacher-led activities and a great deal of direction over what to read, what to think and what to write. You might have been studying in an international context, and so you are now seen as an international student. There is a chapter which focuses specifically on international students, but the whole book is useful for all categories of student.

For many students, particularly some international students, knowledge is seen as being already established, so that you gain knowledge by listening to and deferring to authority in the form of the teacher and texts. It could seem disrespectful to question established knowledge and known authorities, and you might feel you need to be told what it is important to learn about, and that the established facts are there to be gathered and repeated in your work. In UK, US, much European, and Australasian higher education, established knowledge is to be questioned, as are those who claim to be authorities, and you are expected to construct knowledge to add to arguments, ideas and information. Some of this enquiring and knowledge construction might well seem quite daunting.

Students used to taking a good set of notes from teachers and textbooks will find these skills to be very helpful in higher education, as they gather the notes upon which to start to build an argument. But you might be less used to asking questions, developing your own knowledge, and seeing that there are always debates about knowledge and interpretation. You need to recognise that your work can contribute to the debate when founded upon a questioning attitude, good fieldwork and information acquisition, with your own ideas and arguments backed up by research evidence.

For students more used to depending on practical questions and practical, work-oriented projects, the kind of theorising which is required in higher education research might also seem daunting. As we discover in Chapter 5, theory helps us to explore the world, and is closely linked to practice, informs our practice, helps us to interpret it and to understand why we do or should do various things in particular ways, and to understand various phenomena and how they are linked, in context. Theory informs practice and practice can be understood and developed through the use of theory.

Learning leaps

You are making a 'learning leap' in moving into higher education, and finding out how to explore, problematise, enquire, recognise, add to the debate about knowledge and contribute your own ideas and your own knowledge. These are all part of the rich experience of studying. They are also skills that employers expect from you after your degree, so it is a good idea to develop these skills as early as possible in your time as a student.

Of course, you might also have been used to making up your own questions for essays, constructing your own project titles, constructing and carrying out your own fieldwork for projects or longer essays, and finding out about the views of theorists, critics and experts in the subjects you have been studying, in order to write essays at school or college, or address problems at work. You can now build on these skills for longer and conceptually critically deeper pieces of work during your degree study. Previous experience is useful, and some of your practices might have to develop further to really make use of and improve your research skills.

Activity

Please reflect and consider the following.

When you carried out research or enquiry before your university study,

- How did you ask your research question, *or* develop a hypothesis to test or identify a problem?
- How did you plan the research or enquiry?
- How did you go about any reading or background theorising and ideas-gathering?
- How did you go about gathering data or information?
- What did you find out?
- Were there any surprises, good or bad, along the way while you did your research?
- What have you learned from the process about what to do or not to do? What works and what should be avoided?

Assessing and planning the research for learning, assessments, essays, presentations and larger-scale projects

Work at university level [...] ask questions of established ideas and knowledge. [...] to be expected to consult a number of primary and [...] ully and selectively, take notes and identify key points, [...] hen to develop your own views and arguments. Universi[...] ied, increasingly complex, and more dependent upon y[...] es and skills of research than anything you've been in[...] orkplace.

Whatever the kind, si[...] ork, you will be bound to use some research pr[...] question and the scope of the work.

You will need to:

[handwritten note: 1 main goals of conducting research / how to present your findings 2 "presenting facts to build or intro to a new argument" 3 ... 4]

- Identify a probl[...] hat you can investigate. This could be gi[...] worked out by you. You need to find so[...] researched, or ask a new question of a w[...] entify a gap in knowledge which your rese[...] bout the different definitions of problems, qu[...] es are more usually used in scientific resear[...] rmed by a positivist research paradigm. They are assumptions to be tested. Research questions enable you to explore, ask and answer questions about the world.
- Find out about work which has already been done in your field, related to this problem, question, hypothesis, whether highly theorised or practical work which has been written up. Some of this work will be directly related to your own research, while some will ask similar questions of other related areas. Some of the other reading you will need to do will be in theories which can help you to underpin your research investigations and enquiries and also to work out why it matters, what it can say, how we can understand it, i.e. theorise it, and what theories help to interpret and understand it. Your research will involve reading the literature and using it to help you clarify your own version of what the arguments are, what your contribution can be and where your work fits in.
- Identify the research design – the methodology and the methods by which you can gather your information – and, if you are conducting a research project, your data from the field, and how you can analyse this data and interpret it.
- Engage with ideas, develop an argument, and write clearly and well, whether detailing what the issues are or presenting an argument. You will find that identifying, gathering and sorting facts and information are essential. So is stepping back, working out the ideas, using theories to help you ask and address your question, and making them work for you so that you can develop something that is your own, and in which others will be interested.

Carrying out research for short assignments

The many short pieces of work that your tutors might well set you at the start of your degree study should help you develop research skills. Some of these may involve you in exploring questions and addressing problems that have been set by your tutors, appear in the literature, or have been decided on by yourself. Sometimes it is very useful to draw on your own experience, and to use reading to underpin your research and research data-gathering in order to test your assumptions You can ask questions based on thoughts and experiences you have had already, and underpin or inform these with theory and the work of others in the field. Sometimes your work is going to involve research practices in an entirely new field for you. Either way, it is a good idea to consider the range of skills needed and the ways of going about the research in practice. Short early assignments give you some practice in the various forms of research, from determining the field to asking questions and defining problems, drawing up a research design or plan and carrying it out, and gathering data and asking questions about what it can tell you in relation to your research question or problem. They also give you the opportunity to develop skills in writing up or presenting an argument.

Information and data-gathering

You could be asked to find out and practise how you would go about gathering information or data. This information could come from a number of sources and in a number of forms.

It could be already-discovered facts in the form of data gathered through, for example, surveys, the census, experiments, questionnaires, or other forms of investigation carried out by someone and recorded in a formal database or publication; or the facts and information gathered for a report or a publication in order to determine an issue or address a problem as defined by someone else, such as information which is already documented in the publication.

Also, it could be in the form of information or data that you're gathering yourself first-hand, using any one of a number of methods that are explored in Chapter 12, such as through questionnaires, interviews, observation and analysis of documents, asking questions in relation to your research, and gathering information from several sources in order to address a particular question or problem.

As you can see, these data-gathering processes, whether you are gathering facts, perceptions, behaviours, statistics, etc., enable you to gather data that has been already collected by someone else, in order to establish the field, or to ask new questions and address new problems using this established data. You might, instead, gather original data using interviews, surveys and observations, and so on, asking your specific questions or to solve your specific problems.

Library activities

Many tutors set students exercises individually, in pairs or in groups that involve finding out how the library collects, catalogues and stores its sources of information. The sources of information include textbooks, key books in your subject area, encyclopaedias, CDs, DVDs, images, journals, and perhaps a range of special collections, which might have archive material such as letters and reports. Some straightforward exercises that aim to enable you to learn how to use the library appropriately give you:

- a facility with the geography and layout of the library;
- a sense of the ways in which it gathers, stores and enables access to the information it holds, including online information databases and connections to the larger information bases outside the library;
- ways of searching for information from these various storage sources;
- experience in selecting the appropriate information from these sources and taking note of it, so that it can be used to address the questions you've been set;
- ways of learning to make note of where you found the material, in other words, learning to build up your own references so that you can return to such material to find out more or tell other people about it;
- access to librarians, who can be very helpful in your search for information to carry out these assignments. Many librarians have not only first but higher degrees and are researchers in their own right. Subject specialists are usually very happy to help you in your quest. If your tutor has properly alerted them that you and your colleagues are carrying out a library-based exercise, they might well be prepared for you with information and strategies to help you find the sources that you seek. One of the things you will learn from this exercise is that it's helpful to work closely with librarians and, since they are very busy people, to request some time in advance with them, so that they can use their skills to help you.

Fieldwork

Tutors quite often ask students to carry out some early fieldwork in order to practise some of the gathering methods that you will be using if you're carrying out research in a social science or related subject area which uses social science techniques and methods. You could well be asked to get into pairs or threes and interview each other. This will give you practice in developing interview questions which help you answer the question related to the task that you have been set. You will discover some of the strategies of engaging your interviewee's interest in answering your questions, wording the questions so that they are not too long, contradictory or complicated, asking them carefully and clearly, and listening to the replies. You will also learn about managing the time and taking appropriate notes from the short interview. If you carry out this kind of practice activity, you will learn a lot about the construction of interviews and the management of them. The next thing you will need to consider is what you do with the information you gain from the interviews. Here you will find that you select and extract some excerpts from what your interviewee has said as evidence in a discussion which aims to address your question. What's important about interviews is selecting from them, and using them to back up your argument.

Critical work

Your tutor may ask you to carry out one or more sorts of critical work. In a literature course, they might, for example, ask you to select a poem from your course, and to present it to the rest of the class. While you might need to read the poem out loud, what is wanted in this exercise is to read it carefully, and to critically analyse it, exploring how it works: the argument, storyline, themes, rhythm, rhyme, metre, language chosen, imagery, patterns of language and sound, context, both cultural and historical, ways in which it comments on issues or experiences, and how we might read it in context and in relation to other works by this poet, or other poets on the course. Your research will inform your critical analysis. You will be expected to have some idea of what critics have said about the poem and to engage in your own analysis and discussion, which takes note of what they have said, agreeing, disagreeing and using evidence from the poem to back up your arguments.

You might also be asked to compare and contrast the critical views of two people who have written about your poem. If you are studying in another subject, you can critically analyse and compare what two critics have argued about your topic. In these examples, you will be expected to read carefully, identify their main points, take notes on these points, with evidence from the texts, summarise the main points, identify where they agree or differ, and develop a short argument that explores what they are saying, agreeing or differing about and how and where this appears in the text. This kind of contrastive reading is explored in Chapter 7, and it helps you to develop a sense of there being debates about all forms of knowledge. You can get involved in this construction of knowledge and be a critical voice yourself, but to do so you need to explore what other people say, to read very closely, and to have evidence wherever you argue from the sources, whether it is a poem, the critics, other documents or online sources, as appropriate.

Useful ways of thinking and working

Useful ways of thinking and working when undertaking research include developing critical thinking skills and developing reflective skills. Stella Cottrell's *Critical Thinking Skills* (2005) starts by defining critical thinking in this way: 'Critical thinking is a cognitive activity, associated with using the mind. Learning to think in critically analytical and evaluative ways means using mental processes such as attention, categorisation, selection, and judgement' (Cottrell, 2005, p. 1).

R. H. Ennis (1987) identifies as important to critical thinking the ability to reflect scep-
tically and the ability to think in a reasoned way. Scepticism is culturally defined as polite
doubt, rather than not believing in things, and it enables you to question and to wish to
explore more thoroughly all the activities in which you engage, the reading to underpin
your research and the findings from research. Much of the critical thinking process can
help you with your research, because it engages you in questioning, evaluating and
developing arguments. Cottrell argues that it involves:

- identifying other people's positions, arguments and conclusions;
- evaluating the evidence for alternative points of view;
- weighing up opposing arguments and evidence fairly;
- being able to read between the lines, seeing behind surfaces, and identifying
  false or unfair assumptions;
- recognising techniques used to make certain positions more appealing than
  others, such as false logic and persuasive devices;
- reflecting on issues in a structured way, bringing logic and insight to bear;
- drawing conclusions about whether arguments are valid and justifiable, based
  on good evidence and sensible assumptions;
- presenting a point of view in a structured, clear, well-reasoned way that
  convinces others.

(Cottrell, 2005, p. 2)

Other people's arguments

When you are reading the theoretical background and critical literature for your
research, you will need to be able to identify other people's arguments and evaluate the
ways in which they are using evidence. This is in order to use the evidence in relation to
your own developing arguments, and to show that you have read fully in the appropriate
literature. In reading a variety of different sources you will need to weigh up their arguments and evaluate their evidence:

- How persuasive are they?
- Are their arguments logical and well backed up with evidence?
- Or are they trying to draw you in emotionally to agree with them when they
  actually don't really have any evidence?
- Do they seem to draw conclusions and make assertions without having led
  you carefully through an argument and presented the reasons for those
  conclusions and assertions from the evidence?

When reading the work of others, part of what you do in your research is to ask questions so that you can better evaluate, reflect on and relate to their work in your own
work. You can also develop the skills of evaluating evidence, weighing up arguments,
unpicking false assumptions, and being logical in the structure of your writing. You need

to be logical in the way you use evidence to set out an argument and back up your points, your interpretation of findings, the issues you want to emphasise and, finally, to draw conclusions which are valid and justifiable, based on good evidence and sensible assumptions. You also need to use language effectively to present your reasoning and deal with that of others.

Critical thinking

Critical thinking is useful to all of us as students, academics, and beyond in the world of employment, because we depend on the research of others to inform our own under-standing and our own research and we need to be able to critically evaluate that research. We need to be able not just to repeat what we've read and take everything in as if it was proven fact, but to engage with it, think about it, test it out, identify whether what we're being told is presented in such a way as to trick us into agreement, or whether it is logical, reasoned and backed by evidence. We need to understand it, not just 'know' – i.e. learn up, repeat, depend uncritically upon – facts and information which we are told by others in our reading, or verbally.

Bodner (1988) argues that some chemistry students are unable to 'apply their knowl-edge outside the narrow domain in which it was learnt. They "know" without under-standing' (pp. 212–13). He goes on to argue that students shouldn't focus on standard chemical calculations in books, but instead should look for answers to questions and so take more of a problematising approach; they should be asking: How do we know? Why do we believe? Cottrell rightly argues that this is not true just of a chemistry student but for all students in all subjects. As you listen to your lecturers, your fellow students, as you read your various textbooks and source materials or watch the TV, you need to be not just asking and taking notes about what they said as if it were irrefutable fact, but also asking: How do we know that? How did they know that? What are they basing their argument on? Is it that convincing? Why does this matter? What are the implications of this if it's true? Why do we believe them? So what? What next? How does this relate to my work?

This questioning can enable you to critically reflect on and think about what they're saying, so that you don't take just any information, you are also placing it in your own frame of understanding and working out how it relates to what you need to know and want to know. You are creating your own understanding and your own knowledge.

Reflection

Life as a student seems to be so busy that you have little time for reflection. But it's when you reflect or think back over what you've been doing, learning and reading, and consider how it has added to, enhanced or developed your thinking and under-standing of what else needs to be done, that you are really starting to learn and own your own learning. Reflection is the necessary skill for research and one which doing research will help you develop. You can reflect during several stages in your study activity (see Figure 2.1). There are different forms of reflection including reflection on action (before you start), reflection in action (while you are doing something – a constant check) and reflection after action (evaluating and re-planning take place here).

- Reflect **before** you start to identify and then answer the question, take notes, read a book, and develop your own argument. Think –

  - What is the question or problem here and why does it matter?
  - What am I looking for?
  - What do I think the main aims and issues are going to be?
  - What is the best way to go about this?
  - How is it best to go about searching for ideas and information, and enquiring?

  This helps you to plan your research enquiry, reflecting throughout.

- Reflect **in action/during** the research process.

  While you're busy interviewing, reading through critical sources, primary sources and secondary sources, writing your notes, analysing your data, and listening to other students and lecturers, stop for a minute, think back and reflect – think about: What am I hearing? What am I seeing? How does this relate to my question? What am I looking for? How is it related to what I already know? What is directly or indirectly related to this new area of information, these new arguments, or is engaged, perhaps, in an unusual way, a parallel, a contrast, or a surprising alternative? How can I add what I already know to what I'm reading or hearing? Can it improve what I know? Can it question it? Does it change my arguments and points of view? And what do I think about what I know and am learning to know now?

- Reflect **after** a learning experience, after you've carried out a careful reading through of a crucial piece of literature, or carried out a piece of research of any kind, conducted an interview, read through a questionnaire, observed something you are researching, carried out some documentary analysis, had a discussion with your supervisor or your tutor about your work, talked with your peers in a group or informally, or written up new notes. Again, step back and think: What are the main ideas here? What have I just learnt? How does what I have just been reading, hearing, noting, or thinking about, work or contribute so as to develop, change, undercut, or problematise what I'm working on, my research question, assignment, or research-underpinned piece of work, and, more importantly, what I understand about what I'm learning, writing and arguing about here?

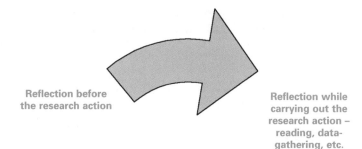

Reflection before
the research action

Reflection while
carrying out the
research action –
reading, data-
gathering, etc.

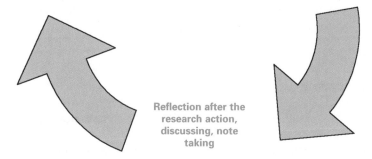

Reflection after the
research action,
discussing, note
taking

Figure 2.1

- Reflecting before action, in action, and after action, and writing down the responses to those reflections in a journal or a notebook can be quite brief, just a few lines, but can maximise your learning and understanding from the work you're doing.

- Reflection is essential in research because it helps you to focus, plan, think clearly, know what you know and how you know it, enhance your understanding, and therefore help you to really remember not just the facts but the reason in the arguments in which those facts are nested. Then you should be able to use those facts, that evidence, and those arguments in your own argument, and really understand, to have what is called by the learning theorists, deep learning, not just surface learning (Entwistle and Ramsden, 1983).

Summary

In this chapter we have considered:

- When you are likely to use research, and undertaking the planning and actioning of different forms of research for different outcomes including essays, projects, group work, presentations and other assessments.
- The processes of research introduced from library activities, information and data gathering, fieldwork onwards.
- Your research, reflection, critical thinking, your learning background and development including the learning leaps involved in working conceptually and critically through your research.

Further reading

Bodner, G. M. (1988) 'Consumer Chemistry: Critical Thinking at the Concrete Level', *Journal of Chemistry Education*, 65(3), pp. 212–13.

Cottrell, S. (2005) *Critical Thinking Skills* (Basingstoke: Palgrave Macmillan).

Ennis, R. H. (1987) 'A Taxonomy of Critical Thinking Dispositions and Abilities'. In: J. B. Baron and J. J. Sternberg (eds), *Teaching Thinking Skills: Theory and Practice* (New York: Freeman), pp. 9–26.

Entwistle, N. J. and Ramsden, P. (1983) *Understanding Student Learning* (London: Croom Helm).

3 Good Research: The Essentials

This chapter considers:

► principles and values necessary in good research;
► essential approaches, and underlying planning;
► everyday good practice;
► thinking about the underpinning conceptual, critical, and creative elements of research.

This chapter looks at a range of basic ideas and approaches for good practice in research. It considers a variety of underpinning principles, approaches, and values in action which you should find useful whatever discipline or interdisciplinary area you are working in, in your research. It builds on a variety of fundamentally good ideas from a range of other books on carrying out research, including my own *The Postgraduate Research Handbook* (2008), interprets these good ideas in a broader range of subject areas, and adds to them. Instead of 'Activities', it uses prompt 'Questions' at the end of each section for you to reflect on your own developing research. It should be useful to you throughout your research at university and beyond.

What this chapter *doesn't* do is to take you through the practical steps of devising research methods and vehicles, or writing. This kind of practical advice, with activities, you'll find in the rest of the book.

Many of the books on research methods or completing a project, focus in the main on social science processes. Some take a very detailed approach to data entry and data analysis from questionnaires and surveys. This book refers you to those more detailed books which look at the practical and specialised areas of social science research, but does not try to repeat what they say. Most of the books on research are for postgraduates rather than undergraduates. Some of the books helpfully indicate the approaches and ground rules that you need, to ensure that your research is of good quality.

In this chapter we are going to collect some of these elements of good advice, add to them and focus them on the range of discipline areas which are the subject of this book, i.e. social sciences, humanities, arts, business, subjects such as nursing and health (non-clinical), which use social science research processes, hospitality, leisure, travel and tourism, among others – in other words, expand the reach of the discipline areas to which such good advice usually refers, focus on a range of examples and expand the good advice.

Martin Denscombe's *Ground Rules for Good Research* (2002) is a good example of this overall approach. He provides a 10-point guide to underpin the research that you do, asking you to consider:

- purpose
- relevance
- resources
- originality

- accuracy
- accountability
- generalisations
- objectivity
- ethics
- proof

Some of these are values which drive the research, and we shall be looking throughout the book at these issues and values in practice. Denscombe points out that social science-related researchers need to have clearly stated aims related to existing knowledge, and themes or questions which can be investigated within the limitations of time, money and opportunity. He argues that research needs to contribute something new to knowledge which already exists, using 'precise and valid data, collected and used in a justifiable way, to produce findings from which generalisations can be made' (p. 2), and that researchers need particular attitudes and approaches to be successful in their research. These attitudes and approaches, he says,

- are open-minded and self-reflective;
- recognise the rights and interest of participants; and
- are cautious about claims based on findings (p. 3).

These are all equally true for much of the research carried out in the humanities, business and health-related areas. They also relate to the research carried out in the creative arts and the media. However, I would like to add the three key indicators of good research which I have found in addition to those identified by Denscombe and others; good research is:

- critical,
- conceptual,
- creative.

These are approaches, and they describe a kind of quality of mind and of the research product and outcomes. Let us look at some of these points in brief, consider how they apply to a variety of subject areas and points on the research journey, and make suggestions as to where you might find the research activities which action them where appropriate throughout the book.

See Chapter 13 on exploring what kind of research you might be doing, whether it is exploratory, predictive, experimental, action, and so on.

Purpose

There needs to be a purpose to the research. Perhaps you are explaining the causes or consequence of something; criticising or evaluating and working out how something works; developing and celebrating good practice for practitioners who wish to explore how something they are already doing or beginning to do works well; exploring, detailing and describing processes and events; or attempting to predict things that might happen in the future. Business and health researchers sometimes are trying to find out whether practices are working, for example, whether a nursing curriculum really does produce nurses who can solve problems and not just carry out efficient actions under orders. For humanities and arts researchers, sometimes the purpose is trying to find out what happened, why it happened and what the debates are about how it happened (possibly in history, archaeology, social geography). A historian might be looking for the debates about the causes of the First World War, and their purpose might be to clarify what the different arguments and evidence could be. An arts researcher, somebody working in the visual arts for instance, might be setting out to explore what working on a theme in a particular medium can produce and what sort of art processes it engages.

Chapter 4 on developing research questions, and Chapter 5 on developing a conceptual framework of the theory for your research, ask questions about what the purpose of your research is.

You will need to define your aims, your research questions and your expected outcomes. As we explore in Chapter 5, the kind of research you carry out is based on your worldview and the worldview popular in research undertakings in your discipline area. Some researchers (positivists) believe that the world is knowable and facts discoverable and provable. Others (post-positivists and interpretivists – see the continuum in Chapter 5) believe that knowledge is constructed, interpreted and in relation to context, researcher and question. While the world itself is ultimately unknowable, we move towards finding out answers to questions, being aware of constructing the research and contextualising the answers. Some research is more focused on exploring and acquiring information, facts, data, in order to establish a situation so that someone else can make some decisions based on your data and, if you produce any, your recommendations. By the time you reach the recommendations section of a report or a dissertation (if there is one), you will have analysed the data and thought about its impact and effect.

If you are writing a formal report in business, social policy or health, for example, which explores factual information, sets out to enquire *what?, when?, how?, to what effect?*, and perhaps to make suggestions or recommendations for change, you would need to summarise your aims and define your context at the beginning of such a report. Some of the wording might look like this:

This report was commissioned by the Cambridge Housing Association to discover what the proportion is of families with young children aged six and under living in housing association property in properties with or without gardens and access to park facilities. The aim of the report is to identify the numbers of such families, and their access to gardens or park facilities, in order to provide information for a larger study which will consider the proper provision of green and play spaces for children under six in housing association accommodation.

If you were writing an assignment, a project or a dissertation which *explores a situation, asks questions and constructs knowledge,* some of the wording might look like this:

> The aims of this project are to explore the effectiveness of a programme which works to develop education and social behaviour outcomes with young offenders. It addresses the research question 'Can young offenders benefit in terms of education and social behaviour from a programme of interaction with students who are studying criminology?'

Its objectives would be to see whether such an intervention programme had a positive effect, what kind of effect it had on the young offenders and also on the students, and what the characteristics of the programme were that had such effects. Its aim overall would be to suggest that programmes like this might be useful for other people to adopt and adapt. This would recognise the limitations, among others, of context and participants.

There are purposes to both of these pieces of work and their purposes affect the kind of research question or topic, and the research design, as well as how the research is expressed when written up. The first report largely discovers facts and answers the question 'what?' It will also contribute these facts towards other people's decisions and probably make recommendations about the decisions. The second project or dissertation asks more exploratory questions about which there might be no final factual answers, and looks at perceptions, experiences, attitudes and opinions to construct knowledge about the process and interaction, as well as perhaps some assessable outcomes. Both have purposes which could lead to finding out information to inform change, but they asked different questions, in different ways, and have different views about what knowledge is ie whether it is facts, or ideas and perceptions.

Questions

- What are your aims?
- What are your research questions?
- What are your expected outcomes?
- What is the purpose of your research?

Relevance

You can ask research questions about almost anything. But not all research questions would be either relevant or of interest to other people. Research needs to contribute to, question, and develop existing knowledge. And it needs to construct new knowledge, new interpretations, new creative explorations and solutions. You could ask a question about the number of tiles on my kitchen floor (descriptive research based on factual information-gathering to answer a simple *what?* or *how many?* question). It would make this descriptive research more complex if you asked about the relationship of the number and kind of those tiles to my sense of satisfaction with my new kitchen floor (this research would be more interpretative and would rely upon relating perceptions and opinions to these facts about the tiles). The first would be relevant if someone was working out how many tiles would fit a particular space, a factually based piece of research which a simple equation should answer. The second piece of research constructs some new knowledge based on interpretation of relationships between things and people's views, so it would be relevant if we were enquiring about customer satisfaction, for instance. However, not very many people would be interested in either of these sets of research questions, perhaps only the people who sell the tiles, or my close friends. They are relevant to a point.

Questions

When considering relevance in a more complex manner, you need to think about the following – think now:

- Does it matter that this research takes place? And if so, why does It matter?
- What is its contribution to knowledge, understanding, development, change, and creativity?
- Why is it important to do it now? Why is it relevant to current issues, concerns and questions?
- Does it address particular concerns and needs?
- Does it fit in with my own personal agenda?
- Is it relevant to my interests?
- My work?
- To my development?
- To the benefit of the world, i.e. does it really matter?

Relevance also relates to the perceived real-world relationship of the subject. You might be carrying out a piece of research exploring housing policy in relation to single mothers to find out whether there are differences in the way they are treated in terms of housing policy compared with mothers in families with partners. You would need to know, if so, what the differences are in policy and practice in relation to issues of, for example, gender, marital status, numbers of children, income support and earning power, and other social issues. You might be asking these questions in order to feed into current thoughts about the relative equality and inequality of housing policies and practices for single mothers and this report or project could contribute towards decisions made at a local or national level. This would depend on where it went once you had finished it and who asked you to carry it out in the first place. Or it could inform your own practice if you are working in housing, or it could develop your thoughts and understanding about gender difference in policy and practice if you're working in social policy or women's studies. This is obviously relevant, as much social research is, to the real world.

If you are exploring the ways in which three Beat writers from the Beat counterculture of the 1950s, 1960s and 1970s offered a critique of the American way of life, then this piece of research towards an essay might look less socially relevant. It could, however, be relevant to your own interests in poetry and the engagement with social movements and pressure groups' philosophies and context. It could be that it is relevant in reopening contemporary literary discussions of the relationship between literature, in this case, poetry, and society, and that you are adding a fresh new view to ongoing thoughts about the relationships between literature and society.

Both projects are relevant in different ways and both make a contribution to existing and developing knowledge. One possibly has an immediately practical application, the other one is a new spin on established themes in a different context and advances knowledge and thinking.

Relevance also concerns a way of going about your research. There are chapters in this book about conducting a literature review, developing a research design, conducting research and analysing research data. One area of relevance relates to the choice of theories and critical reading from theorists and from both primary and secondary sources. Another is the choice, the methodology and the methods, appropriate choice of data collection, of analysis and of your interpretation of your findings, whether statistical, interview data, visual data, literary quotations or whatever your data happens to be. It is here that you probably first immerse yourself in a lot of reading, wide and deep, within which you locate your project. If it's a creative project, it is at this point that you immerse yourself in a mixture of reading and perhaps visual stimulation such as collections, TV footage, or fashion images or sounds. Gradually, as your research question takes shape you start to identify what's really relevant to this research and what might be less centrally relevant but might have informed your broader or deeper understanding, and what is not going to be directly related to the research at all in terms of its conduct – methods, vehicles, data analysis – or its outcomes.

Chapter 7 on the literature review and Chapter 14 on the discussion of analysing your findings focus further on these issues of relevance when considering stages of the development of your research design. We look there at the analogy of a piece of cake. Think of the whole field of reading or influences as the whole piece of cake, and what you are going to focus on and use, then your research as part of your slice of the cake so that you have a manageable, boundaried and do-able piece of research that you can explain and defend, and which does not try ot look at everything – however interesting everything is (because you will never be able to say anything in a focused fashion if you try and look at too much).

The same kind of selection process of what is relevant to your research question and your argument takes place when you look at all the reading you've done, all the data you collected, all these sketchbooks, all the statistics you've gathered and wonder 'what on earth do I do with all this data?' At this point, you also need to focus on what is relevant to your research question, your intended outcome, and to be ruthless with what you cut out and things which don't fit this research agenda and format. (However, you can save them 'for later research' in another file.)

The ways in which you critically review information and data used, choose theory to underpin the research questions you are asking, and select which elements of what you are discovering to focus on in your writing, are all guided by their *relevance*. This relevance is to your research question, contribution to knowledge in the field, the need for this piece of research, and your own interests at this point.

Resources

You need resources in order to carry out any piece of research. If you were working on the effectiveness of magnetic resonance imaging scanners, for instance, you would need access to an MRIS, which is a large piece of equipment, and the access or otherwise to this piece of equipment would certainly affect your ability to carry out the research (or not). We are looking at social science, business, health, leisure, travel and tourism, humanities and arts research, which do not usually require access to large machinery. However, there are still many resource implications that you might need to take into account in carrying out your research.

If you are writing an essay on audience response to the TV series *Friends*, for instance, your resource needs would probably be access to TV and video-taped material of *Friends*; access to the Internet to engage with the chat rooms, audience response and social networking areas there in relation to *Friends*; access to a library and the Internet again for journals, including online journals, and books; access to photocopying and to computers for the word processing of your work and a printer to print off your final piece of work.

If you are carrying out research in the social sciences where, for example, you need to conduct a study of first-year students and their engagement with the induction process at University, you would need fewer hardware resources, similar access to the Internet and the library, but you will also need access to a sample of students and perhaps also staff. Issues of ethics, i.e. participant consent, confidentiality ethics and legal issues, might also need to be taken into consideration and you might require some support with this. Paper-based participant consent forms would also be needed.

Whatever the size and shape of your research to whatever ends, there will be resource needs. One of these is always time. You will need to consider how much time it will take to conduct research. Do look at Chapter 16 on time management. You will need physical resources such as a library, photocopying, Internet; financial resources such as travel funding, for example, to visit museums; and you will need access to the sample and to the data. These are major resources without which you might have nothing to write about.

One resource question you might ask is how you gain access to your sample. You need to be well placed to gain access, for example, to religious schools if they are what you're studying, or the Victoria and Albert Museum fashion collection if that's what you're studying. One will require probably a letter from your tutor to the V&A (not a very big job), while the other one could involve a great deal of time spent working with the religious schools so that they see that you are acceptable and will not disrupt their daily practices and can be trusted to represent them fairly. Both of these forms of research involve people as a resource, ethics and confidentiality. See Chapter 17 concerning ethics.

Your biggest resource of course is yourself. Do you have the energy, the stamina, the money, the time, and the resilience to carry out a piece of research? Don't set yourself such a big piece of research, for whatever assignment or dissertation, that it would be unmanageable and cause you a lot of stress. Do be careful of your health. Sleep, eat, take exercise, ensure you have a good social life, as well as carrying out research. Leave yourself enough time to do the research and to write up the piece of work.

Questions

What resources will you need?

- Time?
- Space?
- Funding?
- Samples?
- Computers?
- Any special technology?
- Any special technology packages?
- Letters of recommendation?
- Other support from other people?
- Other resources?

Originality

Originality is to some extent the aim of all research. Your research needs to be original enough without having to totally change the face of human knowledge. Scientific experimental research relies on the repetition of experiments to ensure that results are identical and therefore as reliable and generalisable as they can be. Research which uses social science, humanities and arts practices, however, is less likely to produce studies which can be replicable in this manner because they deal with human subjects and develop knowledge through interpretation. In a sense, then, it is always fairly original. When you identify a gap in knowledge, a problem that needs addressing, or a question you would like to answer, you do need to make sure you are doing more than just repeating what has been done before, although it will always be a little different from what has gone before because the context will be different. If you are looking at human interactions or working with human subjects, your work is always going to be relatively original because you have identified a need for research at this time and place and with this group of people, this human interaction, this state of affairs, this set of documents in relation to these views. The sample you use, the population, will always be different in some respects from those used by previous research even if you ask the same questions, use the same survey or interview instrument. It is the *variation* in what you're doing from previous research and the *variation* in what you discover which would be original in these instances.

For example, if you are asking questions about the underachievement of young men in college, there will be a wealth of similar studies (but not about the young men you are studying, in the context in which you are studying them) so you will need to consider which part of the topic is particularly new to you. It might be the context your work is conducted in. For example, if most work is being conducted in the industrial North of England then your work on young men from refugee backgrounds in Hastings would use many of the same questions and underpinning theories but would probably produce some variance in the reasons for their underachievement. Or it might be that you're looking at a slightly different population; young white male middle-class students as opposed to Afro-Caribbean students. As long as there is an element of originality, you won't be completely repeating some work and you can refer to and build on previous work and so make a contribution to knowledge.

You might be using a new method to investigate. So if, previously, people might have used documentary evidence in order to research the way businesses manage their pension schemes, you might decide to interview people who have added extra amounts to their pension schemes in practice, and explore their hopes and concerns in relation to their pension. You would be looking at issues to do with pension schemes but using a different method (perceptions and behaviours rather than paper-based practices).

You might carry out a new form of analysis on relatively familiar information. So you might compare or contrast it with other information, use different strategies to interpret it, and so on.

For example, a researcher exploring fashion students' use of a fashion exhibit at the Victoria and Albert Museum could go about this in several different ways. Other people are looking at students' use of collections to inspire their work, but if you as a researcher asked the students how they used collections to cause reflection, for example, or how they directly translated them into a creative product, you would be using the same theories and context but asking different questions. You can also/alternatively be creative in your own right and perhaps study your own responses to such sources of inspiration (cf. the Centre for Excellence in Teaching and Learning through Design (CETLD)-funded Sources of Inspiration project at the University of Brighton).

So, your originality might be in the topic, your context, your methods, your method of analysis, your findings, your contribution to knowledge, or your mode of presentation such as a creative product as opposed to a report. It is important to indicate what is new and original and to recognise that it does not have to be earth shatteringly original.

Questions

- How original is your work?
- In what way is it original?
- New ideas?
- New context?
- New sample?
- New combination of subjects?
- New combination of samples?
- New approach?
- New mode of interpretation?
- For new outcomes?

Accuracy

Accuracy is important in all research because otherwise, whatever you argue from it and whatever arguments you build upon it as a basis would be neither dependable nor trustworthy.

You need to be accurate in your account and recognition of what the research question, hypothesis or problem is before you undertake the research, and how your work contributes something new. You need to be as accurate and robust in the choice of your topic, the theory to underpin your conceptual framework, your framework of ideas, the theories you select to underpin and inform your understanding of what you are researching, your methodology and methods. This is so that you've got a strong approach and an appropriate way of asking your research question, testing your hypothesis or dealing with your research problem. You need to be very accurate in the setting up of research in practice. This could include locating information, devising a survey, coding up an interview schedule, taking and charting the photographs that will lead to your own piece of visual research, or logging information about the episodes you are researching of the TV series you've been watching (depending on your research topic). You need to be absolutely accurate in labelling, dating and cataloguing all your data. And you need to be accurate in the data entry, analysis and interpretation if you are using statistics, observation, image, discourse or any other sources for your research. You need to be as accurate and trustworthy as you can in your research and to indicate the limitations of your work, i.e. what limits the asking of the questions, or the sample, or the processes so that it is clear what the results cannot claim to know or prove.

In social science research, this would mean identifying that, for example, the people whose practices you are researching will differ from any other sample anyone else might use. A limitation would be that you cannot generalise from what you have discovered, so that while the results and findings could be used to inform someone else's research, they cannot be seen as identical because no other research would exactly replicate your own, as human actions are never identical, and neither are people.

Another limitation might be the time, so you could say, to be perfectly accurate, that you could have gathered more data on museums, found more creative sketchbooks or analysed episodes of *Friends* more deeply – investigated the circumstances around which audience figures were produced or propaganda delivered – depending on what you were researching at that time and what prevented you from carrying out any more research than you did. Whatever the limitations, as a researcher you still have to be sure that you've taken all the precautions you can so that what you are reporting and the basis upon which you are interpreting the findings from your research are as accurate as you can make them. You need to be able to show that you have taken every care to check your sources and recordings and set up robust analysis practices where appropriate. You have to be certain that carrying out the process of the research hasn't distorted or damaged the data and therefore what you can say about it.

As Martyn Hammersley (1987) points out, some of the key terms in testing the accuracy of research involve the words 'reliability' and 'validity', which are sometimes used erroneously in much research literature as though they were interchangeable.

Reliability depends on your research design and is possible in both scientific and social science research. A piece of quantitative research which is experimental in mode, repeated many times to ensure absolute accuracy so that the same results are obtained under the same conditions each time, is considered to be reliable. We hope that a similar accuracy and reliability can underpin the social sciences, humanities and other areas of research when we use quantitative methods such as surveys. But it is not so easy to ensure this because if you are using human subjects, they vary, their experiences and circumstances vary and so do the social contexts in which you are conducting the research. You cannot replicate the outcomes of this research with people either exactly or repeatedly. If you set up what seem to be situations to produce artwork as research, results will also differ because of the creative process, which effects (causes) and affects (influences) change. So, reliability in social science and related research must rely on the rigour of 'the methods of data collection and the concern that they should be consistent and not distort the findings. Generally it entails an evaluation of methods and techniques used to collect the data' (Denscombe, 2002, p. 100). If you want to claim reliability and generalisability (in other words, your research can be generalised to other research, because others can use this method with similar subjects in similar circumstances and gain similar enough results), you would need to be very specific in your methods. You would probably use a large-scale survey, carefully tested to ensure that the questions cannot be misunderstood, can effectively ask exactly what you are seeking, can be answered without error, and can produce statistically significant results. The Household Census in the UK is an example of such a large-scale survey with tested questions, delivered to millions of homes. A recent survey with which I was involved was completed by 400 students. We feel we can argue that it is reliable because of its design, testing and sample.

Design and testing – it was tried and tested, piloted, analysed, improved using rigorous tests on the questions.

Sample – it was completed by large (400) numbers of similar students (postgraduates studying for PhDs) from the same kind of context (UK universities).

Validity concerns a kind of internal coherence and considers the following: Have you asked the right research questions? Do you have the right research design (methodology, and methods) to ask your research questions? Have you asked the right questions of your data and been rigorous in theorising what you ask, i.e. relating it to the underpinning theories of your work, and finding patterns or variation in the data which you are then able to interpret in relation to your research question? And have you interpreted your findings from your data appropriately, making claims based on evidence?

Is the piece internally coherent and are the findings you've drawn appropriate to the research? This makes it valid. Although what it finds cannot be reliable and generalisable, the research design and methods are internally coherent and so the research is valid. You can draw valid conclusions and others can trust what you have found out. If they want to carry out similar research, they need to realise that identical results cannot be guaranteed, but that your research can inform their work, and results might be quite similar if the design, sample and context are similar.

You would argue validity in terms of an artistic product by ensuring that you have explained why you used the practices you did in order to investigate or ask the question that is answered in the artwork or musical piece.

Questions

- How can you ensure accuracy in your work?
- Is it robust in its design?
- Is it well planned and appropriate in its data gathering and analysis?
- Is it reliable?
- Is it valid?
- Is it generalisable?

Accountability

This section considers issues to do with the credibility and expressiveness of the research and the ways in which decisions, strategies, method and analysis have been justified so that an evaluation of the conclusions can be drawn which ensures they are trustworthy.

Reports of research need to contain enough information to make some kind of judgement about their trustworthiness, their credibility and the importance of their contribution as well as about the safety and rigour of the methods which underpin their findings and claims.

Denscombe (2002) considers accountability to be a kind of assurance of the value and the robustness of the research design, methods and analysis in practice. He talks about issues to do with authenticity, verification, and reliability. This is not about how account-able it is to the participants, for instance, although that should be important also; it's more an issue of the quality of the actual research in terms of the design and analysis because of the robustness and trustworthiness of the research. Accountability relies on the consideration of an audit trail to check the research results.

In order to ensure the robustness and accountability of your research, you need to consider:

- the question, hypothesis, or problem;
- the underpinning theories as explored in the literature review or theoretical perspectives;
- the research design itself and the appropriateness of the methodology and methods being used;
- the data – how well it has been collected, labelled and stored;
- the first review and analysis of the data, which starts to identify some themes, patterns and ideas;
- any reports before the end of the project;
- notes on the research process and background materials.

There is also the issue of matching the claims made in the interpretation of the find-ings and conclusions against the actual evidence provided. The mapping between these two is an issue of accountability and quality.

These aspects of undertaking research are each considered in the chapters following.

Generalisations

An important reason to carry out research is that you can suggest that there are patterns of behaviour or of results that you have discovered. In research based on social science practices, where knowledge is constructed in a social context which differs in each instance, it is not possible to directly generalise from one piece of research to another and it's important in your work that you acknowledge that as a limitation. However, though you cannot completely replicate the situation and the sample with which you conducted your own research, so that the research can be generalisable, it should be possible that others who wish to ask similar or the same questions of similar samples in a similar context feel that there will be some similarity or correlation between your findings and theirs even though they will not be identical.

Objectivity

Objectivity is sought by researchers because we do not want to contaminate our research findings with our opinions and personal feelings, our subjectivity. It is not possible to completely remove the human elements from research based in the social sciences, arts, humanities or related subjects, and indeed, often it is those very human interactions and interpretations that we are seeking in the first place. However, we do not want to tamper with the information and misrepresent the data and findings, so we seek objectivity in our research processes and acknowledge any effects of our own subject position.

This is a very vexed area. Scientists might claim that because they are not dealing with human subjects and they do not bring their own personal opinions into the research, then their work is entirely objective. However, it can be argued that what has been chosen to be researched in the first place is dependent upon the opinion, historical context, needs of the moment. The data is collected rigorously and interpreted without the involvement of personal opinion. The objectivity lies in such an instance in the conduct of the research and the interpretation of the data. It can be argued that social science, humanities and arts research are never truly objective because what is acknowledged is that there is a human interaction in a social context taking place which affects the questions being asked, the data being gathered and interpretation of that data.

To be really subjective means to involve your own opinions and your own interpretations, probably against what is being shown to you by the data. It's because of this contamination of data and interpretation by the subjective, the personal, in the interpretations of an individual or group carrying out the research that subjectivity is seen to be such a bad thing. It is, however, in some measure always unavoidable. Some research in business and other areas, for example, uses the self as a case study, and/or uses reflective journalling accompanying longer pieces of research as part of the findings. In feminist research, the effects of the researcher's experience, gender and position are often openly taken into account and discussed, or made part of or even the subject of the research itself. In your research, you need to acknowledge your own context, involvement, and the extent to which subjectivity could affect your questions, methods, analysis and interpretations. You need to make sure you acknowledge the ways in which your own experience and position could affect your research, and ensure that your own subjectivity, opinion, perceptions or experiences do not alter, or misinterpret the data. You must be rigorous in collecting and analysing the data, so that interpretation can be trustworthy, valid or reliable depending on the design, and useful to other people.

We want research which provides a fair and balanced picture, detached in terms of discovering the truth, and open-minded.

There could be other issues about objectivity or bias in practitioner-based professional research where you might be carrying out research in your job or a business context, or when research is sponsored by, for example, your manager or a funding body. If they want your findings to uphold, emphasise, bolster up some kind of decision already made, you would need to protect the rigour of your work, and not be influenced in your findings by the results they want. Your results and findings need to be unbiased and pure, so that those commissioning a report can base their decisions upon them and others can also make use of them.

It is also important in research to consider alternative interpretations which might be culturally conditioned and to consider different points of view.

You need to take into account your own background, and the context or background of those who answer the questions and those who are receiving the research findings, in order to work out how your work might be received and how it might be acted on. All of this might look as though it is peripheral to the research itself but in fact it can enable and allow the research to be heard and acted on, or silence, condition, and constrain it.

Ethics

We have a whole chapter (Chapter 17) on ethics. Ensure that anybody who is participating in the research has been given full information about it and how the data and findings arising from the research will be used and where. Any participants should be asked to give their informed consent to take part. If they cannot give this informed consent because of their age or level of ability then it's important that someone who can give it for them is consulted. Ethics in practice ensures confidentiality, the preservation of the rights of those involved in the research, and also issues to do with access to information.

Proof

One of my key maxims in research is that there should be no claim without evidence or proof and that it is pointless to use any kind of evidence unless you have attached a claim to it, in other words made plain where it fits into your argument.

Denscombe's issues about proof cover questions such as:

- How can you prove you're right?
- How can you ensure your explanations are better than 'dogma or common sense'? (p. 195)

In order to prove your research findings, your research design has to be watertight and appropriate to the question that you're asking, the problem you are considering or the hypothesis you are proving/disproving. You need to have thought about alternative theories, alternative methodologies and alternative methods and to be able to argue about why you've chosen the ones you have. You need to recognise the limitations of your own study in terms of access, availability, research practices, and the possibility of interpreting data. You need to be able to argue that the conclusions you've drawn are the best that can be drawn based on the evidence in this context, underpinned by these theories in relation to this research design.

All of these aspects of the research process aim to make it fit for your purposes, so others can access and make use of your findings, and you make a contribution to knowledge.

Critical

Carrying out research involves taking a critical approach. Nothing is taken for granted. Everything is questioned. This does not mean that everything is criticised. What it means is that statements of value, interpretations of findings, arguments and the evidence of others are all questioned and need proof before they can be accepted as truths. Take an example in the literature review. Here you consider the ideas and arguments of the theorists and other researchers, critics and writers who have used theory in their own work to argue the case, present a point of view subject to questioning, or made a critical appraisal. You make sure that their ideas and arguments are clear, backed up by evidence. Developing a critical approach also involves looking at different points of view and different arguments, bringing these into dialogue with your own work. Look at Chapter 2 and the discussion of critical thinking.

Conceptual

Your work as a researcher will involve a range of ideas, activities and approaches, some of which are very 'busy' such as the gathering of data, locating of documents, cataloguing and filing of results, identification of patterns and thematic analysis. But all of this is underpinned by the conceptual work that you are also doing, starting right at the beginning and running throughout your research. This involves working at the level of concepts, of theory and of ideas, questioning what is implied in words and taken for granted. Concepts and assumptions should be unpicked in order to be problematised and theorised, to deepen our understanding, the gaining of new knowledge. Problematising involves questioning, unpicking, rather than assuming we understand a term, or a concept. Being conceptual in research involves questioning, thinking about and putting into action or operationalising ideas, concepts, values, perceptions and interpretations.

When you begin to undertake research you will need to find out what the main concepts or ideas are with which you are dealing and ask questions about them. If you are researching an issue which involves the concept of 'value for money', for example, you will need to explore what this concept means in different or changing economic contexts. Something which seems to be value for money in one economic context might seem overpriced in another; what you can sell goods for changes in relation to time, place, the cost of production, and market forces, which all affect what people will pay for them and what seems value for money. Value for money is therefore variable, it's not a fixed fact.

A concept that a student working in cultural studies might question, for example, is that of 'the monstrous'. We probably think we know what monsters would be like and consider the creature that Dr Frankenstein put together in Mary Shelley's novel of the same name to be a monster. But if we are going to use this concept in research and writing about monsters in film and text, we will need to ask what makes something a monster, why it is, sometimes, that creatures including humans are portrayed as monstrous. Asking these questions will cause us to use theories which derive from psychoanalysis, cultural studies, gender studies and a range of other areas which combine into the notion of the 'abject', or that which is rejected because it is seen as disgusting. Through this kind of problematising what seems to be a simple concept, we discover that society itself defines what is monstrous and possibly creates monsters, that is, the application of the term varies. In the films and texts we are investigating, that kind of creation of the monstrous is dramatised and expressed. We can then question why these monsters are created, and what they might represent.

Thinking, understanding and threshold concepts

We have unpicked and so can now question and use the concept of the monstrous, but there is something else going on here in the level of the thinking and learning activities expected of you at degree level. What is involved in this particular discussion is what Meyer and Land (2006) call a 'threshold concept'. A threshold concept affects the level of your thinking and so your understanding and construction of knowledge. It is an essential concept which needs to be understood in order that the discipline (cultural studies, in this example) can be understood and worked with. Threshold concepts are difficult to understand, and change your perceptions of the subject, the world and the self. They are both 'troublesome', and 'transformational'. In literature, art and the media, the concept of *representation* is one of the threshold concepts. Character, place, image, event are not merely records of the real world but stand for something other than they seem to be. They represent, symbolise, suggest values, interpretations, something in addition to the real thing. A monster in a film is not merely there to frighten the viewer; it represents ways in which the society, the film maker, the audience construct what they are disgusted by and frightened of.

In your research, you will also need to develop a conceptual framework or framework of concepts and the ideas which underpin a research project. Do look at Chapter 5 for further ideas on this. You will discover that your tutor or supervisor expects you to deal with the ideas or concepts throughout your piece of research and occasionally might put in comments on your work to encourage or nudge you to conceptualise and theorise. They might ask questions such as:

'and so what does this mean?',

'how does this add to our understanding?',

'please develop these ideas to move you on from merely detailing the factual to ensuring that you are using theory and ideas'.

Any conclusions you draw in your research will also need to use ideas and concepts and not merely state the facts found.

Creative

In a sense, all good research is in some ways creative because it is producing new knowledge, new interpretations, new views. Seeing things anew and creating new solutions to old problems are part of your approach, as researcher, to asking your original question, conducting your research and then interpreting your findings. However, if you are conducting creative research itself then you will probably also end up with a creative product such as an art work, creative writing, or a piece of music. How people become creative and how what we produce can be seen as creative are the subject of many books. It can be argued that everyone is in some ways creative and what we need to do is to harness and nurture this creativity, part of which can be explored and expressed through research.

Are you combining ideas or the questions you are asking across established areas of knowledge in order to produce something new? Then you are being creative.

If you are responding to a range of influences such as a museum collection, words overheard on the subway, images, diaries, buildings, and using these as notes, commenting and building on them, bringing them together and turning them into something else affected by your own thoughts, arguments and imagination, then you are being creative in the more artistic sense.

Those conducting creative research would aim to recognise where the creativity is a product as well as a process. You need to be able to articulate what this process is, this identifying, gathering together and fusing into something new, and to be able to reflect on how you went about this, as well as what it might mean or say about your own arguments, ideas, views and processes.

Questions

How:

- critical
- conceptual
- and creative

is your work? And in what ways?

Summary

In this chapter we have considered:

- A range of values, behaviours, processes, and even some of the products of research and ways we might study them.
- The essentials of good research.

Further reading

Denscombe, M. (2002) *Ground Rules for Good Research* (Buckingham: Open University Press).

Hammersley, M. (1987) 'Some Notes on the Terms "Validity" and "Reliability" ', *British Educational Research Journal*, 13(1), pp. 73–81.

Meyer, E. and Land, R. (2006) *Overcoming Barriers to Student Understanding: Threshold Concepts and Troublesome Knowledge* (London: Routledge Falmer).

4 Carrying Out Research for a Project or Dissertation

This chapter will consider:

▶ focusing on research questions and areas of interest;
▶ moving from topic to title;
▶ research approaches: which are yours?

Research is an everyday part of all your work at university whether reading round for a lecture or seminar, placement or fieldwork, or researching a topic or question for an assignment.

You are expected to carry out research for a variety of assignments and also to inform your study more generally. Towards the end of your second year or in your third year you will normally be expected to carry out a longer, more complex project or dissertation which requires you to develop and use more complex and thorough research skills, over time. This research could involve developing and engaging with a project brief, finding out the answer to an exploratory question, collecting evidence and analysing it, and then making recommendations. Or it could be for a dissertation and involve in-depth research using primary and secondary sources, fieldwork, perhaps your own professional practice, perhaps the production of a creative piece. Some dissertations and projects combine across subject areas, where reading your way into parts of a discipline new to you will be necessary. Some dissertations or project reports involve engagement in a placement. In these cases, the report writes up process, experience and the research undertaken.

For these longer pieces of research, you need to build on the good research habits you have developed so far in shorter work, and to be able to work longer, in more depth, conceptually, critically and creatively, engaging with and using more or more complex theory. Such larger, longer pieces of work are not only more time consuming, often spread out over a year or more, but also more demanding in terms of your complex thinking. They will really help you to develop useful research skills and a thorough exploration of a discussion or an area of interest in your specialism. The report or dissertation will be evidence of these skills.

Focusing on research questions – areas of interest

From topic to title

Start with an area of research and a real interest. This is a long-term project which could last for up to or over a year and you will need to pick something both 'meaty' or complex enough and which addresses a 'gap' in knowledge; in other words, it is an area not already fully covered by other people in their work, and is more than merely descriptive: it asks questions and problematises some given beliefs.

- What interests you?

Your research question needs to be of interest to you and to others. In a long-term project, interest sustains enthusiasm and hard work and if it is also of interest to others this could be useful to you in the future. It could lead to a job and it could persuade people that you are well informed about your specialisms.

- What is the current state of research and discussion in this field/area? What are the key debates and issues? What does the literature say?

Sometimes it seems that there is absolutely no information on the area in which you are interested, and that no one has written on the area in which you wish to research. This is actually unlikely. While it is important that you identify an issue, angle or area which is under-researched, there will be researchers who have gone before you and looked at similar issues or questions, maybe in different contexts and from different angles, or maybe not directly. There will be theorists and critics, experts and other researchers who will have written about similar themes, used similar theories or methods, approached similar questions perhaps from different angles. You need to establish both that your work contributes to these ongoing discoveries and debates so you can enter the dialogue and contribute to the arguments about them, and that you have found a 'gap', an area or angle which has not yet been directly or fully researched. This makes your work part of the ongoing discussion and also original enough in its contribution.

- Why is it topical?

Even if the area you are researching is ancient history there needs to be a reason why you and others might want to look at this anew, or for the first time in the light of other developments and interests. Examiners will also want to know why your work is topical.

- Hypothesis or research question?
    - Are you going to develop a hypothesis which you will be testing?
    - Or will you be asking a research question?

If you are undertaking scientific or science-related, social science or clinical health research you might well be testing a hypothesis, an assumption which needs to be tested rigorously and proved or disproved. Testing, experimentation and large-scale surveys are often used in such research designs which are based on a positivist research paradigm. An hypothesis is an assumption, a suggestion, a belief which can be tested through empirical (real-world) research. Testing a hypothesis involves methodology and methods so that the hypothesis can be tested through an experiment or other way of gathering data which is factual and reliable. 'Reliable' is a term which means that other people would come to the same conclusions if they set out to test this hypothesis, ask these questions, in this context and in this way. It means the research has been rigorously tested many times and so the research design and processes are replicable (others can replicate or reproduce your findings under the same conditions) and generalisable (your findings can be generalised to the work of others). It holds true (will always produce the same results).

Most social science, non-clinical health, business, humanities and arts research is more likely to be developing research questions in a post-positivist or interpretivist paradigm. **Research questions** problematise accepted versions of events or situations, explore and question relationships between **variables** which are the elements of the research context, such as characteristics of the population (for example, variables of age and gender) or a broader context (for example, variables of time and location). They are based on the understanding that human interactions cannot be proven as such, or accurately measured, and that we interpret reality and information rather than fixing and measuring facts. (See Chapter 12 for further exploration.)

A research question is a question which causes you to find out more about an area of interest, an idea, what current arguments are, how established beliefs relate to reality, how a problem can be identified and dealt with, how things work in the world. Asking a research question involves think about methodology and methods, as well as about your discipline or subject area. How would asking your research question and carrying out research contribute to debates about it in the field and contribute to knowledge?

The acquisition and analysis of varieties of data are explored in Chapter 1, and the ways in which hypotheses or research questions grow from worldviews and research paradigms are explored in Chapter 5.

It is important to identify the difference your research will make to ongoing academic discussion, debates about knowledge construction and interests, and depths of understanding. Maybe it is a new view, a new field, a new question?

You need to be aware of where your work will fit in and advance discussion and understanding, which gaps in knowledge your work will fill, the importance of filling those gaps, and your unique contribution to academic and related debates.

- Why is it worth asking this question?

How up to date is your area of work? Why does answering your question matter? Topicality, significance and your enthusiasm are all important. How does addressing your question contribute to humankind and the future of knowledge development? Answering this helps maintain your enthusiasm, gives you a vision and convinces others the research is worthwhile.

Boundaries and gaps

As you develop your research area and question, you need to define the **gap** in knowledge which your work will fill and the **boundaries** to your work.

It might help to do a mind map or a visual diagram which identifies (i) the whole possible field of study, and (ii) the area in which your work will fit, the gaps it will fill. Here is an example.

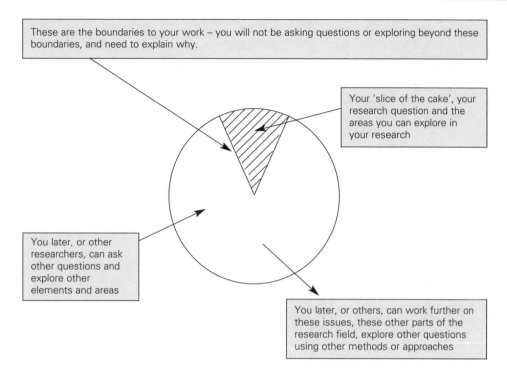

These are the boundaries to your work – you will not be asking questions or exploring beyond these boundaries, and need to explain why.

Your 'slice of the cake', your research question and the areas you can explore in your research

You later, or other researchers, can ask other questions and explore other elements and areas

You later, or others, can work further on these issues, these other parts of the research field, explore other questions using other methods or approaches

Figure 4.1   This is the 'whole cake'

Think about your whole field and all the questions you can ask of it as a 'whole cake', and the part you are going to work on, the do-able, manageable piece of research for your project or dissertation, as if it were a 'slice of cake' (see Figure 4.1).

You need:

- to open your question up more in order to ask it;
- to identify the concepts or key ideas or terms that you are using – this is called 'operationalising the concept', which involves finding the important concepts underpinning your work, then asking questions about them, putting them into action;
- to consider the theorists whose work underpins the way in which you can theorise and so understand more fully both your question and the kind of information and interpretation of the data and findings, the information and issues that your research will produce;
- to identify what sources you can use: both **primary** – immediate, from the time and place under research, exactly what is being researched, such as people, archives, documents, media footage, objects – and **secondary** – others commenting upon these sources in relation to ideas and questions and arguments (see Chapter 9 on sources).

> ### Example
>
> A student of history and media studies wants to explore 'How, why and in what ways did the representations of war in London change during the London Blitz?' They find other people's research in the different subject areas of history and media, and where they intersect, and then look in the thematic areas of:
>
> - The London Blitz – historical details, dates and events
> - War imaging – themes and topics used in representing war
> - The role of the media – identifying and representing values, propaganda, changes in media representation of war at different stages in a war.
>
> See Figure 4.2 for a mind map.

Primary sources used could be:

newspapers,
newsreel footage.

Theories would include those on media and representation more broadly (such as those of Marshall McLuhan).

Narrowing it down to focus the theories on the sources, they would be looking at history reporting; more specifically, war reporting; then very specifically, media coverage and change in reporting the Blitz. They would be using **secondary sources** in terms of other critics' and historians' comments on the Blitz, such as the book *Our Longest Days* by the writers of the Mass Observation.

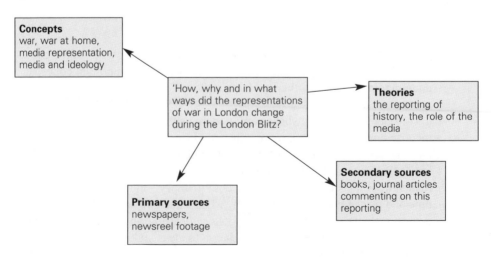

Figure 4.2

When someone else, an examiner perhaps, or the reader of your book (!) looks at your research question, they will probably think of interpreting it according to their own interests and discipline area, and with the methodology and the methods which they are used to. They might well think of asking it in ways that differ a great deal from those you intend to use. Bear this in mind as you refine your question and use questions, and develop the research methodology and design which will enable you to address the question – you will need to defend and explain these in your thesis or dissertation, and understanding that there are many different ways of approaching a question helps you to appreciate the best ways for you in your research. See below for some thoughts about the kind of research you might be undertaking.

What kind of research is yours going to be?

You need to think about the kind or kinds of research you will carry out, what your research approaches are going to be, before finally deciding on your methodology and methods. Some of this will depend, as does the choice of methodology, on the way you see the world – as problems filled with facts, testable, or to be interpreted differently by different people, explored, responded to with an individualistic or social response, a creative response, and so on. Do please look at some of the views and approaches below. Your research in this instance might well be a combination of some of these. If it is merely *descriptive*, however, it will not be at the right level for your degree because in effect the question it would be asking would just be of factual record without conceptualising or problematising – it could add to the sum of knowledge but it would not really expand our understanding; it would not be conceptualised. There is a deal of description in the early stages of research during note taking, investigating and collecting data and even in writing up, but your work will need to move beyond this eventually to be of degree level.

Research approaches: Which are yours?

- Descriptive?
- Exploratory?
- Predictive?
- Explanatory?
- Theoretical?
- Empirical?
- Experimental?

You do need to determine what your research approaches are, and your research could be a combination of some of these.

Read on through the following descriptions and see if you can define your research type(s). What kind of research is yours? It will probably be a mixture of two or more of the following kinds of research.

Descriptive research

Descriptive research aims to find out more about a phenomenon and to capture it with detailed information. It tends to produce factual detail and to answer the question 'what?'

Often the capturing and description of information is only true for that moment in time, but it still helps us to understand and know more about the phenomenon. The description might have to be repeated several times and then further exploratory questions asked about the reasons for its change or stability. An example of (completed) descriptive research might be:

> *Rehabilitation of offenders*:
>
> In 2007 the Government released details of the number of offenders who re-offended in the first year following their release. 45% of offenders were found to re-offend within the first two years of release.

Clearly this description would have to be repeated, probably yearly, so that stability or change could be noted.

A piece of descriptive research is often the first stage in more complex research which then goes on to ask questions about why? So what? To what effect? How can this be interpreted in a specific context of change? It tells us something about the effectiveness of the system of prisons and the likelihood of offenders re-offending. The research which led to the data collection and publication was not aimed at asking 'why?' questions but 'what?' questions, and so these tables and results tell us about a situation, but not its causes. This data does not tell us anything about why offenders re-offend. What is going on in the prison system, what happens to support them upon release, would have to be discovered using other questions and something as complex as this would be the basis for more then merely descriptive research, it would also have to look at 'why' questions. This questioning would lead us into exploratory research, which often goes alongside descriptive research.

Descriptive research also often contributes to **evaluative research**, which is designed to deal with complex social and cultural issues and to go beyond the collection of facts. The outcomes of evaluation do not try to capture and describe the real world as it is (if that is possible) but aim instead to produce interpretations and constructions that place value on views, which would differ in different contexts. Education studies use evaluative research, for example, to find out students' responses to different learning experiences, or to contexts. Walliman (2001, pp. 94–5) talks of two sorts of evaluative research. One is *systems analysis*, which explains systems to understand complicated situations and often uses models and diagrams to do so and to see how a project, system, or programme is working. The other is *responsive*, which seeks people's feelings and responses to an event, situation, or development.

Exploratory research

Exploratory research asks both 'what?' and 'why?' questions. It begins with the factual question: 'Does X happen?' and then moves on to consider reasons for this, situations, contexts, implications; it asks, for instance, 'Why does X happen?' and sets out, using a variety of methods, to discover whether what is in question is true or not. It can be used to explore both simple and sometimes also complex issues. Sometimes what seem to be simple issues turn out to be complex because a seemingly straightforward question such as:

> Do parents take their children to school on foot more often or more commonly than they take them by car?

has many underlying subsidiary questions and complex causes.

This might seem a straightforward question, but it is quite complex. Other factors than choice are involved and these factors affect or bias any other questions you could ask or experiments you might carry out to explore your research question. For example, in this instance, the reason for taking children to school on foot could be related to how close the school is to the homes of most of the people who use it, or how dangerous the area is or what social class the people using the school are – or any combination of these issues and more. An exploratory study which could gather information about these variables (and others) would be both more interesting and more useful for anyone making decisions or coming to conclusions.

Exploratory research is used when we are looking for new knowledge or we are trying to determine reasons for certain behaviours. It can be aided by explanatory research, which sets out to explain how, why, to what effect, and so on.

Predictive research

Predictive research asks 'what if?' questions and looks often at the relationships between several variables, trying to predict an answer or outcome. It usually works with a hypothesis – or an assumption – based on data already collected and considered; this is based on knowledge and its interpretation using ideas and theories, and often it is also based on past experience. You start with a hypothesis –

> I suggest that . . . if this happens then that is likely to happen –

or

> îf this is the case, if this is the situation, then these kinds of results or events might follow.

Predictive research is based on probability (or the likelihood of something being the case or happening).

For instance, predictive research can be used to predict the likelihood on a Saturday night in the middle of a city that there will be some people drinking too much and causing fights. It is based on predictions which grow out of repeated actions and events that have been studied, and a mixture of experience and research by others. Predictive research takes several variables into account. For example, as above, the relationship between Saturday night when people tend to go out, public houses being open and serving drinks, people drinking too much being on the increase, alcohol lowering self-control and often being present when people get involved in fights – all of these act as variables which all add up to a predictable result. If the prediction, in the event, was unfulfilled, other variables would have to be questioned.

Predictive research works by using knowledge gained from past research and events and is based on identification of relationships between variables, so changing one or more variables could, it is predicted, change the outcomes. You can then deduce the effect of those variable on the outcomes, to some extent.

Explanatory research

Explanatory research also asks 'why?' questions but asks 'how?', 'why not' and 'if so, what?' kinds of questions, seeking explanations for events and actions. It specifically seeks to look at the cause/effect relationships between two or more phenomena. It can be really helpful if your earlier descriptive and exploratory research has just produced some data and facts but no connections between events and causes or people and actions. Description and simple exploration might come up with a number of variables which confuse rather than clarify the assumptions and hypotheses. Explanatory research might, in the case of the prison re-offenders, compare different sets of variables to see what might be the really important variable. So it might ask about provision of education in prison and the connection between that provision and re-offence, or the provision of support schemes which help offenders to get jobs once they leave prison and the relationship between such schemes and the likelihood of re-offence. All of these variables such as education and job support are not present in every prison so if it was discovered that prisons which had both education and job schemes for prisoners immediately upon release had lower re-offence rates than those without such schemes and provision then you might be able to see an explanation for the difference in re-offence as lying in the variables of education and job support. The sets of variables need matching against each other before conclusions can begin to be drawn.

Such research, which involves taking several variables into consideration, might be carried out to answer questions about:

Why hoteliers in country X find they need to charge lower prices than those who operate in country Y, where there might be some political histories and issues about who travels and takes their holidays where, the cost of living and the costs of travel.

Or, for example,

Why with the government's drive for widening participation so that more working-class pupils can go to university, the increase in numbers at university has actually been among middle-class pupils, and whether this could in any way be related to the implementation of a fee structure which has meant not only that fees need to be paid for higher education but that they have grown over the past few years.

Asking research questions which take related variables into consideration could try to determine something rather more subtle than a description or a straightforward link between cause and effect. Clearly this kind of research could grow from and also cause social and political argument! But it is certainly fascinating and much more complex than merely stating something about numbers travelling where, or numbers re-offending. It starts to ask 'why?' 'what is involved?' questions. It can also lead into or relate to predictive research.

Theoretical research

It is perfectly acceptable to carry out a *theoretical* research project. A dissertation or thesis expanding and arguing about the different ideological constructions underlying our perceptions of, for instance, something as serious as the position of refugees, would produce several different angles and so, different theoretical perspectives, for example, being a refugee/the refugee problem is a social construct; it is due to political clashes and problems/defects; it is a choice of freedom from oppression, or could be to gain the bene-fits of a society which is not the one you were born into; the refugee problem is one which cannot be cleared up by social policies; it is a symptom of an uncaring global society; the refugee problem is humanitarian and needs dealing with in humanitarian ways.

You can engage with questions as theoretical and philosophical as the contested views about the existence of God, or arguments within different theorised approaches to learning. Each of these can be approached using different theoretical perspectives. With a *theoretical* piece of research you are involved in debating between theories, and discussing the different beliefs, views, arguments, rather than testing anything in the real world or asking people directly for their opinions.

Empirical research

Empirical research is research which is based on the belief that the world is knowable and can be discovered through the gathering of hard facts from experience, observation and experimentation. It is fact-based, evidence-based research rather than theorising. However, often part of what we do as researchers is first to gather empirical data from experiments or from observations during fieldwork, then to interpret these, using theory.

Experimental research

Experimental research seeks to control the objects of study and to answer the questions 'What if?' 'If . . . then . . . ?' It is based on cause and effect where one variable is changed and the effect is studied. Experimental research is based in a positivistic paradigm, i.e. on the belief that the world is knowable, fixable, testable and much of its effects are identi-fiable and provable. The research does not always have to take place in a laboratory. It follows scientific methods and has several stages: development of a hypothesis or prediction of cause and effect, the assumption that these are linked, which is to be tested; design of the experiment, which identifies the variables to be tested, controlled and measured. Pre-tests are usually then carried out and any problems which might be detected in the procedure are addressed, and the design altered accordingly. Then, the experiment is carried out under strict conditions with carefully managed procedures and rigorous application, data collection and management. Next, the data is analysed, processed, and interpreted so that the findings can be identified and evaluated. Experimental research is based on cause and effect, is reliable, and generalisable; in other words, it can be repeated under the same conditions to produce the same results, so much experimental research requires repeated experiments to test the reliability.

Activity

Take an area you might be interested in researching into, for example, the popularity of holiday resorts, binge drinking, international students studying in the UK, the relationship between religious differences and subject choice at university.

1   How can you 'operationalise the concept' – that is, break down the concepts of, for example, 'popularity' and 'the holiday resort' into fundamental issues and underlying elements and questions?
2   How can you ask research questions and take the different research approaches which would produce data about this area of interest? Where would you find the primary sources for your question about binge drinking? (Young people who acknowledge they do this?) And the secondary sources? (Journal articles and TV programmes on the phenomenon…)
3   What would be the questions you would ask? What variables might you take into account? How might you gather information and data using:

  - descriptive research
  - exploratory research
  - predictive research
  - explanatory research
  - theoretical research
  - action research?

Would you use a mixture of these? If so, why? If not, why not?

Which methods could you use?

Look at Chapter 8 on methodology and research methods.

The decisions about approaches depend on the kind of question you are asking, your belief about how knowledge is discovered or interpreted and created, and how you can ask your question. If you are asking a research question about the existence of God, for example, you would find it somewhat difficult to carry out *empirical research* that considered God's existence in the real world, or *experimental research* testing God's existence scientifically through repeated experiments. You could remain at the level of *theoretical research*, at first *describing* the different theories and then setting them in a debate, or you could decide to *explore* people's views and to use interviews to ask people about their belief systems, practices, the social role of religion.

If you were looking at the experiences of refugees you would be less likely to carry out *theoretical* research because it would be richer to find out about the refugees and their experiences first hand if you could. However, it would be inappropriate to carry out *experimental research* testing various changes in experience through repeated experiments, as this better suits elements, objects, and (this is contested) animals. Perhaps you might carry out a piece of empirical research in the real world, using field data about how refugees survive, their numbers, their views, views of others about them, social provision, prejudices, practical resolutions, politics. This might use observation, or interviews, or focus groups.

Summary

In this chapter we have considered:

- The early stages of establishing and carrying out research specifically for a dissertation or a project.
- Turning a fascination or area of interest into a research topic and title.
- Identifing the underlying ideas or concepts – and questioning or problematising them so you can research – in order to answer those questions, address the problems, test the hypothesis.
- Identifying a conceptual framework of these underlying ideas to drive your research.
- Identifying theories and theorists to help underpin your research, inform your thinking, ask your questions in a theorised way, inform analysis, interpretation, findings and conclusions.
- Considering which paradigms you are working within – positivist or post-positivist or interpretivist?
- Deciding what kind of research it is – experimental, descriptive, exploratory etc.
- What questions you might ask?
- How you will ask your research questions, or test your hypothesis.
- How you will gather information and data when using different kinds of research approaches.

Further reading

Bell, J. (1998) *Doing Your Research Project* (Buckingham: Open University Press).

Cormack, D. F. S. (1991) *The Research Process in Nursing*, 2nd edn (Oxford: Blackwell Scientific).

Koa Wing, Sandra (2008) *Our Longest Days: A People's History of the Second World War* (London: Profile Books).

Walliman, N. (2001) *Your Research Project* (London: Sage).

5 Research Paradigms, Theorising and Conceptual Frameworks

Your research grows out of how you see the world, believe knowledge is revealed or constructed, and how you can structure your approach to making sense of that knowledge. As you develop your research, this involves research paradigms, theory, and constructing a conceptual framework. In this chapter we are looking at research paradigms based on how you see the world and what knowledge is believed to be, how it is discovered or created. We are also looking at how you structure your understanding of that knowledge, the role of the theory you use to select, structure and make sense of your research.

The theories you are likely to use in your work will spring from a mixture of your own worldview and sense of yourself in the world (ontology); ways in which you believe that knowledge is constructed or discovered (epistemology) and the discipline within which your research is being undertaken, since disciplines have their own ways of asking their own questions about the world, and interpreting what is discovered or created (see Figure 5.1).

Ontology

Ontology is the theory of being and existence, your worldview, and your sense of yourself in the world, how you and other living things exist in the world. What you believe is out there in the world and how you can relate to it are affected by your ontological position.

Epistemology

Epistemology is knowledge, what can be known, and the construction of knowledge. Ontology and epistemology underlie the research paradigms which inform your research, and the theory you use to structure, make sense of, the knowledge which is revealed (positivistic research paradigm – knowledge exists to be discovered and revealed) or constructed and interpreted (post-positivistic, or interpretivist research

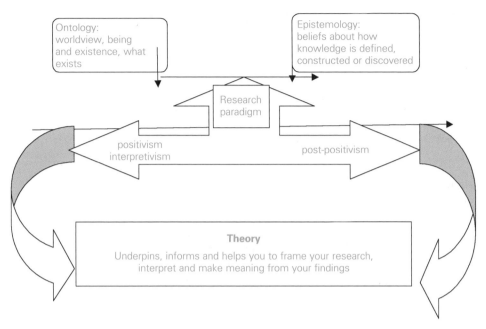

Figure 5.1

paradigm). From the basis in these research paradigms, you identify the appropriate theories to help you to manage, structure, and carry out your research either to test your hypothesis (natural sciences, some social sciences with a more positivistic basis) or ask your research question (social sciences, humanities and arts). You do so, using the appropriate methodology (belief systems about how the world and knowledge are constructed or revealed, which underpin, inform and are actioned by the research methods, as developed within the overall research design).

Different, appropriate theories, based in research paradigms, based on ontology and epistemology, enable you to underpin your testing of your hypothesis or asking of your research question, and to make sense of the data and so interpret the findings.

Research paradigms

Research paradigms are, like theory, based on ways in which we view the world, and believe that it is understandable, can be explored, fixed, or interpreted. Your research will grow from and be based in research paradigms. Any attempt to discuss these is going to be a gross oversimplification. But you do need to be aware of the debates, and so I hope here to provide a straightforward map through the debates and the paradigms. Following this, the use of theory based on those paradigms will, hopefully, help you in your research or at least provide a starting point. Beware, some books are so heavily influenced by one paradigm that they undermine the others as if they were wrong, or

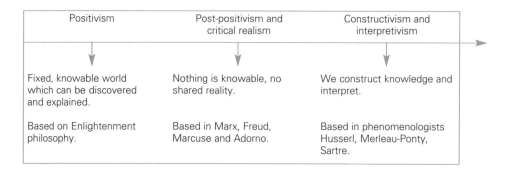

Positivism	Post-positivism and critical realism	Constructivism and interpretivism
Fixed, knowable world which can be discovered and explained.	Nothing is knowable, no shared reality.	We construct knowledge and interpret.
Based on Enlightenment philosophy.	Based in Marx, Freud, Marcuse and Adorno.	Based in phenomenologists Husserl, Merleau-Ponty, Sartre.

Figure 5.2

only used by people who had not seen the light, i.e. could not yet appreciate the absolute rightness of the paradigm that the author believes in and uses.

Figure 5.2 suggests there is a continuum of research paradigms which reflect philosophical views of the world, and influence research design and the discovery or construction and interpretation of knowledge. The philosophers and movements are also indicated.

On the left of the continuum, **positivism** is influenced by the philosophers of the Enlightenment (18th century in the West), René Descartes, David Hume, Francis Bacon, John Locke, Émile Durkheim, whose work, broadly speaking, is based on a belief that the world is knowable and it exists independently of our experience of it (Guba and Lincoln, 1998, p. 204). In the middle position is **post-positivism**, an example of which is **critical realism**, which Jonathan Grix also places in the middle of his continuum (Grix, 2004, pp. 78, 84) derived from the work of Karl Marx, Theodor Adorno, Herbert Marcuse, Sigmund Freud and the German Frankfurt School. This paradigm recognises agency, that people make meanings, and hermeneutics, relationships between elements in a system. Grix quotes Peter Kerr and one small part of that is helpful here:

> Given that agents are themselves active in interpreting their own structural context and that the meanings which they attach to any given situation are likely to differ, part of the quest for explanation must be the inspiration of the notion of hermeneutics, i.e. an understanding of the differential meaning which agents infer upon their actions.   (Kerr, 2003, p. 123)

This is a mid-position, which already recognises interpretation and a subject carrying out the interpretation, rather than arguing for a fixed real world which is discoverable.

The views of the positivist theorists were significantly questioned by the philosopher Immanuel Kant at the end of the nineteenth century, and at the beginning of the twentieth century by phenomenologists Husserl, Merleau-Ponty and then the existentialists such as Jean-Paul Sartre, who variously explored being in the world, perception, and labelling. Although they make different cases for different perspectives on such views of the world, broadly speaking their work underpins and informs a set of beliefs that the world is essentially only known to us insofar as we place meaning over it, interpret it and choose to share and agree those interpretations with each other. It cannot be fixed: it is experienced through our perception, interpretation and construction of knowledge. In an extreme version of existentialism, you would never be able to say you knew anything or that you could trust these elements of the way we make sense of the world – such as language, values, clocks – to offer any interpretation at all. You can move towards a slightly less unstable or nihilistic position, and one which is more manageable in a shared world, by agreeing to use terms and structures which interpret and communicate. Denscombe (2002, pp. 21–2) notes: 'There is a "relativism" associated with interpretivism that challenged the idea that the researcher's explanation can be taken as the right one – true and correct.' There is always scope for other interpretations. The researcher is not an expert, and 'There is a degree of *uncertainty* contained within interpretivist explanations of the social world that can be uncomfortable for researchers' (p. 21).

At the positivist extreme the research conducted in the natural sciences and positivistically influenced social science research seeks to find and fix the truth, measure and label it, and might therefore be using large-scale survey data which produces replicable results, categories of response to fixed questions, and where the research could be generalisable, i.e. if carried out again, under the same conditions with the same population, it would yield the same results. Already I feel uncomfortable about this because of my own research position and the paradigms within which I feel more comfortable since I believe it is difficult to assert with human subjects that you can ever exactly replicate a context or a population, as people are always shifting and so is the world. However, I am also uncomfortable about a worldview which asserts that nothing is at all knowable, nothing can be interpreted, everything is relative to the point of chaos and lack of communication. My own comfort zone lies with interpretivism and constructionism. Here I should acknowledge that we cannot find out or fix reality, but that we interpret it, having asked certain questions from our own worldview and context, and ensuring the research itself is as rigorous and internally valued as we can make it, then tempering any conclusions with the awareness that they cannot be generalised to other contexts, although they might shed light on similar questions of similar populations in similar contexts.

Grix also recognises two other positions which could be called research paradigms: postmodernism and feminism. Both these relatively new positions are ideologically based, i.e. based in worldviews and value positions, questioning the notion of proof and fixable reality. **Postmodernism** rejects the notion of absolutes, for example that following the right methods produces guaranteed results. Instead, postmodernism, which grows from structuralism in the early twentieth century and the deconstructionism of Derrida in the late twentieth century, sees all constructions of knowledge as dependent on their structure in context, based on choices of question, methods, modes of data analysis and interpretation. **Feminism** is also ideological. Feminist research questions the basis of all knowledge as having been defined and produced by men, recognises the subjective position of the researcher, which can affect any research undertaken, and advocates explicitly using that subject position as a source of research. Feminist researchers tend to deal with questions and issues of gender, or of cultural difference where it is likely to be gender inflected. Feminist researchers also advocate using narratives, story-telling, reflective responses, and are keen to involve those being researched as full co-researchers, so avoiding any sense that you are taking information from people for your own use and possibly disempowering them in the process.

As you decide what you would like to research, and begin to define your research question, you will need to consider which research paradigm your work can best be placed within, and grow from. This will affect the kinds of assumptions you have about what questions you can ask, how you can ask them and how you interpret them.

Developing Conceptual Frameworks

Now that you have the proposal for your project, dissertation or other long piece of research, you need to think about the framework of ideas which underpins the research. This is called the **conceptual framework**. It need not be excessively complex. You are not merely asking research questions, you are problematising – unpicking, questioning – the ideas, values and terms you are using which underpin your question. You are using theories to help you approach, explore, interpret and understand the question, the whole area of thinking in which it fits, and the ways of understanding the information which is produced by asking the question using your methodology and methods (questionnaire, observation, narrative etc.) and the vehicles (interview schedules, observation schedules, diaries etc.) by which the information was obtained.

- Your *conceptual framework* is the scaffold, the framework of ideas, questions and theories, that *help you ask* your questions, develop your ideas, underpinning your research and dissertation. It keeps you focused and on course.
- It ensures that what you find/conclude is underpinned by your questions and theories, is enabled by your methods, arises from these questions and goes some way to addressing them.

The conceptual framework contains, structures, actions, ensures:

- that your *ideas and aims and questions* are underpinned by, enabled by, particular *theories and theorists*;
- that your *research methodology and methods* can actually act as the vehicles by which you ask these theoretically underpinned questions;
- that how you *analyse and interpret what you find* – themes in an author, responses from a focus group, documentary evidence from archives, statistical responses to a questionnaire – relates to the theories and the research question;

- so that you can *draw conclusions*, and make recommendations (depending on the dissertation) which are based on these questions and aims, theories, methods and findings.

For example, if you are asking a question about:

Why are young people homeless? And what can be done about it?

This then focuses into the following questions (notice we have narrowed the focus down to a population sample):

- What are the causes? and
- What solutions are being developed to cope with homelessness among young people in Cambridge?

Once you start to work with concepts, ideas, and then theories you would need to ask:

What do we mean by:

- homelessness?
- the causes of it?
- young people?

Homelessness = not living in a rented or owned home, being without a fixed address . . . (there are different definitions in different contexts).

We will need to do some reading, thinking and talking with others to fully define the meaning of homelessness that we want to explore. If it is left vague, we could have something too nebulous to explore and far too large a sample. A vague definition would be everyone without a fixed address. However, some people are not homeless, they are in transit; some are travellers. Are they homeless? Not really.

Unpick the concept, define it, problematise it. Whether you are homeless depends to some extent on how you define your own situation, and how the council or government define it for benefits or lack of them. To ask the question, you'll need to argue about the definitions, problematising what seems a straightforward concept – homelessness in this case – and then defend how you are defining it and asking the questions about it.

Theorising follows. To understand homelessness we need a number of theories, which will be written about by

- theorists;
- critics who are relating with such theories in action in similar contexts.

One concept might be –

Residence and belonging.
Another, identity.

Theorising the state of mind of the homeless might well bring in theories about

Health and conformity – mental health and fitting in – ability to fit in/conform.

Once you have understood the concepts you are using, and the theories to underpin them, you can start designing your research plan and picking the right methodology and methods and research vehicles to get out there and ask your question. When you analyse your data you will again need to remember the concepts – the ideas you are using, and the theories to underpin them – or you might just repeat exactly what you hear, read and see without theorising and conceptualising – dealing with the ideas, issues and problems, managing the contradictions and the questions.

Putting all of this into action throughout your research is working with a conceptual framework, and doing so ensures your work is at the right kind of level for a degree – not just reporting what there is, without problematising it or conceptualising it.

The role of theory

Linking theory and practice is the key to good research. There is a maxim which is useful in considering the ways in which you might use theory in your work: 'there's nothing so practical as a good theory'. Theories are ways of looking at the world, making sense of it and, in research, they help you to focus on, sift out the knowledge you are producing. Theory underpins and informs the questions we ask, the ways in which we can understand what we are finding out, can interpret and express what our research has discovered and what it can contribute to knowledge and making meaning in the world.

Theory helps to explain the world and to explain the empirical data you collect in scientific and social science research, why what you have sculpted, woven, painted, danced, or written engages with a view of the world and has something to say within the bounds of this view in the humanities and arts.

A few warnings. Theory is a contested term used differently in different research paradigms and research traditions, so you will need to explain how you are using it, and ensure that any section of your dissertation, project, essay, or other piece which uses theory accompanies and helps explain how your work is connected to the data, the findings, the product. A dissertation with a big theory chunk exploring many theorists' work which then does not use those theories to ask the research questions and help understand them, is unlikely to pass because it is divorced, and fragmented. Use your theory to ask your questions and interpret the research.

⬤ Using theory in a piece of professional practice-based research

An example

Lorna is a health promotion tutor. She uses interactive drama with her students in working with them to take health promotion into schools to enable the teenagers to make considered decisions about their choices of eating behaviours. In order to explore the effectiveness of the programme she is running with these students, she will need to read in and use the ways in which several theories construct and interpret knowledge and the world.

In the diagram in Figure 5.3, Lorna's programme and her research are linked, and each is informed by, interpreted by the underpinning theories. These theories are of (1) health promotion (which seeks to encourage people to take positive measures to improve their health); (2) interactive drama (which seeks to involve the participants in acting out scenarios related in this context to health promotion, and to encourage empowerment through the acting out); (3) self-worth and self-image (where these are about identity and empowerment); and (4) healthy eating (where certain kinds of eating are seen as healthier than others). She needs to read in each of the theories in order to develop her work, understand it, ask her questions, link her practice with the research, and interpret the data she produces through her research in practice (she has used observation and focus group interviews to gather her data).

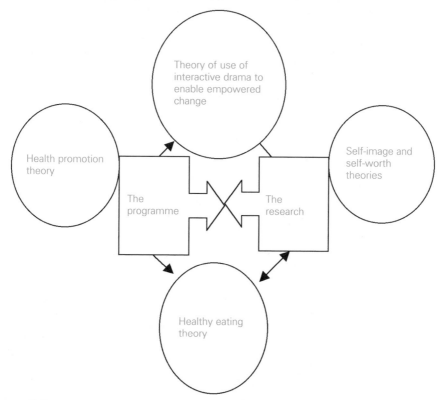

Figure 5.3

You need to find out about the experiences of international students studying in the UK higher education system. You have a few thoughts and assumptions – thoughts that there are increasing numbers, the students seem to be going to some universities rather than others, studying some subjects more than others, doing quite well, and some go home and some stay. They do not always seem to be mixing with the UK home students and often they stick with their own language groups. This is a complex topic. You need a research focus and a question. Please read through and consider the following scenario and decide how you would develop your conceptual framework, and then construct and action your research design.

1 You are a social science researcher from a positivist research paradigm. Your ontological position is one of believing that the world exists and is knowable; we all live in it and have experiences we can define. Your epistemological position is that the world is knowable and research can give you the facts, reveal the knowledge. Your research hypothesis is that the numbers of international students in 2009 have grown since ten years ago, and that they are concentrated in a few subjects in a few institutions. In order to test this hypothesis you have to find the statistics of numbers of students between 1999 and 2009 and measure growth.

   Find the demographic information from the HESA figures or from individual universities to indicate the patterns of choice and the numbers in universities in certain subjects.

   Using this statistical data you can map growth and choice and prove your hypothesis. If you want to find out from the students themselves about their choices, you could conduct a survey which would produce more up-to-date statistics, but not on the full population (central statistics would, hopefully, produce those on the full population, as they are centrally gathered).

2 You are a social science researcher from an interpretivist research paradigm. You are interested in the cultural experience of international students studying in the UK in Higher education and you want to explore their perceptions about their experiences of being international students in different contexts. You need to narrow this down to a manageable question, and sample.

   There is an increasing number of international students from country X; they choose particular subjects; they don't seem to mix in and they take away a qualification and a limited cultural experience. You would like to explore their experiences with them, using inductive methodology within an interpretivist paradigm, and so using methods which ask them to respond about their experiences and their feelings, which methods would most probably be interviews and focus groups.

Once you have your question, and your belief-ontology, epistemology, research paradigm, methodology and approach, you will need to read in the theorists, apply this to your own work, develop the research design and methods, carry out the research. You analyse the data, interpret their responses and construct knowledge from this, adding to our understanding as well as our factual knowledge about international students from country X.

How can *your* actual research be informed by, scaffolded by, helped by such a structured and focused approach?

Summary

In this chapter we have considered:

- Worldviews and approaches to research.
- Research paradigms.
- Conceptual frameworks and theory.

Further reading

Blaikie, N. (2000) *Designing Social Research* (Cambridge: Polity Press).

Denscombe, M. (2002) *Ground Rules for Good Research* (Buckingham: Open University Press).

Grix, J. (2004) *The Foundations of Research* (Basingstoke: Palgrave Macmillan).

Guba, E. G. and Lincoln, Y. S. (1998) 'Competing Paradigms in Qualitative Research'. In N. K. Denzin and Y. S. Lincoln (eds), *The Landscape of Qualitative Research: Theories and Issues* (London, Thousand Oaks, CA, and New Delhi: Sage).

Kerr, P. (2003) 'Keeping it Real! Evolution in Political Science: A Reply to Kay and Curry', *British Journal of Politics and International Relations*, 5(1) (February), pp. 118–28.

6 Writing a Research Proposal

This chapter considers:

▶ what a good research proposal for a dissertation, a project or other longer piece of research work looks like;

▶ stages and elements of a research proposal;

▶ submission.

If you are carrying out a small piece of research to inform an essay or other assignment, you will not need to draw up a full-scale research proposal. However, you will need to identify your research question or hypothesis, the theories you think you will need to use, and key literature. You will also find it useful to develop a time and action plan to work out what parts of the research you need to carry out when and to make sure you get started with your writing as soon as possible. This is a small-scale version of the longer research proposal explored in this chapter, so reading about such a longer proposal for a longer, more complex piece of research will give you some idea of the research planning process, ready for when you undertake your own project or dissertation, normally in the third or final year.

If you are carrying out a piece of research for a project, a dissertation or a community volunteering project or placement, or any other lengthy assignment, you will need to produce a proposal. This shows your tutor or supervisor that you can think through the research from start to finish. You will need to define the question, the concepts or ideas underpinning the research, and the theories (although you might not yet know exactly which theories you will use), the design of the research, in other words the methodology, methods and research vehicles to collect your data and information, and how you think you can analyse and interpret the data you will discover in order to discuss it and write it up. You will need to identify the key literature you think you will use, and plan the time and action of the project to take as much of the elements of the research and writing into consideration as you can. If you are also working part time or carrying out other assignments for other courses or modules you will need a plan that takes these other calls on your time into consideration. Each element of this planning is explored further in the following chapters.

Planning and drawing up a research proposal gives you the opportunity to think through your ideas and decide whether this is a realistic, do-able piece of research, and whether you can draw up a realistic plan, which you can carry out. Research is actually messier than any plan or proposal and although you may not be able to stick to the plan or proposal completely, having a plan is a good way to clarify your ideas and deviating from it with reasons is much better than having no plan at all.

Do consult Chapter 4 on developing research questions, and Chapter 8 on methodology and methods.

Your research proposal is the main basis upon which a supervisor, tutor, research committee placement manager or employer can begin to judge the value or potential of your research work. You need to have more than just a title, because a proposal is really a plan, a design, and shows all concerned how do-able your research is in the time available. The greatest single problem with undergraduate research proposals of all shapes and sizes is that they often indicate that you expect you can do too much in the time and word length available. Look again at the chapter on developing a research question and the idea of your 'slice of the cake'. Don't try and do too much. Research at undergraduate level shows a tutor or employer that you can plan and carry out research, can develop the skills, and action a research proposal, following the design. If it is the right size, well organised, and carried out well it will be enough to show them that you have these skills and can complete a well designed piece of work. With a do-able piece of research which is not unmanageably huge, you will avoid being run off your feet and over-stressed by trying to do too much in too little time.

Please keep this in mind as you develop your proposal along the lines below.

Do check on university regulations very early in advance, as you enter your research, because there will be both restrictions and opportunities. Restrictions include word lengths, due dates, presentation expectations, subject areas you are not expected to research. Opportunities might include interdisciplinary research, or the chance to work alongside other students or employees in the workplace, or your university staff, in order to carry out useful real-world research.

You will need to seek support from your supervisor in the development of a proposal of sufficient quality. Before you submit a research proposal formally, you will need to carry out some early research work, some literature reviewing and searching, and to identify the theoretical and methodological underpinnings to your work. This gives you an idea of what is possible.

You need to work out and focus on the methods, beliefs and ways of constructing and discussing knowledge and ideas that you will need to be familiar with. You need to be able to show you can work with these to achieve your research outcomes.

A fundamental question to keep in mind when developing your research is – so what? That is, what will this piece of research lead to or contribute to? Why carry it out? What does it intend to contribute to our knowledge? Then you could broadly define it, asking: Is it real-world research leading to changes in practice? Or is it theoretical, leading to contributions to theory and understanding?

The research proposal is a carefully crafted piece of work. It is also a very useful foundation from which to develop your ideas and arguments. You will be able to use it to help you plan your work and study programme and to draft your chapters and parts of them, the paragraphs. However, it is always under construction until it is finished. So, for example, some of the problems you might encounter in your early reading or literature review could lead to changing or refining the central underpinning questions running throughout the research.

The proposal highlights the main issues, theories, questions you are going to work with and which will be important in your argument when you write up your project or dissertation, etc. It is a stage and a substantial piece of work from which you will draw in the future. You will also have to recognise that it is a compromise. By producing a detailed plan like this, you could well feel you are in a 'straitjacket'. Actually you are not – it will change as you find out new things and the context in which your work is being carried out. You will discover other information and arguments, you will find that some of what you seek is not there, you will change your mind and your emphases and you will find also that the time changes, and so on. But the proposal is a draft outline and it will be worked with in the future in a dynamic way.

What do you want to research? How can you draw up a good proposal?

First you need to identify your main research questions and sub-questions, to clarify for yourself, and for others if you are working with an employer, a tutor or a group.

Activity

Please consider:

- What are you looking for?
- What do you want to prove or investigate?
- What will you contribute to?
- What will you change?
- What difference will your research make? Why does it 'matter'?
- If you are working with others: how will your work fit in with theirs?
- If you are researching in a real-world related context as an employee or a volunteer, how will the research fit in with the employer's needs as well as your own at the university?

The proposal

In your proposal you will need to address the following areas:

Indicative title

What will you call the dissertation/project? You need a topic title and research questions. See Chapter 4.

Aim and focus of the study

This should suggest the underlying research area and your main question and sub-questions. Eventually it contributes to the abstract of a dissertation and the terms of reference and aims of a project. Think about it carefully. What are you really exploring, arguing, trying to find out and hoping to find out, and then suggest? What links with what in your mind?

Context for the research

- What issues, problems, history, background and others' questions provide a context, a culture, an ongoing set of questions, thoughts and discoveries for your own work?
- How is it contributing to academic work in this area and to the body of research and knowledge in this area?
- How is it contributing to addressing issues and to solving problems in the workplace or the real world?

Theoretical perspectives and interpretations and your conceptual framework

- What are the underpinning theoretical perspectives informing your ideas?
- What theories can help you explore your question?
- Where have you taken your theories from?

For example, you might use feminist or Marxist theoretical perspectives and work on organisational analysis. You might need to use theories about identity or conformity, about sustainable development . . . the theories you use come from the questions you ask in the context of your discipline area, and the workplace or academic context. Show how the theories you are using can help you ask your questions and understand what you find out.

You will need to develop a *conceptual framework*, which is the framework of ideas and concepts underpinning your work, and which you question, explore then use to act as a structure or scaffold for your research design and processes. If, for example, you are investigating 'the effectiveness of tutor support for trainee student teachers in primary schools', your conceptual framework would start to be built by your asking about and defining *tutor support*, *trainee teachers*, *the concept of effectiveness* and even the concept of the context, *primary schools*. The concept of tutor support, for example, could be understood by exploring concepts of power, and of mentoring, as a developmental process, which you would need to theorise starting by reading about power, hierarchies, control – for example, Foucault's theories. You would need to work out which elements of these theories can help you both clarify the concepts you are using and ask your question in a theorised way which helps explore the ideas embedded in power, control, freedom, ownership, development. Developing a conceptual framework using theories and unpicking the concepts means you ask questions which explore: What does this mean? How does it work? And how do we know it works? Why does it matter? What are the implications of this? Rather than: How many? How often? Where is it? Brands of factual questions. Chapter 5 is on conceptual frameworks and theory.

Research methodology and methods

- What is the research methodology or what are the research methodologies underpinning your research?
- What methods are you going to use, and why? How do they link with and help inform and develop each other? Look at Chapter 8 for insights into this.
- What research vehicles (the tools, the questionnaire or the interview schedules etc.) will you use? You will need to know exactly why you have chosen, for example, questionnaires or interviews, because of the way they can help you get to and find out about the answers to your research question.

Research design

How will you go about carrying out literature searches, collecting information and data? Provide an outline of the different activities you will undertake at what points in your research and show how it fits in with the time you have available. This usually shows you that you need to be careful not to carry out several pieces of work at the same time and that you need longer than you think for some elements of the work.

Produce a timeline for your research activities.

Ethical considerations

Much research has ethical considerations, and these will be particularly complex when you are using human subjects. Look up your university's code of ethics for guidance. (See Chapter 17 on ethics.)

Outline plan of study

This part of the proposal asks you to indicate what you think would be the main features of each of your chapters. Do look back at this once you have got on with the research as it could well change.

Finally, describe and discuss what you feel your research will contribute to the field of knowledge, the development of arguments and the research culture.

- What kinds of practices or thoughts and arguments can it move forward?
- How can it make a difference?

- Why does it matter and why is it obviously at this level?
- Is it serious, broad, deep-questioning and original enough?

Primary references

If your submission is a project or dissertation, 10 or 12 of these will be included. Do make sure they represent key texts, the range of your theoretical areas, and some up-to-date examples.

You need to be in agreement with your supervisor, tutor or employer, whoever you relate to, about your proposal, as it forms the basis of your future work.

Projects

If you are carrying out a project you will probably produce an outline which is shaped in the following way:

- Terms of reference: who is it for? Why is it being commissioned?
- Context: what is the situation in which it will be carried out? What will it contribute to?
- The theory underpinning your work.
- Plan and design of the study.
- Data analysis, discussion and interpretations.
- Recommendations: what will the result of this research recommend (you do not know, of course, at the proposal stage but could suggest what it is expected that recommendations will relate to or contribute to).
- References.

Activity

- Look carefully through this draft proposal and discuss it with a reliable colleague or friend.
- Produce a draft proposal.
- See if you can justify and explain each part of it to them/to yourself.
- What questions and gaps do you have?
- What is still to be developed?
- Draw up a plan of action to work on the elements that are not fully developed.
- Draw up your own draft proposal under the following headings. Remember these are just still notes, which you can flesh out.

Draft proposal for a dissertation or long piece of research

- indicative title
- aim and focus of the study
- questions and sub-questions
- context for the research
- theoretical perspectives
- research methodology and research methods
- research design (stages of your work – over time)
- ethical considerations
- outline plan of study

> - timeline for activities in the research
>
>   1 from ...... to ......
>   2 from ...... to ......
>   3 from ...... to ......
>   4 from ...... to ......
>   5 from ...... to ......
>
> - draft chapters and what they might focus on
> - conceptual justification for the research – which will lead to the conclusions - Why does it matter? Why will it make a contribution?
> - important references that you will use
>
> Does this make perfect, coherent sense to you? And to your colleagues? Talk it through with a friend, colleague or family member, and of course, with your supervisor or tutor or employer!
>
> - Talking it through with others helps to shape it and clarify it.
> - Developing the framework of different chapters helps you to see where the conceptual work can run throughout your research.
> - Models – look at models of proposals by others and at essays, dissertations, projects – these all enable you to imagine how your work might develop.

A typical plan of an essay/article/dissertation

- Title
- Abstract
- Introduction
- Theoretical perspectives (containing the literature review - in dialogue with your arguments)
- Methodology and methods (including the design of the study, a sample, timings, choices made)
- Presentation of results/findings/data and discussion of results/findings/data
- Conclusion, containing a summary and possibly recommendations
- Appendices/statistical tables and illustrations
- References

A typical project report

- Abstract
- Terms of reference: Who asked you to produce this piece of research and report? And why?

- Context of the project research and report: What is the situation – the problem, the question, the intervention needed which led you to begin your research and in which it will fit?
- Introduction
- Theoretical perspectives (containing the literature review - in dialogue with your arguments)
- Methodology and methods (including the design of the study, a sample, timings, choices made)
- Presentation of results/findings/data and discussion of results/findings/data
- Conclusion, containing a summary and possibly recommendations
- Appendices/statistical tables and illustrations
- References

Sometimes you might have to resubmit the proposal. This is perfectly normal. You need to get it right, as it informs all you do – so don't be too upset if it is sent back for rewriting – it will encourage you to be clearer, more coherent, and more likely to produce a successful piece of research which matters. Sometimes you might lose sight of the conceptual framework and find yourself busily capturing information and coding it up – the concepts and theories help you raise your research beyond the level of being just descriptive. It is important to remember you are being:

- **conceptual**
- **critical** and
- **creative**

enough.

GOOD LUCK!

Summary

In this chapter we have considered:

- How you put together a research proposal.
- How to develop a conceptual framework to your research.

Further reading

Grix, J. (2004) *The Foundations of Research* (Basingstoke: Palgrave Macmillan).

7 Carrying Out a Literature Review: Engaging with the Literature

There is an early chapter in a dissertation, or section in an essay or project, which is engaged with literature in the field and gives you a sense of theoretical perspectives. It is using the literature to establish context and argument, the perspectives of major theorists whose work informs yours – putting all of this into a dialogue with your work. It is important to remember that a literature review is a dynamic piece of work, not just a dead list of the books you have read, but an engagement with their ideas and arguments in relation to your research questions, problems or hypotheses.

Reading and engaging with the literature

You continue to draw on the literature throughout your work towards a project, dissertation, or long essay. From the literature, you develop the theories, themes and threads running throughout – underpinning and feeding into the conceptual findings.

You need to keep reading, but know where to stop so that you get the right stance and level of engagement from the different reading you are doing and can make sure you haven't just recorded what others say, and instead have noted arguments that have engaged your own ideas and findings and brought them into a debate about previous and current literature, as appropriate.

In order for you to make a contribution to knowledge with your research, however large or small that might be, you will need to know what has already been written in the field, what are the main debates, who the experts are, what the themes are and where your work can be positioned in relation to what's been said before and what is being said at the moment. You have probably read some of the literature that you will need for your literature review even before you developed your research question or hypothesis. Indeed, you could have thought about what your question or problem was, while reading through someone else's work and realising there was an issue they had not covered, or a disagreement between experts, or a gap in the knowledge. As you prepare for your own research you need to think about literature searching, reviewing, and engaging in a critical, conceptual dialogue with the literature.

It is a good idea to read more widely in order to identify your problem or question, the area that you're going to work on, and to narrow down your own focus. If this is in an area in which you have already read widely, look at related fields and issues and review the literature. However, you might not be fully aware of the literature in the field especially if you are moving slightly out of your own discipline or into another context, period or issue. You will need to find a wide range of literature so that you are identifying and then engaging with the key theorists, themes and debates. The work of those researchers and writers who are and have been using the key theorists in their critical research work is already engaged in the debates and provides a good start for your own engagement.

Through your reading, find out where your own work looks as though it will make a contribution, i.e. a gap in knowledge, a new angle, a different combination of ideas and area of thought, and start to engage in a discussion between the experts and the critics in your own writing. This engagement in dialogue is not undermining the authority of those who have already written; it is identifying the lively debate and joining it. It is also ensuring that your own work is not just recording what others say, or summarising, but working at a conceptual level of idea development, ensuring that you have your own voice, something to say in the current debates, can identify the argument, the experts, what they say, and join in with the unique contribution of your work.

Carrying out a literature search and a literature review

Don't forget to involve your tutor or supervisor and any helpful librarian in helping you to identify the key words, areas and arguments through a literature search so that you get the best and the fullest detail out of it. When conducting a literature search you are:

- Discovering what the key theorists are saying in your field and in relation to your question and what they have written about the concepts and the ideas that you are using.
- Discovering what those who have been engaged in the latest work in the field are saying in order to ask questions of their particular part of the subject, or field, what their views are, how they differ, what evidence they are using, and what points they are making.

Literature reviews/theoretical perspectives

Make the role of the theoretical perspectives/literature review chapter absolutely explicit. They are:

- Not a dead list of annotated comments about texts only in an early chapter

BUT

- An ongoing dialogue with the experts, theorists and theories underpinning *your* research.

Hart (p. 13) defines the literature review as 'progressive'. 'It starts with wide reading, narrowing into themes and debates.' Engaging with these themes and disputes, and sharing your work, will ensure you are moving beyond a summary and into a dialogue.

Finding where literature is

Suggestions to students undertaking a literature review:

- Read widely (more than you need) for context and debates.
- Ask your tutor or supervisor for suggestions about reading – they should have a good idea of some of the key reading from the theorists and the critics in your field.
- Talk to a librarian – they are experts in conducting literature searches, and your subject librarian will have a good idea of where to find some of the main sources for the literature search for your literature review. Contact them early and discuss the question you're asking, the problem you're addressing and the area you're working in. They should be able to suggest online subject databases, journals in the library, and some books.
- Find out the relevant abstracting and indexing services for your subject area and look up the abstracts to journal articles. There is usually also another abstract collection which relates to people's PhD theses, some of which might be quite cutting edge for your work. If you're working in an interdisciplinary area, you might need to consult literature and abstracts in more than one subject area. Useful databases for abstracts sometimes link to the whole article. Some of the useful databases are:

  - Eric – the education database
  - SOSSIG – for the social sciences
  - EMB – reviews for medicine
  - Psychlit – for Psychology
  - CINAHL – for Nursing, midwifery and health areas

  Look at Chapter 10 for further ideas on internet database searching.

- Be very systematic. If you can't find what you want by scanning the databases, try asking a librarian or your tutor, and have a look at the books that are next on the shelves to books that you are using. Sometimes these will relate to what you've been reading about although their titles don't necessarily stand out as being obviously useful.
- Have a look at the references that your key books and key journal articles are using, track back through these references and then look up the sources yourself. These leads will give you the fundamental key ideas, and some further suggestions that you can look up and use.
- Keep up to date with the new journal articles if you can. In undergraduate work, very few people will be going beyond some key points and sources, perhaps a journal article, and the online reading. If you really search hard

and read up-to-date journal articles, you will be ahead of the game and your work will look fresh and engaged. If you find some really important journal articles, download them and copy them, properly referenced, into your files for further use, or photocopy them and store them in a ring binder or cardboard wallet carefully labelled. Read them carefully and identify the arguments, and the quotations to back these up, then engage with their arguments in your own work, extract small essential quotations and properly reference your sources.

Whether you are looking at an online source, one in the library or one you have yourself or have borrowed, you need to ask yourself the following question:

- How up-to-date is this? Some of the key texts from the well-established theorists and great names in the field may be quite old but because they established the main arguments in the field they are still relevant to your work. There will also be an absolutely huge range (probably) of people who have used these theorists and experts to underpin their own work, or who have done little more than represent them.

After you have skim read quite a lot of books and journal articles, you should be able to see where people are merely repeating arguments, theories and issues rather than adding to them or indicating debates and new knowledge. You do not really need to read everything. What you do need to read are the key theorists whose thoughts and work underpin the work of the critics or professional practitioner writers, those writers who have established an engagement with the debates and the themes and developed the theory or contradicted the theory, and others' work in their own work, and those who are adding new knowledge and new ideas to the ongoing debate.

For each source:

- You will need to read carefully and to identify the themes and arguments made by the key players (critics, practitioners who write in the field).
- Reflect and think critically about what you are reading, don't just take notes down from it; think about both the case that is being made, and the evidence to back it up. How reliable a source is this?
- Does this fit with what you already know?
- Does it contradict other evidence?
- Have you got any evidence to back up its claim in its argument?
- What is being hidden from us, any viewpoints or information?
- What does not seem to be understood here?
- Are the reasons for the conclusion logical and well argued?
- Does the evidence back up the argument in the claims?
- How can you use it in your own work?

Keeping good notes and references

- Take not just notes of the content of the argument but also extracts from what is said, using key quotations, and referencing and discussing or commenting on them.
- You also need to take down publication details. When you find a source you think is useful or even one you've read that you're not sure will be useful, take down the full publication details, make some contextual and critical comments about the article, book or other source and about the issues it raises and argument it makes, and carefully reference and quote from it so that you can come back to it. You can then also use the quotes, properly referenced, i.e. noting the book, journal article, online source or whatever it is.

It is important to reflect and consider how what you're quoting relates to your own argument. In this way you select and identify the work and decide how you are going to include it in your literature review.

Summarise and synthesise in order to engage in critical debate. Your arguments arise from, relate to, and are underpinned by the experts, in terms of either their content or their methods.

> The main point about a literature review is that it engages in a debate with the critical reading in the field and then engages your own work in this debate.

Activity

Please consider:

What are the problems with what these students are saying? How could you enable them to overcome the difficulties?

1. There are no books in my area, it is a completely new area and question.
2. My theorists are diametrically opposed – help!
3. I know nothing about this topic/area – where can I start?
4. I just need to know who are the RIGHT theorists and critics to use – please tell me (so I don't have to do all this reading).
5. It's all been said before . . . what can I add?
6. I don't want to read those writers because they might disagree with my argument.
7. I've done the literature review – now I can leave it and do all the research.
8. I'm going to do my literature review and work on my theorists after I've gathered my data.

Some thoughts and responses

1   The student might be right – perhaps it is a completely new area. It certainly should be a fairly new question. However, it is probable that they need to use different key words, to look more broadly, to look at work that's been done on similar issues but perhaps in different contexts, and then they will find work in books or journal articles which relates to what they are looking at.

2   This looks like bad news but actually it is good news. Already there are some grounds for debate and discussion here, setting the theorists in relation to or opposition to each other. This can help generate a healthy discussion into which your work might fit.

3   The student needs some guidance about basic reading and a tutor will be able to help here, or a librarian might. However, if the student knows absolutely nothing about the topic, perhaps it's not the best one to pick. Perhaps a topic with which they are slightly familiar, or one where they are familiar with some of the books, and have an idea about what they're interested in, would be more suitable.

4   Well, there won't be 'right' theorists and critics. The issue is that there will be debate and arguments about different points of view in different readings and this student needs to find out what these different arguments are and develop their own route through them. Suggesting that there are just right critics and theorists is a bit simplistic and looks like the student is taking short cuts. However, if we are very new to the area this is often how we respond, thinking there must be a single right way. But there rarely is. The student will have to find out what the debates are and make up their own mind on the evidence of the strength of the argument.

5   If it's really all been said before, then this is probably not a good topic to pick. However, this is probably just a response to a sense that there is an over-whelming amount of literature on the subject, shelves and shelves of books by experts. This student's question is probably quite different from anything that has been asked before, or they could focus it perhaps on a different element of the topic and so by asking something fairly new, they can direct a work by the great experts and the critics in the field to help support them in their own work.

6   If you are to develop a well argued case, you really need to know what the argu-ments are. It's important not to avoid authors, critics and experts who might disagree with your point of view, because their views can give you the opportu-nity to find out how to argue for your views and back them up with evidence.

7   Actually, you never stop doing the literature review until you hand the disserta-tion, project or essay in. Continuing to read in the field is important as you carry out your research because you might miss something that comes out while you are doing the research, or that hasn't turned up from your researching so far. This can give you a new perspective, an edge over other people. So never stop reading, but you might not need to use all of it.

8   This really is not a good idea at all. The idea of reading in the literature is to establish the arguments, the theoretical approaches, ways in which people deal with these sorts of issues. You carry out your own research. If you had not done that kind of reading you might quite easily either work at a much lower level than most of the rest of the literature in the field, or miss the major argu-ments, deliberations and theoretical underpinnings which would inform your own work. Either way, what you could end up doing is producing a lot of data which doesn't really relate to a well focused question based on having read the literature. Don't do it. Start the reading and start to develop new questions and your own work alongside the reading and let them influence each other.

Reading into the field is only one of the tasks

If you are unaware of debates in the field you might merely recreate them.

You need to work out where your research engages with the debates and what it can add.

Writing and engaging with the literature follows this journey:

- Summary
- Synthesis
- Evaluation and reflection
- Engagement in critique
- Argument and dialogue between the experts and critics have worked with their work, and with your own work
- Contribution to meaning – something new which is your own.

Activity

Please consider:

- Who are YOUR main theorists?
- Who are you reading in relation to theory and to method?
- What are the debates in these areas?
- And how does YOUR work engage in a dialogue with these debates?

Good use of the literature

L. Blaxter, C. Hughes and M. Tight (1996, p. 115) differentiate between effective and proper use of references, where they

- justify and support your arguments;
- allow you to make comparisons with other researchers;
- express matters better than you could have done;
- demonstrate your familiarity with your field of research.

(Blaxter et al., 1996, p. 115)

But referencing is not just to impress your readers or fill up the writing with notes, references and quotations.

Vernon Trafford and Shosh Leshem (2008, p. 68) suggest ways of 'exploiting' the literature, which they define as:

- a physical corpus of published work on a specific topic;
- the extended body of writing that relates to a specific corpus of published works;
- the accumulated knowledge that resides within the corpus;
- work in progress that, when finished, will add to the corpus of knowledge.

They note that artefacts are included in this body of work in some subjects. Their book considers PhDs from the vantage point of the Viva at the end so it is at an even higher level than your own work at this stage, but they note how examiners value wide reading which is clearly organised and managed.

Activities to identify the characteristics of a sound use of literature in writing

You can work from models of a key essay and 'process it' in terms of its:

- Introduction of the issues and major developments in the field, in context.
- Introduction and development of the major arguments, conflicts, trends and the work of (1) the major theorists, (2) the major writers/researchers who put the theories into practice.

Activity:
Using theorising to start research and writing

Reading the literature helps you to develop your own thoughts and arguments. You might find it useful to plan this out, visualise it or discuss it with a colleague.

- Visualise – use diagrams to identify contradictions in the literature.
- With colleagues – state your research question.
- Unpick ideas, concepts, problems, theories and contradictions in the literature and your own work.
- Start to build your arguments from the visualisation – explain to colleagues.
- Orally develop the arguments your theorists and experts use in relation to your own.

Modelling an activity

- Read examples of essays which use a wide variety of literature.
- How do they use the literature?
- Is it a dead list? Is it *merely* summarised?
- Is there any organisation into themes? Issues, or developments, or contradictions or arguments in the field?
- Is it vague? Too broad? Too narrow? Disorganised? Leading too widely? (Remember boundaries!)
- Do they summarise *to add to debates*?
- Do the texts read and written about here engage with the arguments developed by the author?
- Is the discussion of the literature working at a summarising level or a conceptual level?
- Is it properly referenced? And does it use quotation and extract appropriately?

Developing critical thinking as part of dealing with the literature

Critical thinking is crucial in research. Much of this involves questioning and problematising accepted ideas and information. Much of it involves engaging in a dialogue with others who have developed theories or carried out research, creating a dialogue between theoretical perspectives and research activity. Critically reviewing the literature involves more than loosely listing a range of writers in support of an argument. For example,

> Smith, K. (1976); Bloor, P., and Baggis, G. (1993); Snow, K., and Cream, C. (2004) all argue that universally women are more likely than men to develop a counselling function, while Orthrop, S., Kittle, P., and Lovel, H. (2004) suggest that this could be due in part to the caring functions more commonly presented by women

indicates the development of an argument, and key thinkers or critical contributors, while:

> Women are more likely to be counsellors than men (Smith, K. (1976); Bloor, P., and Baggis, G. (1993); Snow, K., and Cream, C. (2004); Orthrop, S., Kittle, P., and Lovel, H. (2004))

fails to develop an argument and just looks like a list.

Equally irritating and undiscriminating is the format where every writer on the subject is given the same space of a paragraph, with neither discrimination between major and minor contributors nor any sense of the development of an argument between the contributors.

Reading, arguing and writing in different ways for different purposes

As you read the literature in the field and start to use it in your own work, consider the different ways in which you use your reading in your writing. In this case we are considering the literature review, but this is also important when you start to discuss your methodology and your choice of methods and when you're interpreting your data or engaging with your writers in the middle section of your dissertation or long project. Here you again need to bring the reading on theory and other practice to bear on the work that you've been doing.

- Where do you engage in dialogue? With what main theories and arguments? What are *your* points and arguments? How and where have you been analytical of theorists, research data, and your own findings?

Summary

In this chapter we have considered:

- Ways of developing the literature review or theoretical perspectives chapter, to engage with dialogues in the field.
- Identifying theories, themes and ways in which you can use extracts in your own arguments and so establish your contribution.

Further reading

Blaxter, L., Hughes, C. and Tight, M. (1996) *How to Search* (Buckingham: Open University).
Hart, C. (2000) *Doing a Literature Review* (London: Sage).
Trafford, V. and Leshem, S. (2008) *Stepping Stones to Achieving your Doctorate* (London: McGraw Hill).

8 Research Methodology and Methods

Your research methodology is based on the way you see the world, your beliefs about existence and being in the world, and your relationship to that (ontology), and the way you believe knowledge is produced and constructed or discovered and fixed (epistemology). Methodology is the ideas-based system which can enable you to address your research question/problem/hypothesis. It underpins the research design, i.e., the plan for the research defining, among other things, the methods and the actual research tools or vehicles used to collect the data. 'Research methodologies, therefore, comprise the theoretical frameworks and concepts in which approaches and methods are situated; they provide the rationale and justification (intellectual, epistemological and ethical) for the methods that are selected and the ways in which they are used' (Stierer and Antoniou, 2004; quoted in Burgess, Sieminski and Arthur, 2006).

View of the world and methodology come first. There is a great deal of confusion about the terms 'methodology' and 'methods'. Some people seem to use them interchangeably, which is incorrect – they are not the same. One (method) grows or emerges from the other (the overarching system, methodology) and it is probably better to think of them as related, where **methodology** is a system, an overall approach based on a view of the world, and **methods** are the ways of actioning, putting into practice, the underpinning beliefs, ideas and questions generated by methodology in order to question or test the world and gather data. Jonathan Grix calls it 'a branch of science concerned with methods and the techniques of scientific enquiry; in particular, with investigating the potential and limitations of particular techniques or procedures' (2004, p. 169). He sees methodology as a logical system which in this quotation seems rather self-reflexive.

There are many debates and some contradictions about definitions and practice concerning both methodology and methods. I have tried to be very clear about the worldview (ontology), belief about the construction or discovery of knowledge (epistemology), the system (methodology), and the research design which follows these using research methods to investigate your research question or test your hypothesis. There is what is referred to as the quantitative/qualitative divide, the deductive and inductive divide where views of the world and the methodology and methods which derive from them are seen as utterly incompatible. While it is essential you get your methodology and methods clear and defend them, you might well find that you are building a research design which crosses these divides in order to ask your question.

As a rule of thumb:

If you believe the world can be investigated, reality discovered, fixed facts found, you are most likely testing a hypothesis and using deductive methodology, quantitative research, and so experiments and large-scale surveys might well be the research methods you use.

If you are identifying and exploring a problem or asking a research question and hoping to construct versions of answers, versions of knowledge rather than produce final facts (because you believe knowledge is not discovered and fixed but constructed), you are likely to be using inductive research methodology and qualitative methods such as interviews and focus groups, journalling.

Methodology

Research design
The overall plan of action which will enable you to ask your research questions or test hypotheses, etc. Methods, time, plans, samples, etc.

Methods
Ways of going about asking the research questions or testing the hypotheses, gathering the research data, e.g., quantitative data gathering methods, such as survey methods, or qualitative data gathering methods, such as interviews.

Research vehicles or tools
These are the actual things used to gather the data, such as the experimental apparatus and the large-scale surveys or questionnaires themselves (the tools or vehicles for quantitative methods), or interview schedules, focus group interview schedules, narratives, journals (the tools or vehicles for qualitative methods).

Methodology and Methods

Methodology refers to the overall approach to the research process, from the theoretical underpinning to the collection and analysis of the data.

Methods refer only to the various means by which data can be collected and/or analysed.

(Hussey and Hussey, 1997)

Methodology –

Will inform and lead to:

- Why you collected certain data.
- What kind of data you have collected, and how you collected it.
- Where, and when, you collected the data.
- How you analysed it.

It also leads to the kind of conclusions you can draw from analysing and interpreting your findings (*either*: this proves that . . . based on a version of the world as discoverable, using research designs and deductive methods which lead to *reliable and generalisable* research and findings; *or* this suggests that . . ./it could be argued that . . . based on a version of the world as relative to position, questions asked, context, ways of interpreting which lead to *valid* research designs, inductive methods and valid findings).

Methodology –

Is an underpinning approach which is based on your view of the world. For example:

(A)   Is it fact-based; can we understand it through collecting facts? Can questions be answered through experimentation and systematic practices that are repeated? Is it essentially knowable, i.e., if you keep looking long enough in enough ways thoroughly enough, you will eventually find the truth? Such beliefs and the methodology arising from them can usually be found in science research, some social science research, or health and business research where it resembles social science, because they are using facts and figures, providing some information about large numbers or large samples, fixing the world, and knowing it.

Or

(B)   Do we actually construct meaning, interpret any evidence we come across – through discovery, exploration, asking questions, using a variety of means. This is a constructivist and interpretive worldview, philosophy and methodology.

(A)   The methodology that is based on a fact-based, fact-discovering, fixing, measuring view of the world is often termed a **positivist methodology**. It tends to lead to deductive research methods, i.e., that test theories and hypotheses, and prove that this way or that way is the case. It uses largely quantitative methods to do so, so it is likely to use experiments, surveys or tests, and in science it produces experimental data from carrying out a number of repeated experiments in order to fix the truth, finalise the results, know about the situation, the experience, the existence, through proving the same result time and time again. It often generates statistical data in the social sciences because the questioning or gathering of data has been carried out many times or because the surveys are large and rigorously tested, and reliable results have been achieved. This research is said to be reliable and generalisable, i.e., you can depend on it to happen that way again, to have the same results under the same conditions. These results are replicable in the same way under the same circumstances.

(B) This methodology is often termed either anti-positivist or post-positivist or interpretivist. It tends to lead to inductive research methods that use research vehicles which allow you to build theory.

It's based on a view of the world as not fixable but interpreted by human beings, in context, and the inductive research methods and vehicles that are the tools by which the methods operate such as the actual questionnaires to small numbers, and /or using open-ended or semi-structured questions, the list of questions asked in an interview, i.e., the interview schedule, the observation checklist for a set of observations that are not based on repeating identical processes. These gather data that cannot be identically reproduced even in similar situations. This is because they are based on human situations and interactions, which are always a bit different, non-replicable, and non-identical. This is not sloppy subjective research, it is research which recognises that human experiences and interactions change, and so do interpretations, in context. The methods can be rigorous and should be, so if they have been carefully developed and the questions are appropriate and well worded, the results are valid and the processes said to be internally valid, i.c., they are appropriate for the questions being asked, in context.

It is very important when deciding on what methodology you are using, what research design and methods can actually enable you to address your question, test your hypothesis, or open up, solve or go some way to solve your research problem, that you state the methodology, the methods, research design, and that you indicate why you have chosen them to help you action your research. You also need to indicate what the limitations of this methodology and chosen methods are. Identifying the limitations means you make it clear that nothing can be absolutely stated for certain to be true in every case, and there are necessarily some issues as part of the research which will affect its being utterly dependable and replicable in other circumstances (however many precautions you have taken to ensure the research is well designed and carried out and the data handled well). For example, limitations might refer to the sample – you cannot ask everyone the questions, or the context might hamper people's responses. There are a range of factors affecting the absolute certainty you have about saying that results indicate that something is the case or is always going to be true.

In developing your research design, be very clear and define your choices. Other people might well choose to ask questions in a different way. Most research will be either positivistic and quantitative or post- or anti-positivistic, or interpretivist and qualitative. There are many fine distinctions that other writers and researchers will enter into argument about here, but this is a rough guide.

Using mixed methodology

Despite some popular beliefs and very firm arguments to the contrary, it is possible to use mixed methodologies at different stages of your research, although you do need to be extremely careful.

You can believe both that we can find out facts, and that we can develop and construct knowledge.

This mixed methodology uses mixed methods.

Your work could be:

1   Deductive (theory testing – believes in facts – using, e.g., mass observation according to certain categories).
2   Inductive (developing a theory from the next stage of questioning by, for example, using the interview method and an interview schedule of questions with 20 people or so and growing your theories from the interview results).
3   Deductive again (testing the theory you developed from the interviewing method by turning the key questions into the form of a large-scale survey that gives you further statistics).

Using mixed methodologies, and using mixed methods

From your mixed beliefs about the way in which knowledge is produced in the world and your position in the world, you might develop a research design which uses mixed methods, growing from your belief in mixed methodology (see Entwistle and Ramsden, 1983).

This could take several journeys.

Deductive then inductive

Figure 8.1 shows three possible stages your research might involve.

You might start out by testing a theory with a large survey (this is the method, the actual physical survey itself, the research vehicle). This would be quantitative data gathering, deductive methodology in a positivistic paradigm, i.e., positivist testing of the world based on your belief that if you ask questions which have been rigorously pretested, of large numbers, the statistical data produced can be interpreted according to certain theories, to produce underlying themes and ways of measuring the responses, and the patterns of people's responses show trends. The large number of responses produces statistically viable results which you feel, in the same circumstances, could be replicated, but should the circumstances change, or those whom you ask, or where you ask and why, these variables (population, context, location) might well alter the results, and so you would be able to argue that the change of population, context or location causes such a change in response.

This establishes a basis of statistical 'fact'.

Next you might move into an inductive stage, where you generate interview questions from your own ideas and experience and the responses from the survey – those questions

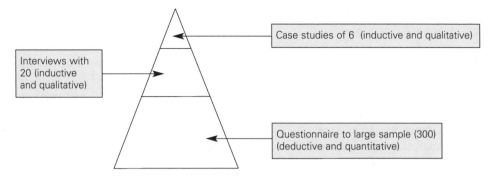

Figure 8.1

which seemed to generate interesting statistics – and ask a few people about the issues that are the focus of the interview. Here you are believing first that some of the world is factual, fixable and calculable, and this stage of the research comes up with reliable and generalisable data, while you know that the second stage of the research is not reliable or generalisable but internally valid in itself and yields rich data about feelings and people's views.

Finally you might build on this inductive stage by narrowing down your focus, and developing deep and rich data by identifying a few case studies from your data.

Or

Inductive then deductive

You might start, for instance, with an exploration – ask questions, carry out semi-structured open-ended interviews around a range of questions, see what your results indicate as important patterns or variations, then start to identify patterns, develop some fixed questions and deliver a large-scale survey with these questions at the heart of it. In the inductive part of this research you would be developing theory based on initial enquiries, and in the deductive part you would be testing those theories using large-scale survey methods and statistics.

One such example is the development and use of the Reflections on Learning Inventory (RoLI), which Professors J. H. F (Erik) Meyer and Gillian Boulton-Lewis developed (1997). They began by asking questions about how students went about their learning, what motivated them, what they thought learning was, what they knew they had learned and the kind of learning outcomes they sought (using interviews, qualitative research on an inductive design). Erik carried out his interviewing and questioning in multicultural South Africa and Gillian among white and Aboriginal students in Australia.

They then built the survey, and it has been tested and used with students from international contexts for over ten years (quantitative and deductive). It keeps being refined as the different survey items are more and more rigorously tested with large-scale usage so that they are arguably really dependable.

Whatever is appropriate for asking your research question, be clear about the different stages and defend your work.

Subjectivity exists in both kinds of research methodologies, although we always try to acknowledge and reduce it. It is clearly present in research methodology that relies on the construction of knowledge, where it is acknowledged that the sample, methods, and design are all in variation and affected by time, place, the researcher, the sample, research practices and interpretative processes, among other things, but that attempts at the removal of bias and opinion are enabled by a robust research design, and triangulation of methods. Subjectivity also exists in what could be termed 'pure' scientific research, where scientists carry out well managed and well documented experiments. Their choice of experiments and, to some extent, the questions they ask of the data produced in order to interpret it are based on essentially subjective research questions and a need to know some things rather than others. This can be determined by different times and places, different needs and abilities, the opportunities for different kinds of study, and different subjects.

Research designs – samples, variables

Once you have defined your methodology you can start to build your research design, which, like a pattern for sewing clothes or an architect's plan for a house, will enable you to plan out how you can ask your research question or test your hypothesis. From your methodology grow the research design and the methods. You will need to develop a time plan, decide on sampling, and the methods in action to make that design real, using tools or vehicles – interviews, surveys, observations, journalling, experiments and so on, much as a craftsman would in making a coat or a house.

Your design will contain methodology and methods, time and plans of action. If it is for a scientific piece of research or a social science (or related subject) piece of research, it will use the term 'sample', which means the items, people, dogs, houses, whatever you are looking at, which have been selected from the whole population of houses, dogs, people, etc. available. The sample is those of which/whom you ask your research questions/test your hypotheses/work out your problem.

Why sample?

Because we cannot test every instance, or ask every person, or try out a procedure on every dog, or observe and define every house, or whatever your population is. Our sample must be defined, chosen for a reason, and will affect the results and the applicability of those results and findings to other instances that you and others might research.

You might choose:

A representative sample   This is a sample taken from a whole population because the sample are typical of the population's characteristics, and so can be said to be representative. The whole population of a specific field, such as those who fly regularly (at least once a month) on Ryanair to Dublin, cannot be asked about their experience of the new Dublin airport, because this group would be too large to ask. However, once the characteristics of such a group have been defined, for instance business travellers, flying at least once a month, staying no more than one night and more usually flying in and out in a day, then a representative sample can be discovered. It needs to be noted whether the sample is a specific proportion of the total number (e.g., total number 20,000, 10% sample taken).

A stratified sample   If the whole population of those you are studying can be sub-divided in categories, according to different strata like rocks, then you might decide it is important to take a sample which represents these strata or categories in relation to their appearance in the total population, for instance, of types of universities. In the UK there are several types of university:

1   Old ones of medieval foundation – Oxford and Cambridge.
2   The Russell group – old, well established, high status, some nearly as old as Oxbridge, some built early in the twentieth century or late nineteenth century, e.g., Durham, Leeds.
3   Red-brick – mostly established before and expanded just after the Second World War, often in the cities. Leeds would fit this category again and so would Nottingham.
4   Greenfield – those established in the 1960s, usually set outside the cities.
5   The ex-polytechnics – those founded as universities in 1994 or close to that date.

You can stratify them differently but this will do for our purposes. They are so stratified because of their age, status, location, date of foundation, where all these elements affect the funding, the range of subjects, and the student experience, so these differences would give us some way of dividing up the range of universities according to their differences.

Opportunistic sample   This is a sample taken from those which are available to you, e.g., all the people who happen to be on the number 19 bus, where you are looking at the experience of bus travellers or commuters, or the number of single mothers who are studying for research degrees in your university, where you are looking at the experiences of single mothers undertaking research degrees.

Random sample   This is not as random as it sounds. It is not just looking, for example, at any dog which turns up, or any headmaster who answers your online questions. You need to set up a mechanism to choose the sample randomly according to a selection of categories of difference, where the individuals of the population have been seen to fit the set categories. Individuals for your research sample can be chosen in relation to these categories, each one of these selected at random.

Your kind of sample affects the results you can produce and how other people can use your results in their own work.

Variation and variables

Variables are categories of difference that can be applied to your sample, the design aspects, such as time, context, researcher, and to the analyses. Grix defines them thus: 'Variables are concepts which vary in amount or kind' (2004, p. 177).

For example, if we return to our travellers to Dublin on Ryanair, we might want to know if there are differences in the responses to the new airport from men or women, younger travellers and older travellers, those in groups or those who travel individually; these differences in the types of traveller are *variables* in our research sample because the differences might well affect the responses to our questions. Independent variables are causal and explanatory, i.e., they cause and explain the differences in your design, and so your results. Dependent variables are caused or affected by the independent variables (see Grix, 2002, pp. 164 and 168).

We might like to look at those who travel at 6 a.m. and return the same day, as compared with those who travel during the day and stay over. This kind of variable is related to the time of travel and length of stay.

We might look at those who use the online check-in or priority services as opposed to those who don't. The use of check-in is the independent variable while the dependent variables, congestion and travel time, are caused by the independent variable.

When we come to analyse the statistical data resulting from this survey, we might be able to cross-tabulate or compare across different variables and so discover for instance that:

(1) 10% of women travelling stay overnight and 60% of men stay overnight;
(2) 30% of all business travellers who stay overnight use the online and priority check-in. Of those who use this form of check-in, 50% are women, and 80% of those women say that this eases congestion and provides a more pleasant business airport experience.

While the first analysis of results just looks at two variables – gender in relation to overnight stay in terms of the whole population of business travellers on Ryanair to Dublin, the second analysis is more complex and relates more variables – (a) gender, (b) stay, (c) form of check-in, and (d) satisfaction with the airport experience.

In any research proposal you will be expected to discuss and defend:

- Your choices of methodology/ies
- Your choices of methods

to indicate which theorists lie behind these and why.

And explain why you did not choose other methodologies and methods.

Activity

Please consider these key questions to ask yourself (based on Fraenkel and Wallen, 1993).

- Which methodology or (less common) methodologies have you chosen for your research and why?
- Which methods have you chosen and why?
- Have you fully described the design and methodology in this study – what was done, why, where, when and how?
- Can you defend the research design? Is it likely to help you test your hypothesis or ask your research question?
- Is the connection between the conceptual framework and the research design and methodology clear?
- Have you described how you analyse the data and why these procedures are appropriate?
- Where are you taking your sample from?
  How will you find them?
  Can you foresee any problems or difficulties in your sampling?
  What are the variables, if any, likely to be?
  What kind of information do you think you might be going to find out, and
  What might it all mean, given your sample and variables?

Summary

In this chapter we have considered:

- Research goals and research questions, the research problem or research hypotheses.
- Methodology.
- Methods.
- Research design.
- Reliability, validity and generalisability in the research.
- Samples – research population – reasons and explanations for how the population was sampled, description of the participants and their characteristics.

Further reading

Burgess, H., Sieminski, S. and Arthur, L. (2006) *Achieving Your Doctorate in Education* (London: Sage).

Fraenkel, J. R. and Wallen, N. E. (1993) *How to Design and Evaluate Research in Education*, 2nd edn (New York: McGraw Hill).

Grix, J. (2004) *The Foundations of Research* (Basingstoke: Palgrave Macmillan).

Hussey, J. and Hussey, R. (1997) *Business Research: A Practical Guide for Undergraduate and Postgraduate Students* (London: Macmillan Press).

Meyer, J. H. F. and Boulton-Lewis, G. (1997) *Reflections on Learning Survey* (Brisbane: Queensland University of Technology).

Stierer, B. and Antoniou, M. (2004) 'Are there Distinctive Methodologies for Pedagogic Research in Higher Education?' *Teaching in Higher Education*, 9(3) (July 2004), pp. 275–85.

Wisker, G. (2008) *The Postgraduate Research Handbook: Succeed with your MA, MPhil, EdD and PhD*, 2nd edn (Basingstoke: Palgrave Macmillan).

9 Finding and Using Sources

This chapter considers:

- ▶ steps on your research journey;
- ▶ searching for sources;
- ▶ using sources;
- ▶ primary sources;
- ▶ secondary sources;
- ▶ working with librarians and others to find and use sources;
- ▶ using the Internet;
- ▶ salvaging, foraging, managing and using your sources appropriately.

Sources are essential in research – without them there are only questions and problems.

Your sources, both primary (originally produced at the time and place that you are studying – historical facts, participants, responses, artefacts) and secondary (usually critical responses and comments on sources or events) are where you get your information, data and the basis of your evidence for your arguments. Of course, you are also using your own imagination and cognitive processes and probably those of others around you.

Seeking out primary sources, locating them, enabling them to provide you with information, ideas, arguments, evidence for your research, is a rich part of your research journey and your skills as a researcher. Secondary sources are others' theorised use of sources, in a research framework, the critical comments on, theorised arguments about the usefulness of, theorised engagement with primary sources and arguments. Working with these secondary sources is largely discussed in the chapter on literature reviewing where you can consider how to engage in a dialogue with others who have something to say about your area of work and who might have worked with similar sources asking the same questions as yours, or with the same sources, asking different questions.

Much research is like foraging for food. You are not sure what you will find even if you set out with some clear ideas and directions. You might believe that certain sources will be easy to get hold of and provide you with all you need, but you might well need to go beyond the obvious sources and ask questions which are quite different from those planned, and you might need to use unusual sources. It is also possible in research that surprising ideas and information emerge from the most unlikely of sources. Letters, photos, maps, visual images, artefacts, videos, diaries, books, posters, music, government documents, prints, dissertations, serials, newspapers, tablets, oral histories and many more are all primary sources.

The main pieces of advice in terms of your location, identification and use of sources are to:

- Seek out sources which will help you address your question, test your hypothesis, identify and approach, even solve your problem.
- Be very focused, organised and directed and keep careful notes of your sources and what they tell you at all times.

- Be very open to alternative sources of ideas, inspiration and information because research is a mixture of hard, directed, organised, managed, documented work, and creative, inspirational work mixed with surprises and revelations.

Seeking out, finding and making use of your primary and secondary sources are part of several steps on your research journey.

Steps on your research journey

Step 1: Decide on your topic

This is based on your broad definition of interests, questions, problems, thoughts and hypotheses to test, or research questions to ask. It is usually a broad, ill-defined area from which you need to select a section for exploration and work that you can really get to grips with, which will lead to a do-able and manageable project.

Step 2: Define your question, problem, hypothesis

Define your research problem, question, or hypothesis and then this will guide and narrow your searching for primary and secondary sources. Basic reference tools like encyclopaedias, bibliographies, and the Subject Guides developed by your university's librarians can help you define the parameters of your topic.

> Before delving too far into the subject area and then the facts, think about what angle you want to take on your topic. What alternate terms are relevant to your topic? Contextualise it in a broader area.

See what is related and relevant as well as the central areas of focus for your topic. This will help you to look at the absolutely obvious central primary sources and also to look around your topic. This looking around helps you to contextualise your topic, see a variety of issues and concerns of importance to it and a variety of angles or approaches you might take, and then perhaps even cast a new light on the topic by contrasting or comparing it with similar or different issues or related subjects, and finding new ideas and approaches to it. See Chapter 4 on the research project to consider ways of developing your question, or hypothesis, and defining the focus of your research.

Step 3: Decide on the kinds of sources you can use

Consider what represents sources in your subject area. You will probably be using both primary sources and secondary sources.

Primary sources are produced in the period and place under study and they are the sources that are the focus for the study, rather than comments by others about the study focus, while secondary sources are usually comments upon, reflections and critiques about events, data, and primary sources. There are some more complex cases that are discussed below, but the main point is that the primary sources are the focus which provide information for your study, and they are produced at the time and place under study either by yourself (through questions, interviews, observations) or by others.

Primary sources will probably comprise:

- witness statements,
- government documents,
- manuscripts and archival material produced at the time and place being studied,
- artefacts – if this is what is under study,
- questionnaire data,
- interview and focus group data,
- audio and video records,
- visual products under study.

For example, history tends to use documents, public and private records and artefacts from the period under study, while sociology tends to use people's responses collected via questionnaires and interviews, their results are presented as data and then organised according to themes and patterns. Literary studies tend to use original writing from the author(s) being studied, and information about context.

If you are working in interdisciplinary subjects and are less used to identifying the sources for the new subjects with which you are working, then seek advice and/or look at significant articles and books in this interdisciplinary subject and work backwards – what did they use as primary and secondary sources? These could be a start to suggest what you will need to use in your own research.

Once you have decided on your research topic, you need to brainstorm the range of sources that you might find useful. Some of the most usual ones might not be the right ones for this particular piece of work.

Ask friends and colleagues; be open to new thoughts and kinds of sources. However, as with focusing on the definition of your topic (remember the slice of cake analogy in Chapter 4), at some point you will need to decide which sources you are going to use among all those available because to some extent this choice determines the kind of answers or responses you will produce.

For instance, if you are looking at the topic of airline terrorism, your sources could be an airline terrorist, whose views and experiences you would gather through interviewing him about his experience/intentions and the subsequent punishment he is experiencing. Who you ask, what your primary sources are, depends on the fine definitions of your research question. You could gain primary source information by:

- Interviewing hostages who have been victims of airline terrorism (if your question is about their experiences).
- Reading documentary sources in the form of letters between terrorists, or between victims and family members (if your question is about communications).

- Looking at the immediate representation by the media, by reading media coverage from newspapers, viewing TV and film footage, and so on (if your question is about media coverage). Here a problem could arise about the value and status of media responses and written records and responses (indeed your question could focus on their value and status).

Reportage is a *primary source* if you are looking at how the events are reported, i.e., the reportage itself is your focus. But if you are looking only at the events and artefacts arising from them, then reportage can be seen as a *secondary source* because it is a comment.

Your sources may also be used to contextualise some specific examples of airline terrorism, for instance, using archival material of various events in order to establish a history, to build a pattern or indicate deviation from patterns.

You could also

- carry out a documentary analysis of the regulations brought in by airlines to try to prevent terrorism;
- interview some of the people who are responsible for these regulations;
- listen to videotapes of confessions;
- view photos taken at the scene;
- access more artistic responses to airline terrorism: analysing the sculptures produced in a park commemorating victims, for example.

Do be sure to be clear about which sources will help you ask your question and whether you are using the sources as primary sources – produced at the time, directly related to your focus – or secondary sources – comments about the time and the events. With the artistic responses, above, they will be primary sources if you are researching artistic and other responses, but they will be secondary sources for the actual airline terrorism events because they are comments.

For any project, whether research to back up an individual essay or report or a fully explored dissertation, you will need to consult primary sources. For some people the main research work is carried out directly engaging with the primary sources as they are produced. For example, students studying archaeology might well need to go on an archaeological dig and actually uncover original pieces of broken pots and artefacts, and to dust around the sides of emerging constructions, which later can be identified as rooms, doorways and parts of ancient homes. This uncovering of primary sources takes place in many different disciplines, not merely archaeology. For instance, those of us researching into the ways in which the media have covered 'fandom' and celebrity, primary sources would be the newspapers, the fanzines, and the TV footage responding to, projecting and creating celebrity for current stars of music, screen or stage. The secondary sources would be the critical comments, the articles and reports theorising these products of fandom.

Please consider your own proposed research. For your use of all primary sources you will need to ask a number of questions, so please think about these now in relation to your own research:

- What do I need to search for?
- What am I allowed or able to search for?
- What sources can I use?
- How can I access them?
- Who or what could help me access them?
- What represents an extract, artefact or primary source, which will stand for evidence?
- How can I have the right to use this source? Are there issues of copyright? Ownership? Are there issues of confidentiality involved in accessing, extracting and reusing these extracts, pieces of evidence, and primary sources?
- How can I extract from the primary source materials to help me explore my topic and ask my question?

Identify primary sources in the context of this piece of research.

Then start to ask questions about how you can use the sources in a theoretical framework, as part of your ongoing, developing, critical, focused explanation in addressing your question. You need to consider:

How can the theories you are using help you to interpret these sources?

Your local university librarian and the online catalogues are very good initial locations for primary source material in text form if you are working with, for example, text produced at a particular point in time or place, or original written material.

You might need to email, write to, phone or visit the place where the data is stored. For example, if you want to know about births, marriages and deaths you can consult local sources – parish records – and national sources – government records. If you want to think about the ownership of land and its changed usage, the local land registry offices could well be the place to start, where your primary sources are maps and deeds of title. Your first point of call is your librarian in the subject in which you are working; they will be able to help you with:

- Online guides.
- Catalogues and other filing and data management of sources, so you can see what there is and start to identify and select in relation to your research area.
- Ways of accessing materials, whether in archives, online or on the shelves.
- Other locations where you might find your sources, such as links to the local government archives, various records held by religious organisations or central organisations. Your librarian can probably help you with suggesting how to gain access to these primary sources online or in person.

You also need to consult the secondary sources.

Step 4: Find out what has already been written on your topic

Once you have chosen a topic, the next step is to search the literature to see what has already been written. You might want to start by looking for *books* and *journal articles*.

You need to consider:

What *types and formats* of material are in the library? Or on the Internet? Or in other collections and information sources such as archives?

Where and how can you search for books and journal articles? Statistics and collections of information to enable you to ask your question or explore your topic?

What other archive sources are there for commentaries and critical responses? Newspapers, documentary films? All of which might be in your local university library or in specialist libraries or collections.

Step 5: Consider other types of materials that might be relevant to your research

You will need to look beyond the obvious, which might well have been thoroughly used by someone else, or might not exactly fit into your research question or topic. Ask yourself, where else might I find useful primary sources? For example, if you were researching the musical influence on an author or the ways in which a writer and music interact, you would need to go beyond the references of the musical sources and some comment on their originals, perhaps, to original music recordings and to the archives that store these. In this way you can both hear them and check up on the response at the time, the reason for their composition and production, and why and where people listened to them. Then you might need to explore the author's journals, blogs, diaries, notes, whatever is publicly available for you to see, to find out what the author says they are using the sources for. Some authors are very explicit about sources, as if they wish you to follow in their footsteps and seek their sources, and others are not even very aware of them. You need to discover what they say about their sources, what and how they wrote and responded to in their time. For this you might need to consult newspaper archives and publicly held music or picture sources (depending on what your research is for).

If you are looking at how certain authors deal with ecological issues you might explore the sources that they consulted, such as material on the politics of the time, scientific discoveries about the impact of social changes. You might also look at their diary and journal entries, in order to evaluate their reasons for their focus and how they have responded to what, and in what ways and why. You might also wish to explore the effects, facts, texts and activities, and look at and listen to radio archives, perhaps, or artists' responses to these events and records, to find out about the reasons behind and response to these productions.

For a major research project, it will often be necessary to locate materials that your university doesn't own and collections outside the obvious and local. You can use library links and other links on the Internet, and track back, record and note the source materials of your authorities and their references, then identify and locate materials which they used.

Library catalogues and databases that you could use include

Internal Internet library source holdings
Center for Research Libraries catalogue
WorldCat
Eureka/RLG Union Catalogue

Bibliographies and Annual Reviews you could use

Scan the bibliographies in books you have already located for additional sources.
Look for book-length bibliographies and annual reviews on your subject.

Periodicals

Periodical articles ('journal articles' or 'magazine articles') can be of two general types, both potentially useful in research:

Scholarly articles: These are written by specialists in their fields of study and are published in journals aimed at specialised audiences, usually identified by academic discipline (such as archaeology, Greek literature, economics, or history) or by broad fields of study (such as the humanities, social sciences, or sciences).

You might want to consult scholarly articles:

- as secondary sources in your research;
- as sources for the identification of primary sources.

There are many indexes that can help you find articles in scholarly journals. Look in your Library's *Research Guides* for sections on 'Locating Journal Articles', on 'Indexes and Abstracts', or on 'Databases' to identify indexing tools most relevant to your topic.

General articles: These are written by a variety of authors and published in journals and magazines aimed at educated but not specialised audiences, or at the general reading public.

You might want to consult general articles:

- for non-specialist treatment of a subject;
- as primary sources, indicative of or reflective on the general or popular culture of a period or for contemporary non-specialist commentary on an event.

The most frequently used resources that index general periodicals and/or offer full-text access to articles are:

- *Academic Search*
- *Academic Universe*
- *Readers' Guide Abstracts*

Consider using alternative types of material

There is a variety of *Book Reviews* material that can help you in your searching and which might not be obvious at first glance. Some of this is provided by others who have carried out previous research and made evaluative studies or have catalogued and evaluated, problematised and explored.

Reviews of books appear in journals and monographs. Books may be reviewed individually, or a group of related books may be reviewed and compared. Though short notices or summaries of a book often appear fairly quickly after its publication, scholarly book reviews usually don't appear in journals until a year or two after, so you will need to keep searching over time. Look at book reviews and then the sources they refer to, and follow up these sources. This sometimes leads you completely off course, so do be selective, and sometimes it leads to exactly the richest and most appropriate piece of information or essay which can help you in your work.

You might want to consult book reviews:

- as shortcuts to learning about the content of books;
- for information about the status and importance of a book;
- as summaries of work in your subject area;
- to lead you to further reading – using their references as a start.

Where you should look for a book review depends on whether the book in question is popular or scholarly, current or historical.

Internet resources

Many of us might not even go into a library for our first exploration of the primary and secondary sources, but instead look them up on the web using one of many search engines, such as Google, or for a more refined search: Google Scholar. Look at Chapter 10 on Internet searching.

Resources on the Internet include websites, electronic texts, information about people and institutions, full texts, extracts from texts, some scanned articles for the period you are studying, and discussion groups.

Usually, your university library, the British Library or similar will have secured Internet sites and selecting from them in a way which helps you to use them more straightforwardly often helps. These often appear behind the university portal or gateway into which you have logged. Their selection also ensures the reliability and authenticity of the sites.

Ask yourself questions like these before using information gathered from Internet sites:

- Who is the author of the website? Are the author's credentials listed?
- What institution or organisation is behind the website?
- When was the website created or last updated?
- Who is the intended audience for the website?

- Is the information provided objective or biased as far as you can tell?
- How does information provided by the website compare with other works, including print works?

Statistics

When you are searching for statistics, consider the following:

- What is your topic? What agency or organisation might have collected statistics on this topic? How reliable are they? Where else might the statistics be found?
- Are you looking for statistics in a specific geographical area, or are you comparing geographical areas – e.g. comparing demographic downturns in Latin America with those in the USA?
- For what time period do you need statistics – the most recent or a time series?
- Are you looking in a single subject/area or across subject/areas?

The following are suggested resources for current statistics about the United States and countries of the world:

- *Statistical Abstract of the United States* (Census Bureau)
    Provides statistics on all economic and social aspects of American society, as well as comparative international statistics.
- *Fedstats* (Federal Interagency Council on Statistical Policy)
    The gateway to statistics from over 100 US Federal agencies. Provides access by topic, geography, subject and alphabetically by agency.
- *World Factbook*
    Provides essential facts and statistics for all areas of the world.
- *OFFSTATS: Official Statistics on the Web*
    Lists websites offering free and easily accessible social, economic and general data from official sources. Listings by country and by subject.
- *United Nations Common Database* (UNCDB)
    UNCDB provides selected series from 30 specialised international data sources for all available countries and areas.

Step 5: Consider using alternate types of material

Images and graphic materials

You might want to use images or graphic materials:

- to study visual evidence for historical or sociological research;
- as primary source materials.

Video recordings

You might want to use videos:

- to study cinema;
- for historical or sociological research;
- as *primary source materials*;
- to supplement work on a particular course.

Whatever you do with your primary sources, do make sound notes about where they came from, what they are, how to locate them. There are comments in Chapter 10 on taking sources from the Internet in particular.

One interesting tip is to see if you can access the holdings of other great libraries such as the British Library, Cambridge University, or Yale, by visiting them. As a university student you can often gain a pass or visitor's ticket to other libraries. Ask your tutor for a letter of recommendation and ring/email ahead to check, or contact them through their websites. Often your university will have an agreement which lets you access some of their materials, some of the library tutorials on how to use primary sources, and some of those sources.

Summary

In this chapter we have considered:

- Definitions of primary and secondary sources.
- What kinds of sources can be found and where.
- How you might access sources.

Further reading

Denzin, N. K. and Lincoln, Y. S. (2003) *Collecting and Interpreting Qualitative Materials* (New York: Sage).

Walliman, N. (2001) *Your Research Project: A Step by Step Guide for the First-time Researcher* (London: Sage).

10 Using the Internet for Research

This chapter considers:

▶ straightforward ways of searching for information on the Internet;
▶ making good use of information available from the Internet;
▶ Google and Wikipedia and beyond;
▶ avoiding plagiarism;
▶ referencing Internet sites;
▶ networking via the net;
▶ Net ethics.

The Internet is a very useful source of much of the secondary and some of the primary information which you might well need in your research. However, you need to become skilled in using it so that you get to the range of appropriate sources, rather than relying on Google (a search engine which can lead you to some of the sources you need, but not all) or Wikipedia (an online encyclopaedia of sorts which is written by anyone and everyone and so is sometimes brilliant and sometimes untrustworthy as a source) alone, and you do need to learn how to use the Internet wisely, in a properly selective, properly referenced fashion just like any other information source.

In Jorge Luis Borges's story of 'The Library of Babel', he imagines a library in which everything that has ever been written or could be written in any order in any manner was actually stored somewhere in the library. The Internet or World Wide Web would make a good subject for a Borges short story. It is probably true that practically everything you might want to find for your research background and much of the critical work you need to read to help focus your own research and engage it in a dialogue with other people's work in the field is out there somewhere on the net, and much more besides.

The problem is that you need to know how to ask questions, search sensitively and appropriately, and manage the information you find and incorporate it where useful, as just part of the elements of your research work, whether underpinning critical reading, or the management of original data.

One of the great temptations with a heavy work and life schedule and very little time to go about the painstaking enquiry and thinking processes which make for good research is to look it all up on the net. Much of the reading that you need will be available there and if your library has bought subscriptions to places which store journal articles, such as JSTOR or Muse, depending on your subject area, many of the journal articles you need will be there.

But actually it isn't all on the net. Whole books are unlikely to be on the net, for instance, and many primary sources (historical documents like diaries, or parish registers, novels, statues or paintings, questionnaire results and the questionnaires themselves) are most frequently not on the net either.

Of course what is *definitely* not on the net is the answer to the particular research question that you have set yourself, or to the particular problem on which your research is based. If your research design involves you in gathering original data through your fieldwork; if it involves you engaging the critical theory and other critical work by other critics in a dialogue with your own work on a particular research issue, question, problem or body of work such as, for instance, a range of novels by African American women writers, or data about widening participation in Israel, then you will find that you can use some of the things you read on the Internet but that nobody has addressed your question or your problem directly. Your work is a unique exploration in a dialogue with critical work and some other work which has been done by others, just as is the case with all sources in hard copy as well as those on the net.

Some ways of using the Internet

Suggested reading

Your lecturer may include Internet sites in the suggested reading on your course or for your essay or research project. You need to access these sites and sources in the normal way, and treat them as if they were of the same trustworthiness as any hardcopy source would be. Read carefully to identify what of the information, argument, quotations or examples are useful in addressing your research question or dealing with your problem. Then take notes and gather some of the information from these sources, extract it as you would any other reading but using net referencing, and make sure it's part of your overall argument and is referenced at the end of your essay, project or dissertation. It is unlikely that you will be safe merely referencing Wikipedia. In fact, you could be penalised in any essay, project or dissertation you produce which relies heavily on Wikipedia. Although some of the information there is very useful, it is an unmediated, un-peer-reviewed and unchecked source and some of the information is actually wrong. It is also true that relying on Google or Wikipedia is a rather lazy way of conducting research. You are not doing either the searching or the processing.

Primary sources on the web

The Internet has much data stored on it such as statistics, records, images, sounds, texts and text extracts, and all of these can be used as primary sources, properly referenced. See Chapter 9 on primary sources.

As a data source

Your lecturer may suggest Internet sites and sources of data in the same way as they might suggest that you visit the records office or the Mass Observation project at Sussex University or consult the diaries of eighteenth-century poets, depending on what your topic is and what primary or secondary sources you are using. Again, use the data to relate to and answer your question, and reference its sources.

Secondary sources on the web

It also has a great deal of secondary sources stored on it in the form of journal articles, lectures, interviews, extracts from books, reviews, conference papers, videos, and public reports of all kinds. These secondary sources engage with primary information such as images, quotations, data and so on and comment on them critically, using theory and a dialogue between the author, the theory, the question and the data or work. You too can use these secondary sources as part of your own dialogue and engagement with your question or problem. To do so, as with a printed text, you would read carefully, identify and analyse their arguments or the ways in which they viewed the primary sources of data, engage with their arguments and select from them appropriately using short extracts and referencing after the extract as you would if it were a print source.

Specialist searches and refining your search

There are many general search engines, such as Google and Altavista or Yahoo or Ask, which store vast quantities of information, and they often tend to store information which has been selected differently, so do try more than one engine in your quest for information. There are also subject-specific search engines which collect and store information specific to subjects and topics, and these might be appropriate for a more specific search. The Web of Knowledge, www.tile.net or JSTOR at jstor.org/search are examples of these subject-specific search engines. If you are unsure of such engines' existence, ask your tutor, the librarians, your peers, and look at the Internet references at the end of a couple of books or articles in your field. You will soon find the ones you can learn to trust, because their information is full, properly sourced, accessible and seems as correct as can be managed.

Subject-specific search engines can also really help you refine your search. For example, if you're looking for a literary topic you might search the Voice of the Shuttle at vos.ucsb.edu/, which has been developed by Alan Liu and is based at the University of California Santa Barbara in the English department, on their server. Most subjects or professional areas of study (e.g., occupational therapy, legal services, optometry, and social work) will have such refined and focused engines. Within the data they store and offer, you will find rich databases compiled by subject specialists.

For instance, if you are looking for Native American women writers you will find a literary database on their work nested within the Voice of the Shuttle's database collection. On some databases you can click on the hyperlink to take you to primary sources, in this instance the poems, or secondary sources, in this instance, critical works on the poems and the poet, and biographical details of the poet. Some also provide links to the writer's website.

So you will be foraging and borrowing deep through a search engine and databases to find the rich specific sources you need to engage with your own question and help evidence or develop your argument in your own research. Once you have carried out such a search a few times you will find you can transfer your searching skills to a whole variety of other searches where necessary. Don't just stick with Google!

If you are looking for a person, you can search Advanced People Search on
http://web.icq.com/whitepages/search

What not to do

Poor practice and ethics on the net

1 Don't launch into Google or Yahoo or another search engine with a broad and ill-defined topic or statement and expect to find carefully sifted appropriate information. You won't. You might find a million entries or none at all.

   In the first instance there is so much there it will take forever to find anything even vaguely relevant to your topic. In the second instance you're given a false sense that no one has addressed your topic.

2 Don't just download chunks of information from the Internet, referenced or not, without commenting on them and engaging them in your dialogue with the critics in relation to your question or problem.

3 Don't download someone else's essays, for sale or free, and pass them off as your own (this is plagiarism! and will be punished by the university authorities as other forms of cheating). Cutting and pasting from the Internet is no different from copying straight from any other text source. You need to select carefully and reference properly and ensure that what you are extracting and quoting engages in your argument.

Next

1 Do refine your search and be absolutely accurate about your key words when looking through Google or Yahoo and other search engines. You will probably find that the more refined 'Google Scholar' can help you with more specific questions, which will produce journal articles and other data sources. If your key words produce very little response, try thinking of similar words. It could be that an item labelled by one term in the UK is called something else quite different on the continent or in Australasia. For example, 'regional colleges' in the UK usually means further education colleges in the countryside or towns. In Israel they are part of a programme to extend university education into rural areas where a variety of ethnic groups reside. There is some similarity but we might not be using the same terminology. If in doubt, consult a thesaurus for similar words to the one you're searching for.

2 Read electronic texts as carefully as if you are reading a text source which is not online, and engage what you read in your debate. Quote from it appropriately and as part of your ongoing discussion and argument where relevant, and then reference in the normal way – to both the title and the website source – including information on when you accessed it because sometimes sites are updated, e.g.

   'Domestic Dissection: Mike Arnzen's Domestic Horror', Gina Wisker at www.simegen.com/writers/dissections/ (accessed 23 June 2008).

3   Plagiarism and cheating: You wouldn't think to hand copy out someone else's essay, so why would you buy one off the Internet or copy one off the Internet? You will not have done the learning yourself, it's cheating and if you're discovered you will gain a zero mark and could lose your degree. There is another problem that some of the sources on the Internet include essays of very poor quality. Just because something has been uploaded onto the Internet is not an indication that it is right. Wikipedia is a wonderful source of descriptive information and some quality comments on the issues in many topic areas. However, because it is a relatively unmediated, under critically and peer moderated location of explanations and state-ments, some of it is just plain wrong. You cannot be sure that getting your informa-tion from the unmediated and non peer reviewed sources on the Internet (this does not include journal articles or book extracts obviously – they have been critically finessed before being uploaded) that you have actually got information of quality. They could just have been uploaded by anyone at all. Some students place their essays on the Internet as a matter of course and you don't know whether they got a third class mark for this essay, or if it was even passed. Beware.

A sample search

Search A, in the Humanities and Arts

I'm trying to find out some information and some essays on postcolonial writing and gender for an essay that I'm doing. My key words would be:

Postcolonial, gender, women, contemporary, and after that the authors that I expect to be using, i.e., Erna Brodber and Nalo Hopkinson.

Searching on the Internet is like playing the board game 'Snakes and Ladders'. You find nothing, or you find things, then they turn out to be empty shells, which is like falling down a snake, then suddenly you find something really rich and can pursue it, which is like climbing a ladder – but suddenly you realise it is not the quality you want or it's copied from somewhere else – down the snake again – only to suddenly discover a rich source secreted away behind a term you had not thought of – and up another ladder. If you play hard and put up with the misleading or blank parts, you should reach your destination!

Step 1

Look up the key terms and the names of the authors on Google. A series of recent surveys amongst undergraduates found that this is the first thing that everybody does, so that's what I'll try.

Oh dear, this could be difficult. 'Postcolonial' returned 2,400,000 entries. Luckily the first one is Wikipedia – however, can I trust what it says about 'postcolonial'? This does seem to be quite a well written entry with a series of links so I can follow some of these links through to the theorists, find out more about postcolonial criticism, history, literature this way, but this does not get me very far in the intersection of the postcolonial and gender because again there are far too many potential sites to look at . . .

Step 2

Now, looking at 'postcolonial and gender', I've just ended up on a fascinating site about women writers in Singapore and found a theorist whose work I've opened and followed, and found something he's written about postcolonial writing and the hypertext, which sets me off thinking on some very interesting areas. However, this is not about my essay so I need to store these ideas and this link in a file under 'postcolonial ideas' on my computer to come back to later if I want to follow the idea up properly.

Step 3

And now to go back and read some of the articles recommended on Wikipedia and on other sites labelled 'postcolonial', see how much of the theory is useful, extract some of it, copy some of the references to some of it where it is relevant to the gathering together of ideas and other people's comments on areas in the development of my argument.

This has been quite a broad exploration but it has unearthed a series of essays, some of which I'm allowed to look at and some of which are inaccessible to me because my library does not have a subscription, or if it has a subscription they are inaccessible because I'm working from home so I still can't get into them.

Step 4

Now let us approach this topic from another angle.

I'm going to use a subject-specific search engine, 'Voice of the Shuttle', and see what this turns up.

Directly asking it about my author Nalo Hopkinson turns up no result at all. Clearly they do not have a specific entry on her so my question is too defined. It is a gamble. They might have an entry on her but neither the 'Voice of the Shuttle' nor the 'Literary Encyclopaedia' (online) do have one yet. I could give up at this point but I won't because I think I probably need to ask the question differently or to go in a little less directly, anyway I'll try.

I will use the terms of the search engine, hoping that they map onto what I am looking for. So I will look under 'minority literatures', then 'voices from the gaps', then 'Canadian women' in 'writers of colour'.

In these sections, the website deals with those women writers who are not living in America or the Caribbean or Africa etc. but elsewhere.

Step 5

When I open this I find another such opportunity and type the name in. This time it comes up with a wealth of information including biographies, digital works, interviews and links to other sites, a fan page, current interview and so on. Now I can choose what I need, to some extent. Really, it looks like a rich source. Then I can see a range of essays, all links in relation to the question which informs my thoughts.

I follow a few of the links and now need to use some of the text that I discover.

I need to see what I can quote and reference properly from the website and whether it has published the text and page number and published the references so that I can use this text, as it has been put on the web as if in a journal, not repaginated or re-laid out. If it is a PDF file, page numbers will be as the original but it's not a file that you can cut and paste from. Some files lend themselves to this more easily than a PDF file. In order to quote selective quotes and reference them, if it does not have the page numbers of the original text, I either reference it to the website giving the date of my accessing the website or I have to go off and find the hardcopy text again.

One of the problems with the Internet is that your information is only as good as the sites you can access. You need all your problem-solving and creative abilities to think of new ways to search it, and keep foraging and so eventually to find what you want. I just explored, and I am dependent on the last person who updated the site.

Step 6

Dates – this particular site was updated four years ago and so in order to get criticism about my author's most recent work to inform my own readings of it and to help me explore my research question about how she can be read through the notions or theories of the postcolonial, and issues of gender in particular, I shall have to find something more up-to-date.

Step 7

Being a bit smarter with the search. If you are looking for a specific set of words you can use what is called Boolean operators, i.e., +, –, AND, OR, NOT, between the words and phrases you're searching for, or you can put the words and phrases in inverted commas and this forces the search engine to be more precise.

Step 8

Perhaps I would like to find primary sources of data on the web as well as, or instead of, critical articles. I might want to look for my author's blog or search the homepage of the University for courses on one of my authors. All of this could reveal some useful insider information about what they have been doing, and how people are receiving and discussing their work.

My last step looking for Nalo Hopkinson reveals that just a fortnight ago she did a reading at Yale University. I settle down to watch it online as a video stream – although this won't actually help my essays, it gives me a flavour of her work and life.

And you have to have the odd moment off searching!

Search B, in the social sciences (quicker and different)

Another area I'm interested in researching is in the social sciences, in education in fact. I'm exploring an interest in numbers of international students studying in UK universities, where they come from, where they are likely to be studying, and what they're likely to be studying. My question is:

'What are the trends of international student choice in UK universities? And what might these trends suggest in relation to reasons for university and subject choice?'

Some of the questions I want to ask are 'what' or factual questions, e.g.

What universities are international students attending in larger numbers? Where did the students come from? What subjects are they likely to be studying?

I then become a little more complex in my 'what' questions:

Is there a correlation between their subjects of study and country of origin? Is there a correlation between where they study and the popularity of certain subjects offered? Is there a correlation between where they study and the cost of living? Or the existence of an established community from their country of origin?

Now I have established both my main question, which looks up trends, and my sub-questions, which are both 'what' questions and questions which start to answer my speculations about why students choose the subject and the locations, by suggesting correlations (which might be wrong – these are just hunches on my part).

When I actually explore the data when I can find it, I might well be surprised at the trends that I discover, and then I will have to ask more 'why' questions. Of course my questioning is underpinned by theories that I have been identifying and these are to do with:

- academic migration;
- internationalisation;
- course provision and popularity in a changing world.

I need really up-to-date statistics.

One of my sources in the UK should be HESA, the Higher Education Statistics Agency at www.hesa.ac.uk. I type that into the web browser and go into their webpage.

Unfortunately there isn't a category that says 'international student numbers according to university choice' (no one has done the work for me), so I'm going to have to explore a way in which this website stores its data in order to ask my question.

There is a 'students and qualifiers data table' on the left-hand side which looks promising.

On the right-hand side, on the navigation bar, is a series of other titles which also look promising: under the heading 'statistics' there is:

'How to find data'.

This might be a good start. There is also a: 'View statistics online' and something called 'heidi', which is a mystery to me; I probably need to stop myself from looking at this first because I don't know what it is and I need to keep focused.

And 'data collection' is also a major subset on the right-hand-side navigation bar.

- Students and Qualifiers Data Tables
- Staff Data Tables
- Finance Data Tables
- Destinations Data Tables

Performance indicators

Performance Indicators for UK universities and higher education cover widening participation, non-continuation rates, module completion rates, research output and the employment of graduates.

- View performance indicators

Publications archive

To improve access to our data, we have made earlier versions of our products available to download.

- **Management information tables and HOLISCompare**

Management information tables and HOLISCompare have now been superceded by the new heidi system.

heidi is a web-based management information service that provides easy access to a rich source of quantitative data about higher education.

If your institution does not currently subscribe to heidi, you can take part in a free four week trial of the system. Email heidi@hesa.ac.uk to request a free trial account.

You can find out more about heidi at www.heidi.ac.uk.

Other data on this site

- A lot of data is available freely on this site: how to find data on the HESA site.

© 2008 HESA – Higher Education Statistics Agency. www.hesa.ac.uk/index.php

I have deliberately included the site information here to indicate how you might find it, and how to reference it.

I think I shall be smart before I start wandering. There is a link at the bottom called 'How to find the information you need on the HESA website'. Just in case the publication on exactly what I'm looking for is there, I will look at this first.

Under the latest student data, there is Statistical First Release 117, which deals with 'All students, first years and qualifiers'. The range is of 'Institution, Subject, Level of study (undergraduate/postgraduate), Mode of study (full time/part time)', and 'Domicile (UK/EU/Non-EU), Qualifications obtained'. Under that there is one called 'Press Release 120 – Non-UK domiciled students in UK HE institutions'. This looks hopeful. I shall look at both of these.

The data is from 2006 to 2007 so it is quite up-to-date although I would like to know what is happening this year, 2008–9. What I'm told is that there had been no increase of UK domiciled students between 2005/6 and 2006/7 (from 2,006,035 to 2,011,345) then that European Union and non-EU domiciled students have increased the numbers:

Between 2005/06 and 2006/07, the number of enrolments of UK domiciled students showed no percentage increase (from 2,006,035 to 2,011,345). The number of all other European Union (EU) domiciled students increased by 6% (from 106,225 to 112,260) and the number of Non-EU domiciled students increased by 7% (from 223,855 to 239,210). www.hesa.ac.uk (accessed 25 May 2008)

I now want to look at some of the specific tables so that I can start to cross-refer between location of institution, mode of study and domicile, enrolment numbers, subjects chosen. The data is arranged to show trends and increase in 2002–03 to 2006–07, so I had to look at several tables. I expected the table on first-year student enrolments on courses by level of study, mode of study and domicile to help me in my search. It's important also to look at the notes to editors which have been provided and indicate that the 2006–07 enrolments in further education colleges in the UK are not included in the list although they will be published in September 2008, so I'm not going to know if there are any international students who are starting degree courses in England in FE, which could be a reasonable number. I might expect that those students who are on foundation courses which are started in a further education college and finished in the university might well be part of this record. I need to find this out and I'll have to phone someone up to do so. So I can access statistics, but they are not collected to answer my question so I need both to work with them, see how far they can yield information I can cross-tabulate and correlate with other information, and then might have to ring someone up and ask them further questions because there could be some analyses already carried out and not reported here, or the people with their hands on the statistics might be willing to carry out the analyses and cross-tabulate for me (for free or if I pay).

These are some of the tables I am working with. They provide data and I need to ask it the questions I have outlined, above.

All modes	2002–3	2003–4	2004–5	2005–6	2006–7	Percentage change 2005–06 to 2006–07
UK	173720	181005	175165	184085	183320	0%
Other EU	20760	20195	22840	22935	23535	3%
Non-EU	54635	61755	63465	63380	72315	14%
Total	**249115**	**262955**	**261465**	**270405**	**279170**	**3%**

Table 2 First-year student enrolments on HE courses by level of study, mode of study and domicile, 2002–03 to 2006–07 (1)

This is a start but gives me nothing about institution, origin, subject studied.

Another table indicates origins, so ethnicity (although this cannot be guaranteed), and numbers studying where – but not subject area.

Moving on – it seems that 'heidi' is a data management system and might well be able to answer my question. In order to use it, however, I have to be an institutional member with a password. I have gathered a rich amount of primary data from the website and will probably need to go the next step in order to ask it a specific question about this correlation in case it can answer my research question.

Gathering data via the net

There are many opportunities to gather information using the Internet because it can reach so many people. There is also a great deal of potential for misuse of the information gathered so ethical procedures are very important. See ethics in Chapter 17.

If I want to collect quantitative or qualitative data I could, for instance, put out a set of questions on the net by a survey such as SurveyMonkey. I would have to make sure that contact and responses were kept confidential and came into a university website which is password protected.

All research is subject to ethical approval and participant consent. It is possible to gather qualitative data also through using newsgroups and lists, and many groups and participants might well be willing to take part in a discussion survey. Again, you would need to make sure you had their consent and that the information they provided you was kept confidentially password protected and the names changed.

Contacting individuals

It is possible that in order to gather the data, you need to address your research question, you need to contact someone who is giving a lecture, has written a book, is another kind of expert in their field, is part of your past, holds a responsible position and so would be able to provide you with the data that you need. Whether you have located them using the web, other networks, or personal contact, you still need to be very clear about the confidentiality of your contact and the use of anything they tell you in your research.

Ethics on the web: netiquette

Whether you are contacting people to ask their permission to use what they say, or to interview them online, to form contacts or ask for presentations they've given which relate to your research, or to put you in touch with other students working in a similar area – you need to think about what is called 'netiquette', i.e., etiquette online. When you first approach people, provide them with a basic introduction to the background to your research, your research questions, the context in which it's being done and what you will use the information for. Describe briefly what information you are looking for.

- Identify yourself and your institutional affiliation and give them ways of contacting you.
- Never use any information they provide without their permission,
- and never forward any information they provide to a third party.
- Always be polite to a contact, which means not sending any flame mails, and be careful with the tone. Humour does not always translate.
- Put clear subject headings in any emails to people so that they know what you are seeking.
- It's important to ensure that you use the computer responsibly and don't steal other people's work, lie about them and their work, hack into their work, use or copy any software you have not paid for.
- Do not use anyone's Internet and computer resources without asking them, and at the same time, if you are asking for their use on behalf of a third person, you have to clearly explain how you are using it to anyone who is helping you with your work through that connection.
- You must ensure you are respectful of other people's ideas, their work and their privacy.
- Ensure you gain consent when you are going to use what they have said or written online. When you quote from sources you should reference them fully. Do ensure you never use the work of others and pass it on as your own.

Summary

In this chapter we have considered:

- A range of methods of gaining information using the Internet – searches and how to manage and handle them.
- Good practice in using the Internet.
- Confidentiality and ethics, and the avoidance of plagiarism.

Useful websites

The Web of Knowledge www.tile.net
JSTOR http://jstor.org/search
Voice of the shuttle http://vos.ucsb.edu/
ICQ people search http://web.icq.com/whitepages/search
Google Scholar http://scholar.google.co.uk/
Literary Encyclopaedia (online) www.litencyc.com/
HESA, The Higher Education Statistics Agency www.hesa.ac.uk

11 Quantitative Methods in Action: Questionnaires, Observation

This chapter considers:
► quantitative research design;
► questionnaires;
► observations.

As we have discussed in the chapter on methodology and methods, quantitative methods are usually chosen for positivist research that is based in the belief that there are facts which can be gathered about the world, and that large numbers and repetition guarantee the reliability of such facts. It seeks to prove certain things about a world believed knowable, in which knowledge is to be discovered rather than constructed. Such research would use a deductive research design which proves and tests theory rather than building it, and would be likely to use quantitative research methods and research vehicles such as surveys of large numbers, and observation of a number of activities mapped against a schedule.

This chapter does not intend to discuss all the quantitative methods used by social scientists and others but instead will look at questionnaires and observation schedules.

Quantitative research methods include questionnaires and observation.

Questionnaires

Questionnaires often seem a logical and easy option as a way of collecting information from people because they can be sent out or handed out to large numbers and the data they produce can be analysed and produce statistically sound responses which stand for patterns of belief, behaviour, or whatever you are asking about. They are actually rather difficult to design because what often seem like straightforward questions can lead people, produce unexpected answers, miss out on the important elements of what you really want to ask and cannot ask directly. Because of the frequency of the use of questionnaires in all contexts in the modern world, the response rate is nearly always going to be a problem (low) unless you have ways of making people complete them and hand them in on the spot (and this of course limits your sample, how long the questionnaire can be and the kinds of questions asked).

As with interviews, you can decide to use closed or open questions, and can also offer respondents multiple choice questions from which to choose the statement which most closely describes their response to a statement or item.

The layout is important, to lead respondents from the straightforward informative questions about name and age etc., if relevant; agreement, i.e., Yes/No questions; and then perhaps some more complex questions of response on a scale 1–5, a Lickert scale, which indicates a variety of responses.

You need to take expert advice in setting up a questionnaire, ensure that all the information about the respondents which you need is included, and ensure that you actually get the questionnaires returned.

If you send the questionnaires out in the post you need to include a stamped addressed envelope and this might have a reasonable response rate, but you could lose money on the unused stamps. If you ask people to complete them in a closed space you can collect them in on the spot, and will get a high response rate. If you send out an email survey the response rate is usually quite low, but you can send them out cheaply or for free, and could use an electronic survey mode to do so, e.g. SurveyMonkey.

You will need to ensure that questions are clear, and that you have reliable ways of collecting and managing the data.

Setting up a questionnaire that can be read by an optical mark reader is a good idea if you wish to collect large numbers of responses and analyse them statistically rather than reading each questionnaire and entering data manually.

Whatever questionnaire you use, you will need to pilot it first and then refine the questions as needed. Please consider:

- Why use questionnaires?
- What are their pros and cons?
- How can you use them?
- Analysing questionnaires.
- Managing and presenting data from questionnaires.

Questionnaires gather information directly by asking people questions and using the answers as data for analysis. They are often used to gather information about attitudes, behaviours, activities, and responses to events, and usually consist of a list of written questions. Respondents can complete questionnaires in timed circumstances, by post, or by responding to researchers directly who, armed with the questionnaire, can actually *ask* them the questions in person. It is a method of gathering large numbers of responses, although the response rates are quite frequently not high because so many people become rather irritated by questionnaires and refuse to fill them out. You need to ensure that your questionnaire is perfect when you use it with your sample, so it is important to take advice, pilot questions thoroughly and then use the questionnaire with your samples. It is not usually possible to return to the sample with a further developed version of a questionnaire, not least because having completed it once they will not be able to respond in a natural and genuine manner.

You need to ensure that your questionnaire is:

- kept confidential;
- trialled, piloted and refined;
- really able to ask the questions you want;
- unambiguous and avoids multiple questions;
- composed of entirely clear questions.

When setting out a questionnaire you need to:

- clear the use of it with your sponsor or whoever is allowing you to use it;
- ensure you can code up the questions after the response has been collected so that you can analyse the data. Yes/No and Lickert-scale-type questions (on a range of 1–5, where, for example, 1 = strongly agree and 5 = strongly disagree) are easier to code up. While open-ended questions produce fuller responses, you will need to have an idea of the trends for which you are looking and to develop a code to deal with expected areas of answers so that when the open-ended question responses come in, you can code them up. The coding is so that you can handle the amount of data and carry out some statistical analysis, since questionnaires are most often used to suggest the response of a significant number of people in terms of percentage and proportions.

When sending out questionnaires you need to:

- explain what the purpose is and guarantee confidentiality;
- explain who the sponsor is/who it is for;
- provide a return address and a time for the return (if it is posted);
- explain that the responses are voluntary;
- thank the respondents for their time in completing the questionnaire.

Layout

Questionnaires should not be too long or they will get a lower response rate because people become bored and irritated and fail to complete them.

- Use single-sided paper.
- Do not crowd the questionnaire.
- Start with information questions, then questions can become more complicated if necessary, about beliefs, feelings and values.
- Try not to repeat questions too often (although this can be useful for cross-checking, it irritates respondents).
- Number your pages as well as your questions.
- Include a coding box, on the right-hand side, so that you can code responses.
- Make sure your questions are clear and unambiguous.
- Ensure questions are not insulting, not vague; avoid unnecessary assumptions.
- Provide consistent kinds of questions with a consistent scale, such as 1–4, so your respondents are more able to focus on the questions without worrying about the format. But spot respondent boredom.

Examples of kinds of questions

(A)   Closed questions – these are easier to code

1   Yes/no answers

> Q.   Do you eat Indian food?
>
> A.   Yes/no

2   Agree/disagree answers
Please indicate whether you agree or disagree with the following statements:

> Q.   It is always better to eat at a restaurant than at home.
>
> A.   Agree/disagree

3   Choosing from options
Please indicate your chosen option by circling the item which relates to your choice:

> Q.   Which kind of cooking do you feel is acceptable to the largest number of people who eat outside their homes in the UK?
>
> A.   Mediterranean, French, Indian, Chinese

4   Putting items in order
Please place the following holiday locations in order of your choice:

> 1 = the most preferred, 5 = the least preferred
>
> Cyprus, France, Greece, Spain, Australia

5   Rating responses
Please rate the following statements on a scale of 1 to 5 where 1 is 'strongly agree' and 5 is 'strongly disagree':

(a) The Armed forces are underpaid given the risks and
dangers involved.   1   2   3   4   5

(b) Conscription is necessary in peacetime as well as
wartime.   1   2   3   4   5

(c) Serving in the Forces helps young men develop a range
of qualities.   1   2   3   4   5

(B) Open-ended questions

6 The relatively simple answer

Q. How important do you think it is to stay in touch with current affairs?

A ....

7 The longer, more complex, more varied answer

Q. In the complex modern state, how far can anyone have a real voice in political
developments?

A ....

....

....

Question types 6 and 7 will also need coding, or there is no way in a long questionnaire
that you can draw any conclusions and sum anything up.

Once you have gathered in and labelled up your questionnaires, you remove those
which are incomplete and code the responses on the completed ones.

Enter the coded and numerical responses into the computer manually or using statistical packages such as SPSS, which then work to produce a frequency analysis for you.
Ask the package to produce responses in relation to variables and to produce responses
which relate variables so that you can match up frequencies.

Decide on a topic unrelated to your research such as asking people about preferred holiday destinations and reasons for this.

Draw up a questionnaire which has at least one question of each of the seven kinds illustrated above, making sure you word them carefully.

Code them (1 for yes, 2 for no, 1, 2, 3, 4, 5, for the Lickert scale, and so on).

Try them out on a friend.

Which ones can they answer? Which ones don't work? What kind of insight do you get about holiday choices from this questionnaire? What do these holiday choices correlate with? Age? Previous choices? Weather? Kind of entertainment available?

How can you change the items of the questionnaire to make the results you get more interesting, closer to the question you are asking?

Now you need to take all of this learning into consideration when drawing up your OWN questionnaire.

Consider how to word these questions very carefully and which ones would be better as closed choices or open choices, on a scale, yes/no, and so on. Defend your reasons for those choices.

You will soon discover that some questions are considered too insulting or awkward and cannot be asked directly, such as those about personal hygiene, sexual relations, spending habits, and bad habits. This is because people will not want to be entirely honest and will boast or lie to some extent.

Observation as a quantitative research vehicle

There are many kinds of observation – and we have looked at the participant observation – which are part of qualitative research methods. More quantitative observation looks at a large number of actions and charts and organises them into patterns of behaviour, probably using time charts and movement charts.

Large-scale observations would include the work of the Mass Observation research which takes place at the University of Sussex. This is more concerned with collecting data about behaviour of many people in the war and afterwards.

Smaller quantitative observations might look, for instance, at behaviours in context, over time, to identify characteristics, and so an example could be:

The behaviour of holidaymakers travelling on Ryanair over the summer season, to Ireland and from Ireland on Friday evenings.

Such an observation research would:

Look at the behaviour of thousands of travellers over a period of, for instance, 10 weeks, on Fridays, leaving from UK airports (Stansted, Heathrow, Gatwick, Birmingham) or Irish airports (Dublin, Shannon) and using Ryanair.

To make any sense it would need to ask some specific questions about behaviour based on observations of that behaviour, and focusing on some interactions and actions. It would also need to categorise the behaviours and probably to time them in order to differentiate between them.

Observation schedule of types of traveller and numbers

Types of travellers

	business travellers	hen and stag nights	family groups	individuals
Shannon				
Dublin				
Stansted				
Heathrow				
Gatwick				

Behaviour of travellers

	focused on work	quiet	celebrating	a little wild
Shannon				
Dublin				
Stansted				
Heathrow				
Gatwick				

Observation
- Field notes.
- Keep a diary, log or journal.

Summary

In this chapter we have considered:

- Two methods of gathering quantitative data, questionnaires and observations, both of which depend on large enough numbers and identifying categories of focus and then of analysis.
- How to categorise the participants and their behaviours, code these up and make some comparative statements at the end of the analysis.

Further reading

Oppenheim, A. N. (1992) *Questionnaire Design, Interviewing and Attitude Measurement*, 2nd edn (London: Continuum).

12 Qualitative Methods in Action

This chapter considers:

▶ interviews, focus groups and qualitative observation;
▶ developing, carrying out, writing up and analysing interviews;
▶ when and how to use focus groups, running them, writing up and analysing;
▶ kinds of observation – planning, managing, analysing and writing up.

Qualitative research methods are usually chosen when conducting research which is related to the social sciences, arts and humanities, and if you believe that:

● knowledge is constructed;
● knowledge is gained through exploring and interpreting human interactions, rather than that
● it is factual, defined, provable.

You are likely to be using qualitative research methods if you are working with an inductive research methodology and research design.

Chapter 11 focuses on quantitative methods. However, there are many research designs which use mixed methods in order to ask and address their research questions, and some methods which can have either a quantitative or a qualitative intent and effect depending on how they are constructed and used. You can use large surveys or questionnaires for large quantitative pieces of research and small, more qualitative questionnaires for in-depth qualitative research, for example. You might gather factual statistical data from a large-scale survey with mostly closed questions producing statistically valid results, and gather in-depth rich data from a small-scale survey with open ended questions where respondents can develop their thoughts, but there are few respondents and others would not be able to replicate the survey in an identical set of circumstances. Similarly, you can have an observation schedule which looks at activities and categorises them moment by moment, over large numbers, and an observation that records rich responses about feelings and interactions over smaller numbers. The first is collecting more quantitative, the second more qualitative data.

Kinds of research methods in brief: introduction

Please look at the very brief outlines of different methods below. Consider which you intend using and whether you could also find it more useful to combine the *quantitative* with the *qualitative*. You might be familiar with these methods or they may be new to you.

Qualitative research methods include interviews, focus groups and observation.

Interviews

Interviews enable face-to-face discussion with human subjects. You can explore people's thoughts and feelings when you meet with them, in context, and capture this rich information. You need to organise an interview schedule of questions which enables you to first capture any essential contextual information such as:

- name, gender, age, context,

and then to move on to the deeper questions about:

- attitudes, responses, choices,

or whatever it is you are seeking. If you are using interviews, you will probably be carrying out only a few rather than the large numbers usually sought in surveys. You will need to be very careful to identify, contact and recruit your respondents; then prepare and inform them of how their responses will be used. Be clear about what you are asking them, and find sound ways of recording their responses so that you can analyse this data later using your theories and relating it to your arguments.

How to record information

If you are going to use interviews, you will have to decide how to record what you hear as answers so that you can then analyse and interpret the responses afterwards. You need to decide what method of recording suits you, your context and your interviewees and decide whether you will take notes (distracting), tape the interview (accurate but time-consuming when being transcribed – six hours transcription for one hour of tape, usually), rely on your memory (foolish), or write in their answers (can lead to closed questioning for time's sake).

What kind of questions?

If you decide to interview you will need to draw up an interview schedule of questions, which can be either *closed* or *open* questions, *structured* or *semi-structured* or a mixture of these.

Closed questions

These tend to be used for asking about and receiving answers concerning fixed facts such as name, numbers, and so on. They do not require speculation and they tend to produce short answers. With closed questions you could even give your interviewees a small selection of possible answers from which to choose. If you do this you will be able to manage the data and quantify the responses quite easily. The Household Survey and Census ask closed questions, and often market researchers who stop you in the street do too. You might ask your interviewees to indicate how true for them a certain statement was felt to be, and this too can provide both a closed response, and one which can be quantified (30% of those asked said they never ate rice, while 45% said they did so regularly at least once a week . . . and so on).

The problem with closed questions is that they limit the response the interviewee can give and do not enable them to think deeply, or test their real feelings or values. What is useful about them is that they are fairly easy to administer and can give you a large number of responses that you can treat sometimes as statistically significant if there are enough of them.

Closed questions could look like this:

1   Are you currently working in paid employment?   Yes/No

2   If so, is this

    (a)   part time?

    (b)   full time?

Open questions

These can produce thoughtful, longer, in-depth answers that you need to read through carefully and categorise, then code up afterwards.

Open questions could look like this:

1   What are the modes of travel you use to get to work?

(This could produce a range of answers that you can code up afterwards – or you could ask them to choose between – train, car, foot, bike, bus – and code them in relation to those choices.)

A longer question is:

What are your views about increasing the compensation for troops who are injured in action?

(This will produce an answer that could be rich and extensive or rambling and difficult to categorise.)

If you ask open questions such as 'What do you think about the increase in traffic?' you could elicit an almost endless number of responses. This would give you a very good idea of the variety of ideas and feelings people have; it would enable them to think and talk for longer and so show their feelings and views more fully. But it is very difficult to quantify these results. You will find that you will need to read all the comments through and to categorise them after you have received them, or merely report them in their diversity and make general statements, or pick out particular comments if they seem to fit your purpose.

What kind of interview?

There are many different kinds of interview, each of which provides different quality and kinds of responses that you can then analyse, categorise, and use as evidence in your argument (see Figure 12.1).

Structured interviews

These are limited and controlled. You structure the questions you want to ask and when you will ask them, even developing a time chart of when to ask which questions in which order.

They move through categories of questions, leading the interviewee logically. For example, they might move from informational questions through more opinion-oriented questions.

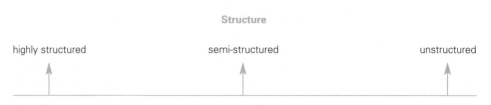

Structure

highly structured   semi-structured   unstructured

Figure 12.1

Semi-structured open-ended interviews

This comprises a series of set questions and space for divergence. You have some responses that are easy to categorise afterwards and then some varied flow of ideas and answers.

There are categories of questions but they are not directive and the respondent explores ideas, which you record with tape, or notes.

> If you decide to use interviews, draw up a set of questions that seem appropriate and try them out with a colleague before you pilot them, then refine the questions so that they are genuinely engaged with your research object.

The unstructured interview

Many interviews are relatively unstructured, although a real interview will not just be a disorganised ramble. You can have interviews that are like a real conversation and these are naturalistic, autobiographical, in-depth, narrative or non-directive, like conversation.

Whatever interview you develop, you need to think about how to organise it; how to conduct the questioning; ethics, i.e. participant consent and keeping responses confidential (see Chapter 17 on ethics); and then whether you will be able to both let your respondent answer fully, and also categorise and code up what he or she says so that you can analyse and use it in your agreement.

> Note the interactional rules of interviews:
>
> Organisation
>
> - Organise the interview – decide on its kind, aims, content, questions, the sample of respondents, time and place
> - Contact respondents
> - Agree time and place
> - Record the interview
> - Write up as soon as possible
> - Send the interviewees a copy of their responses if they want them
>
> Asking interview questions
>
> You need to be sensitive in the questions you ask and responsive with empathetic comments, such as 'yes', 'that's interesting', 'do go on' and mirroring what the person says back to him or her to persuade the person to continue, e.g.:

'I sell cabbages.'

'You sell cabbages?'

'Yes, and I believe that selling cabbages is very important in a market town.'

'You believe it is important?'

'Yes because market towns . . .'

What's said, what's not said

Often respondents indicate responses that go beyond what they say, by body language, or they might retain their information either deliberately or without being aware of it. You need to decide whether you can write interpretative notes about that body language, or need to prompt them by rephrasing your question.

Honesty

This is important in interviewing to gain and retain the trust of your respondents.

- Don't make any promises you cannot keep.
- Do not mislead.
- Share a transcript if this suits them.
- Sum up your notes and check with the interviewee.
- Be polite, pleasant, and thank them for their time.

Questions and behaviours to avoid

- Don't appear threatened or bored.
- Don't ask questions that are
  - excessively long;
  - with excessive jargon or technical terms;
  - leading or suggesting bias and prejudice.

Questions and behaviours to use – DO

- Stay in control and appear friendly and responsive.
- Use prompts and probes.

All of these and, in fact, everything in an interview and how you can then interpret responses are affected by age, gender, ability, ethnicity, religion, class and a number of cultural differences, so do be careful.

The shape of interviews

Interviews have both a momentum and a rhythm. Some typical elements would be:

- Introductions.
- Social comments about time and place.
- Background information to the interview about how it is being conducted, what you are seeking, etc.

The interview itself. Do ensure:

- Variety of appropriate questions and some space to let answers develop.
- Ways of prompting and probing to expand the range of the interview, if answers seem to be leading in an interesting and useful direction.
- A way of closing down and moving on if they are rambling or not focused.
- Formal movements between necessary questions.
- Rephrasing/returning if misunderstood or ignored.
- Winding down.
- A few straightforward questions to finish the interview off, information about use and contacts.
- Closing down – thanks and goodbyes.

Activity:
Mock interview

- Draw up a series of questions for your own interview *for your own research.*
- Try out a couple of key questions. Pilot them with a colleague and ask:
  - Are these too vague?
  - Too probing?
  - Embarrassing?
  - Closed?
  - Will they cause the interviewee to ramble?
  - Are they clear?
  - Do they follow on from questions already asked?
  - Can they really give me the information I am after?
  - Are they not really going to capture that information?
  - Are they misleading?
- Discuss and advise each other on exact wording.

Creative interviewing

It is possible to be even more creative in your interviewing if you are seeking responses aimed at feelings, interactions, emotions, deeply hidden fears and desires. It is possible to ask reflective questions or to prompt interviewees with pictures or synectics – the use of creative metaphors.

Focus groups

Focus groups are small groups brought together specifically to focus on certain issues, for example, the uses of the library and how library facilities might be improved, or how international students' learning is aided (or not) by teaching and learning strategies and resources, or how a group of people respond over time to a *particular* project, TV show, etc. Focus groups enable close scrutiny and lengthy discussion. They can be repeated over time and used to test out ideas. Like any other research sample, if studied over time, the group will actually change in responses and attitudes and so this will affect any random sample quality it initially had. The focus group is also constantly affected by the presence of the researcher, and this will need to be taken into consideration. Discussions can, as with interviews, be either noted down or recorded and transcribed. They are very useful indeed for capturing people's responses and feelings, their records of experiences, and so on. With several people present in a focus group, ideas and issues tend to shape themselves as people speak, and the subjects start to form an understanding as participants debate certain points. This is really helpful as you deal with different areas and issues in your research.

Focus groups as group interviews

If you use focus groups, you need to follow all the guidelines also suited to an interview, such as considering the size of group, layout of the room, timing and questions.

It is important to record accurately what people say, without losing the flow of the discussion, so it is a good idea to give names before or after speaking. What is particularly useful about focus groups is the way in which by encouraging dialogue they build and grow meaning. There is overlapping discussion/dialogue that helps build ideas and arguments. It is like exploratory talk, but is hard to transcribe. The probable resolution to this is to tape – test it out – and ensure that people have some sense of rules of response. Transcription needs to identify speakers.

Thematic analysis can then be conducted and extracts written up.

> There are many other forms of qualitative data gathering. Some are explored in separate chapters. Ethnography and action research are explored in Chapter 13.

Qualitative versions of observation

Observation can be used to gather quantitative data about frequency of activities, length, gaps between actions, regularity etc. of certain behaviours in order, for example, to identify where a road is overused at key times in the day and needs to be widened, or whether shoppers tend to use the park-and-ride more on market days. However, much observation is also quite qualitative in nature. It depends on whether you are looking at frequency, regularity and amount – i.e. the kind of measurements used in large samples, to make statistical or large-scale statements. Even with those large-scale observations, such as the Mass Observation study at the University of Sussex, there are still subject choices about what to observe, how to observe, and what to observe for, i.e. the reason for the observation. However, qualitative observation will need to be very frank about the effect of the observer and the focus or even potential bias. In some kinds of observation, it is essential that the observer identifies the effect he or she makes on the people observed. They might even write about their experience as part of the research data. **Non-participant but semi-immersive observation** is where the observer is not part of the background observed but familiarises him- or herself with the groups to reduce the effect the observer's presence has on the groups' actions.

Participant observation

Participant observation is immersive, i.e. you are immersed in it, fully involved in it, and you also need to be one of the group. In participant observation, the researcher joins the group he or she is studying. This is much more straightforward if the group is similar in kind to the researcher, as the researcher will stand out less, and so affect the responses and results less. If you are observing 'Hell's Angels' as a participant observer then you have to ride a bike, i.e. be a member of the group, which involves some pretence or perhaps a position as an insider already. However, if you are observing kindergarten children you cannot be a fully fledged participant observer because you are not a kindergarten child! But you can be a participant in the situation in which you observe the children insofar as you resemble or act as, or indeed are, an adult working with the children. You are just not one of the group of children.

However, this is essentially a very subjective form of research and great care has to be taken in recognising what is subjective, what objective fact, when considering data and responses. Historically, various sociologists have joined biker gangs and lumber camps, mixed in with hardened criminals, or even changed their skin colour to experience what it is like to be on the receiving end of racism, and so on. It is clearly not so easy to be involved fully in participant observation if you are of a very different ethnic group, age, class, gender, from your subjects. It is rather like 'going undercover'.

Using the self as data

It is possible to use yourself as data, as a case, a participant, or a source if you are a participant observer. If you represent an example of what is under study, then, in the process of the research, you might be using yourself as part of the data. Whatever instance in which you are part of your own research data, you need to discuss the limitation of this, i.e. that there could be subjectivity which sways what you see and say (there is certainly a subjective element in your experience as subject), but stress that you will ensure that what you argue, claim, prove is not totally altered and influenced by your presence. The word 'subjectivity' is often used only to suggest bias. You can minimise bias by discussing the steps you have taken to ensure that your own presence or views do not affect what you see, hear, record and note, and that you are not tampering with or falsely prioritising certain responses or reactions. When recording or reporting on your own responses you need to acknowledge reflectively what is happening and how your mood and prior experiences might be affecting what you see and express.

Personal learning logs or blogs used as data

Many researchers use learning logs or blogs but these do not necessarily form part of the research data; instead they are space to record decisions, 'stuck' moments, to question achievements and so give an outlet to personal reflective response to the research and the events and feelings that it produces. However, it is also possible to use these forms of reflective writing as data themselves if your own response is part of your research focus. The researcher using a personal learning log or a blog as their own experiences and responses as research data is recording his or her observations and experiences and reflecting on them. Researchers can use themselves as an example of the body of people being studied as a case, and need to ensure when they do see themselves in this way that they indicate the differences between their own experiences and reflections and those of the people in the sample, or whether they include themselves in the same categories. The log is a space, location or outlet for recording response, moment by moment, so tracking changing attitudes and building up knowledge and understanding. It can be used as a research vehicle in itself to record, for example, how the researcher is feeling about undertaking the research, and here it is especially helpful if the research is very personally related, ethically testing, involves emotions, and so on. It can also be used like a captain's log to record what is experienced and what effects are noted, what data collected. Usually it is a mixture of discovered detail and personal response.

While further chapters explore research methods in greater detail, you would find it useful to consult the range of full and excellent research books available. These will deal in much greater depth with the reasons for, processes of holding, and processes of analysing data from the variety of research methods available to you.

Activity

Please consider:

- What kind of research methods are you going to use? Are they mostly:
  - quantitative, or
  - qualitative, or
  - a mixture of both?
- What do you think your methods will enable you to discover?
- What might they prevent you from discovering?
- What kinds of research methods would be best suited to the kind of research you are undertaking and the research questions you are pursuing?
- What sort of problems do you envisage in setting up these methods?
- What are their benefits?
- What will you need to do to ensure they gather useful data?

Summary

In this chapter we have considered:

- Choice of research type and methodologies.
- Choice of research methods.

Further reading

Miles, M. and Huberman, M. (1994) *Qualitative Data Analysis* (London: Sage).
Robson, Colin (2002) *Real World Research: A Resource for Social Scientists and Practitioner-Researchers*, 2nd edn (Oxford: Blackwell).

13 Varieties of Research: Practitioner-Based and Action Research, Phenomenography and Ethnography, and other Real-World Research

This chapter considers:

► practitioner-based research;
► practice-related, professional researech;
► action research;
► ethnography;
► phenomenography.

Practitioner-based research, action research, phenomenography and ethnography are all forms of research that work with human subjects without being experimental or based in any kind of clinical practice. They consider that knowledge and understanding are constructed and interpreted, and look at how people behave in context, in time, and often in the workplace or the place where they live. Many universities now also offer the opportunity to practise these forms of real-world research out in business or community contexts. Some offer the opportunities to become engaged in community, commercial or other real-world projects which involve research processes. Many of these could provide both sound grounding and an entrance into employment after graduation.

⬭ Practitioner-based research

Why might you want to carry out practitioner-based and/or practice-based research?
    What kinds of issues and questions would you like to research?
    Practitioner research involves asking research questions about your work practice, perhaps about those who you work with, how you carry out your own practice or how others do, the conditions of working, and many other areas of questioning, all of which intend to discover how work or working lives operate, what a situation, a set of relationships or interactions, a change or an innovation can bring into the workplace. Some people carry out practitioner-based research because they want to research the effectiveness of their own practice, a therapy programme, an empowerment course, the impact of new regulations for healthy eating in the workplace, how managers feel about undertaking complex tasks, and so on.
    It is not a methodology – a set of underpinning beliefs that lead to research practice in

action – it is more about researching your practice or workplace, and so it can use a variety of methodologies or methods to do so.

Normally it will be inductive (theory-building) and based on the ways in which people behave. If you are trying out an innovative work practice or programme and want to see how it develops and causes change over time, you might well combine practitioner-based research with action research so that you can involve everyone concerned in the research as collaborators and persuade the management to take ownership of the development. If you are one of those who are being researched and/or are researching the behaviours of your colleagues, you might be immersed in the people being researched and be carrying out ethnography, which is the study of people's behaviour and beliefs by someone who is relating to them, but does not need to involve collaboration in the whole process and cycles of research building on each other.

If you are using phenomenography you are looking into interactions between certain elements and people, and again do not have to have all your subjects fully collaborated (as in action research), nor do there need to be cycles of the research (action research), and you can study without being part of or really attached to and relating to the group (ethnography).

Practitioner research might well use a mixture of inductive and deductive research methodologies, starting, for example, with exploring the experience of a particular programme introduced into your workplace, then building on the exploration to put the programme in place more firmly, and testing its effectiveness in context (inductive followed by deductive testing). Or it could test the experience and results of a particular phenomenon at work, using deductive methodology and quantitative methods (e.g. observation, survey), and then build a new programme that the participants collaborate in and which is explored inductively and using qualitative methods over time by all involved (deductive and positivist, then inductive, qualitative, post-positivist).

Some methods you might use in practitioner research

Qualitative:

- Interviews
- Focus groups
- Participant observation
- Case studies
- Using yourself as a case
- Storytelling and other narratives

Quantitative:

- Questionnaires/surveys
- Observation

A possible piece of research might ask the question:

1 How do people on the point of retirement respond to the newly introduced retraining for retirement schemes, in the context of local government employment?

or

2 To what extent and in what ways can middle managers in a college of education engage support for implementing change in the college?

or

3 Tensions – How do young representatives perceive and balance their mixture of involvement with the group and responsibility for their health, safety and quality of experience?

Each of these pieces of research could employ a single method or mixture of methods – for example, the third one might just:

(i)   survey their responses to a question about health and safety responsibility; and then
(ii) put in place some change in practice as a result – such as a development/training programme building teams and exploring health and safety, etc.;
(iii) re-survey the same people to see if they perceive improvement.

Quantitative survey methods have been used to diagnose an issue, a change in practice is put in place, then it is tested. This is quite an experimental social science model using quantitative methods.

Or it could:

(i)   survey, to determine responses;
(ii) interview in depth;
(iii) try something out, and continue the research alongside this involving all concerned as collaborators (action research model) to enable effective change to be owned and to stick;
(iv) continue to interview with, for example, focus groups which meet over time;
(v)   keep changing the programme to refine the responses and success; and
(vi) keep the focus groups going;

so determine the response to the changes which have been implemented because of the tensions first noted through the initial survey, and also cause whole organisational change of a sort because everyone is on board. This is more properly called 'action research'.

Action research

Action research is a form of practitioner research that involves all the subjects of the research as collaborators, and engages the management, the whole organisation, in the reflection and the changes related to the research. It:

- is useful in practitioner research;
- resembles reflective practice and innovation plus reflection, but is more rigorous;
- enables partnership and collaboration between the population and researcher, and researcher and colleagues – all share in the research planning, processes, and outcomes;
- involves reflection;
- encourages the development of those involved.

Practical and participatory, action research encourages ownership of the whole research activity and process by those undertaking the research (usually more than one person) and those involved in it as participants. The aim of this is ownership of change because the research fully involves people, and the suggestions arising from the research can be owned and put into action by those involved, particularly if the decision makers such as management are involved.

Action research not only takes snapshots of an activity at a moment in time, it looks over time at change or a situation and interaction, then the results from this change, some part of what is being explored and who is involved, and then another research cycle begins. There are several research cycles, each affected by the previous ones, and the ways in which the situation and participants change is all acknowledged as useful and necessary.

Action research:

- is emancipatory;
- involves emotions and feelings;
- is interpretative;
- has a critical attitude;
- involves self-evaluation;
- has professionalism;
- has accountability;
- uses triangulation;
- uses validity and validation;
- involves ownership;
- feeds into change;
- is NOT scientific.

Action research operates in cycles and addresses problems, interventions, innovations and questions arising from practice.

Steps in a piece of action research

- Focus on and define the problem/intervention/innovation in context.
- Involve participants and colleagues.
- Produce a general action plan.
- Take action – try out an intervention.
- Monitor the effect using qualitative/quantitative methods.
- Collect data.
- Analyse and evaluate results.
- Share and debate with your participants and colleagues.
- Reformulate the plan and repeat the cycle . . .

Make a suggestion for change to your employer/the management, etc., based on the action research results.

(Cycle 1) Experience – reflection – planning the intervention – action – observation of the results and responses

Reflect again and evaluate (Cycle 2), re-plan the action, carry it out, observe and discuss, reflect, and on it can go. The moment of reflection, discussion and evaluation are shared and lead to further refinement of the action, which can be an innovation programme – whatever is appropriate in your workplace for the research.

Ortrun Zuber-Skerritt (1992) suggests that the core research involving action research lies at the heart of the dissertation. What we are focusing on here is how you would start writing the outline of your dissertation early on, would plan it and carry out your field-work, the research, and look at the conclusions. All of this involves discussion with others but the writing is your own – you step back and capture the whole process, both the intervention and the responses of those who are involved. Once you have carried out a couple of cycles of the research you can think of writing up, planning the final drafts, writing, refining and editing them, and then handing it in – but you do not necessarily ever stop there! Some action research in the workplace is so compelling and interesting that constant improvement is the aim, and the changes, the involvement of others and the research continue beyond your writing a dissertation, to other activities, projects or reports. Other people might carry on the research and the changes if that is not your role and you have moved on.

- Much practitioner research is ethnography and is research into people's behaviours and perceptions.
- Much action research takes place in the theoretical framework of phenomenography. This also involves interactions between people and lived experience.

Ethnographic research

Background (Banister et al., 1994)

Ethnography is concerned with experience as it is lived, felt or undergone, and so it involves a concern with your consciousness and that of the participants or subjects. To research perceptions of consciousness, the ethnographer participates in people's daily lives for a period of time, watching what happens, listening to what is said, asking questions, studying documents, and collecting whatever data is available to throw light on the issue with which the research is concerned. They become immersed (Sarantakos, 1993).

- **Ethnographic research** derives its structure from anthropology, which is the study of people. Ethnography and social anthropology are centred around the concept of culture and holism.
- **In-Depth Study** – Relying on information gained by practitioners living in the groups they investigate and experiencing the culture the way their subjects do.

Methodology in ethnographic research

The purpose of ethnographic research depends on the paradigm that underlies the project. If the research employs a positivistic paradigm (testing theory, believing the world can be captured by facts and explanations), the purpose of the ethnographic research may be to describe, explain and categorise social events, whereas if it is an interpretive paradigm (constructing knowledge, inductive, believing that knowledge and understanding are construed and interpreted by people, not fixed), it may aim at understanding the dynamics of the socio-cultural system, as well as how people interpret their world.

Methods

The most common methods are:

- Participant observation and interviewing, conducted while the researcher is living with the people he or she studies.
- Other methods of data collection which rely on the study of documents, such as personal accounts, life histories, diaries, personal letters and reports.

Criteria of ethnographic research

To be a piece of ethnography research it must involve:

- social relationships;
- the researcher as learner;
- first-hand information – the essential information is gained through direct contact with the respondents;
- long-term observation;
- participant observation.

The ethnographer is a research instrument because he or she is present in the research, is capturing the data and affecting the context.

- It uses naturalistic observation – the research captures social life as it unfolds in natural situations.
- An eclectic approach.
- A humanistic perspective.
- A cross-cultural frame of reference (comparative research).

An example might be the long-term study of patterns of involvement in owned housing, housing cooperatives or local authority houses in a town in Northern England, over ten years, concentrating on observing the changing patterns, and talking with a group of participants with whom the researcher becomes very familiar, about their choices, decisions, changes in housing situation over this period of time.

Phenomenology and phenomenography

Phenomenography grows from the philosophical area of argument and perception known as 'phenomenology', also a theory used in research. Phenomenology had a number of theorists, including Martin Heidegger, Edmund Husserl and Jean-Paul Sartre. They debated being in the world, how and when one experienced things and events, and when we label or name them. Both theories attempt to capture beliefs as well as reasons for actions in a social context, and recognise that many of our beliefs and reasons cannot be openly expressed; also that meaning is something which we construct in a social context, it doesn't exist in itself, and all meaning is based in social activity.

Some of the basic assumptions underlying phenomenology, as summarised by Roth et al. (1997), are:

(a) Beliefs and assumptions implicit in everyday practices cannot be made explicit and are discursively constituted for the purposes at hand.

(b) Practical understanding that is observable in the spontaneous activity of people acting in their everyday worlds is more fundamental than detached theoretical understanding.

(c) Meaning is fundamentally social and cannot be reduced to the meaning-giving activity of individual subjects. Social activity is the foundation of intelligibility and existence, not the individual.

(d) In a phenomenological framework, it makes little sense to speak of things that bear individual properties independently of acts of interpretation.

Interpretation in a social context produces meaning. Phenomenology is the study of this. Phenomenography also looks at being in the world, and focuses on interactions between people in a context where most situations are so complicated and full of interactions, preconceptions and interpretations that usually there is a focus on only a couple of those interactions.

For instance, if in a piece of leisure and hospitality research you were looking at how the waiting staff interacted with the customers over time in a variety of service situations in a restaurant, considering attitudes, behaviour and, broadly speaking, customer service, you would need to consider a huge array of issues of context – time, place, location, and events such as dinner or breakfast.

There are customers and their preconceptions of how waiting staff will behave, their own behaviours and attitudes, and the waiting staff's preconceptions of how customers, old and young, will behave in certain contexts. Since it would take a long time to study each interaction you would probably just pick a few.

What is the relationship between customer expectations of waiting staff at a wedding in relation to the actual service experienced by the customers from those staff? You would need to describe the context – time, place, people, event, the interactions and activities, the preconceptions and the experiences – and to capture these using observation, interview, and focus group. For more complex questions comparing the customers' expectations of the waiting staff and the staff's perception of the customers, and how these change over time, you could use the same methods but would have to build a more complex model, charting change and perhaps locating the change around critical incidents – moments when whatever happens seems to cause their perceptions of each other to change.

Phenomenographic research:

- Relates to 'being in the world'.
- Enables recognition and analysis of interactions, influences, feelings, responses, *in context.*
- Involves:
  - people,
  - interactions,
  - and the effects of the context in which people act, experience and interact.
- Focuses on selected interactions out of several – takes 'a slice'.

Is your own work action research?

Can your own work be undertaken within the theoretical framework of phenomenography?

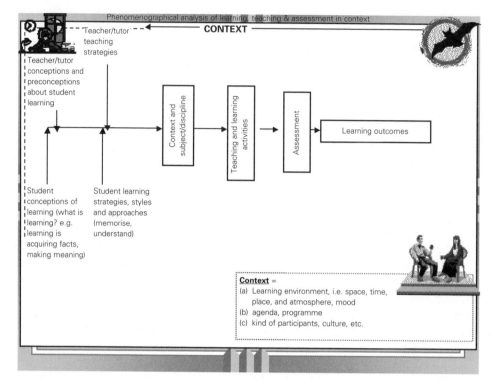

Figure 13.1

The imported PowerPoint® slide (Figure 13.1) shows the relationship between teacher preconceptions of learning, student preconceptions of learning, and the kind of learning activities, experiences and assessments that take place in a learning space such as a classroom or a seminar, all in relation to the curriculum, which is designed as learning outcomes, assessment, and learning activities. If you wanted to study how learning took place in a seminar room where students were looking at Gothic writing (hence the bat in the top corner!), you would need to ensure you knew what they thought Gothic writing was, what they had read before, what the teacher thought it was and what learning outcomes were intended for this class. Then, you would look at interactions in this social space, probably a couple of learning activities, and talk to students and staff about the kind of learning taking place there and what was learned. The smaller the interaction – preconception, activity, change – that is studied, the clearer the way in which you can see how interactions in a learning space lead to socially constructed understandings between people, which are related to that context, i.e., they can be absolutely repeated in another context, and meaning is socially constructed, in context. If you try and look at too much you can't see what relates to what.

Real-world research – working on real-world projects including community research projects – volunteering and credits

Many universities offer the opportunity for you to become engaged in real-world and community oriented projects and to undertake research which involves you in social engagement with the community or with organisations in which you might then work later.

Much university-based research might involve you in highly theorised work where you do not step outside the library, such as if you are undertaking a literature project on Thomas Hardy's representation of women, for example, where visiting Wessex and looking at the memorials is not part of the project, but exploring and critiquing the novels is; or, if you are surveying the responses of your peers in the university as regards their appreciation or otherwise of the customer service in the various food outlets. You might also have the opportunity to take part in real-world research that your tutor is undertaking, or which relates to a funded project, where you are asking and answering research questions, testing a hypothesis or working towards solving a research problem. In all research you often work in a very theorised way, using books and other sources, with a variety of primary sources such as documents and many secondary sources such as critical works about those books and theories. Or you might be largely working in the field with human subjects, or secondary sources such as books. The kind of research you might have the opportunity of carrying out in the community or an organisation is likely to be of use to that community or organisation and to be very real; it could even lead in the future to a job for you, as you solve real-life problems for the community or the organisation with whom you are working.

At the University of the Sunshine Coast in Queensland, Australia, Tania Aspland and her colleagues have a community system where local groups – of which some examples range from people making surfboards to those preserving wildlife, sports clubs to home improvement organisations – place ads for students to work with them and to undertake research for them – market research, research into the effects of advertising, research to solve problems, and a variety of other issues.

Professor Mick Healey of Gloucester University quotes examples of students engaged in real-world research alongside their tutors, such as those at Murdoch University in Western Australia who have been working with staff members in identifying the sources of pollution over shopping centres and working out ways in which the pollution could be halved.

At the University of Brighton thousands of students have undertaken community university placements where they are engaged in working in the community, and many of these are involved in research projects which work to support community groups or volunteer organisations. The project is called CUPP (Community University Partnership Programme). In some of these instances they might well be researching practices for effectiveness, overseeing problems, sorting out the finances, seeking funding sources, whichever of their research skills are needed for the volunteer or community organisation with whom they are working.

The research work of these different students is focused on real-life needs and problems, giving them an excellent idea of how research can be used in everyday working life, and is not just an esoteric activity in a study or attic.

Some of these activities take place on placement, some use mentors, some involve working in student and staff teams, or alone.

If you are placed in a community group, volunteer group or a variety of public organisations, you need to make sure of the following.

Aims and outcomes You are absolutely clear what the aims and outcomes of this research project and this placement are, what you hope to get from it for yourself, what kinds of research it offers opportunities for alongside the other activities in which you might be involved.

Needs and design If you are engaged in real-world research you will need to identify research needs, questions, problems, or a hypothesis, draw up a brief or proposal through which you can agree with the employer how you might take notes, find out from primary and secondary sources the information and data which will feed into the research approach and address or even answer the question, sort out the problem.

Support and resources You will need to find out who can work with you, what kind of support you have, who might be supervising or mentoring you, and what the timescale is and any resources needed, for the outcomes.

Doing the work

You then need to undertake the research as you would any other piece of research, always bearing in mind that this is a real-life situation with people with whom you might work later on and certainly with people who will want to work with the university in the future.

Make sure you keep good notes, keep a log of the activities and the stages of the research as distinct from any other activities with which you might be engaged. This placement in the community could be a useful activity for learning to balance parts of your life as it helps you to sort out the working activity, the research work and your reflection on both and their interactions, in the real world, outside the university.

You need to think of the processes, dissemination, and outcomes. These will probably be both outcomes for the real-world research and the community or volunteer organisation, and outcomes for yourself, such as a module credit following a good project report, for example – whether assessed through a presentation, project report, essay or other form. It might be intended to put forward a case for a financial solution or a marketing proposition, making a case for a development, a change. The situation in such instances is that you are working often from, and in the inside of, a company or organisation, and need the support and engagement of the organisation so that your findings and recommendations at the end of the research are going to be taken seriously and lead to change. Pages 140–4 of this chapter, which looks at practitioner research, also focuses on this.

Working in research with community groups you would need to be very careful about any sensitive issues and their practices, for instance ethics and confidentiality. Details of the work of the company or community group, the practice at work and the interactions with others are all to be kept confidential, in the normal way, but you need to reassure organisations that you will not be revealing any of their secrets or practices to others. As you go about your research you are both a member of this new group and yet an outsider, and issues of gaining confidence and ensuring confidentiality which are explored in the chapter on ethics are very relevant here.

Some rules for working on a real-world community or organisation-based research project:

- Clarify the brief.
- Find a mentor.
- Work with your supervisor/tutor in the university.
- Work out who the stakeholders in the piece of research are, i.e. who would benefit from it and to whom and for whom it is being carried out. There could be many stakeholders and some of them might not be thinking along the same lines, so you will need to negotiate.
- Discover the working patterns and the social interactions and work out how they fit in.
- Define a specific research project to help solve a problem, that leads towards an innovation or evaluation or whatever is suitable.
- Gain confidence and trust.
- Work hard and well.
- Respect differences.
- Plan the research.
- Undertake some reading and early discussions with people working at the community or organisation.
- See the principal issues from their point of view too.
- Use real documents and develop an appropriate research design for finding out what you need to know.
- Manage your time, ensuring you have space to think things through.
- Keep a reflective diary for events and your thoughts, problems and achievements and notes of things you read or heard which are useful to the research.
- Work systematically and share your work with the stakeholders at appropriate opportunities so that there is a sense of ownership of what you're finding out effectively for/with them.
- Deliver outcomes on time in the right form needed for the project and for the community or other organisation.
- Think about how you can build on this project area, these contacts, in the future.

Summary

In this chapter we have considered:

- Undertaking some examples of 'real-world' research – with a super-visor or tutor, in a group or independently.
- A variety of kinds of practice-related, practitioner-based research in a number of different discipline topic areas, around which are built the beliefs about knowledge and understanding being socially constructed in context.
- Relationships between people, in a space and in the context of some form of work or practice.
- Phenomenography, which tends to be used in learning situations, while phenomenology can study interactions in many different situations.
- Ethnography, which involves the researchers being immersed in the group they are studying.
- Action research, which involves collaboration, awareness, and 'buy in' from participants who are fully involved as collaborators.
- Cycles of research.
- Specific examples of undertaking a community- or organisation-located project where the research will seek to solve a problem, develop an innovate answer to a question, and then contribute to the processes and decisions, the developments of that community organisation or other organisation.

Further reading

Banister, P. et al. (1994) *Qualitative Methods in Psychology* (Buckingham: Open University Press).

Hart, A., Maddison E. and Wolff, D. (eds) (2007) *Community – University Partnerships in Practice* (Leicester: NIACE).

Healey, M. (see 'Useful websites', p. 296, 'Linking Research and Teaching', 2005).

Robson, C. (2002) *Real World Research: A Resource for Social Scientists and Practitioner-researchers* (Oxford: Blackwell).

Roth, W. M., McRobbie, C. J., Lucas, K. B. and Boutonné, S. (1997) 'The Local Production of Order in Traditional Science Laboratories: a Phenomenological Analysis', *Learning and Instruction*, 7, pp. 107–36.

Sarantakos, S. (1993) *Social Research* (London: Macmillan).

Zuber-Skerritt, O. (1992) *Action Research in Higher Education* (London: Kogan Page).

Part 2

Managing People and Processes

14 Collecting, Selecting, Organising and Analysing Data, Interpretation

This chapter considers:

▶ ways of categorising and labelling data according to themes and patterns;
▶ analysing and interpreting what you have gathered;
▶ not drowning in data.

Once you have gathered your data you will need to manage it, carefully sort and label it, analyse it, look for patterns and themes then interpret it in a dialogue with the theories underpinning your work, and develop findings. You select from your data and present it as evidence to back up your research claims.

Do look at the full range of more complex books on data analysis (see below for some suggestions), on producing statistics, and on interpreting quantitative data. This book intends to give you a very brief introduction and suggest some straightforward activities.

There are a number of ways to identify, collect, organise, manage and interpret a range of data and this chapter will look at some of them.

> My motto about the use of data in research is:
>
> 'No claim without evidence no evidence without a claim'

It is your data which enables you to say you have found something, some contribution to knowledge and meaning, some answers (however partial) to the question asked, the problem addressed. Without evidence, you have only guesswork and opinion, but handling that evidence is a delicate, robust, rigorous, diligent, and imaginative task all in one. If you merely slot all your data into categories without thinking, you might miss the marvellous moment where a new pattern emerges. Reading through your data, annotating and reflecting, standing back and looking for patterns can lead you to see more complex ideas, overlaps and contradictions all of which might be challenging as you need to say something about this, but make your work more complex, and interesting.

The kind of data you gather depends on your subject area, your research question, your own context and access to the data, and the ways in which you can manage it in order to use it to address your research question or hypothesis.

Your data, once gathered via your research methods and vehicles, will all need managing so that you need to ensure that you are appropriately selective in what you can use, and able to interpret the data you have gathered from whichever variety of appropriate sources. All data, whether scientific facts from experiments or the narrative reflections of participants, needs selection, management and interpretation in order that it can be translated from just data and interpreted in context, to address research questions, contribute to understanding and knowledge.

In the social sciences, you might be using statistics, and these need statistical analysis, involving initial coding up of the categories into which the data falls, such as age, yes/no answers, particular question response categories, phrases found in responses which are not already pre-categorised and coded. Some open-ended responses to questionnaires or semi-structured open-ended interview questions need to be thematically analysed. Segmenting or chunking might be needed, where you cut into manageable segments or chunks, large amounts of data from, for example, a large set of interview or survey question responses. Other forms of management will be necessary so that you can handle the data, see what themes are emerging and start to annotate and comment on it before the final interpretation.

If you have been carrying out visual research or research into the media, literature, and other arts, you might well be gathering developmental examples such as sketchbooks, diaries, poetry in progress and process, or you might be gathering quotations from those who have written about such processes and achievements, and practitioners of some sort.

We often use quotations in literature and the humanities, and in relation to artefacts and artistic processes or products in the arts. This can be either as primary source data, for example, of peoples' responses, if that is what we are looking at, or as secondary sources, information on critical responses to and interpretations of the text/artwork/artefact etc.

Here is an example of using quotation which is a secondary source, a comment on the use of data. (If our study was of things people say about how you use data, this would be a primary source, and data for our study!):

> We thrive in information thick worlds because of our marvellous and everyday capacity to select, edit, single out, structure, highlight, group, pair, merge, harmonize, synthesize, focus, organize, condense, reduce, boil down, choose, categorize, catalogue, classify, refine, abstract, scan, look into, idealize, isolate, discriminate, distinguish, screen, sort, pick over, group, pigeonhole, integrate, blend, average, filter, lump, skip, smooth, chunk, inspect, approximate, cluster, aggregate, outline, summarize, itemize, review, dip into, flip through, browse, glance into, leaf through, skim, list, glean, synopsise, winnow wheat from chaff, and separate things into the sheep from the goats.   (Tufte, 1990, p. 50)

It is doubly useful as the content suggests how we need to identify, manage and analyse the data with which we work.

Data handling, management and analysis

Collecting data is real and exhilarating. You have direct access to your sources, you meet the people, you touch the documents, you carry out the experiment, you send out, receive back and collate the questionnaire, you read the books and take thoughtful notes. One of my research colleagues is currently in Bangladesh collecting data, doing his fieldwork. He is living in a poor community, learning Bengali, and goes out every day to talk with people about how they do or don't educate their children, where they can or can't send them and for what results. It's hard work, it's hot, it's bringing him new experiences every day. He is collecting his data. I'm just putting the final touches to my questions to interview a Caribbean/Canadian speculative fiction writer. It's very exciting to collect hands-on data. It can also be immensely frustrating, tedious, riddled with difficulties and then just a little irritating if:

- what you have gathered is not what you expected at all;
- you lost sight of the research questions;
- much of it is not actually useful or usable in relation to the questions;
- you couldn't get to the data in the first place;
- you collected so little you feel you won't be able to analyse and interpret and say anything much; or
- you collected so much that you don't know where or how to start with dealing with it.

And perhaps you found out some really rich pieces of information that you could never have predicted, and which will take your research to a new level, help you make a real contribution to meaning and knowledge.

These are the joys of data collection, data management and data analysis.

Analysing data, scaffolding and keeping records

Collecting your data

- Remember your research question, problem or hypothesis at all times when putting your research vehicles and tools into action, using your research methods to gather your data.
- Keep careful field notes of when, where and for what reason you collected what data and how you collected it.
- Keep notes of your responses, the problems and surprises of *all* research activities and *particularly* those involving data collection. These details will affect how you can use and interpret it (or not).
- Label/code up/number all questionnaires.
- Label all tapes – dates, occasion.
- Note and file all reading references.

This is all a meticulous activity, which means that you will be able to work with the data you have collected without the irritation of trying to recall where it came from, the reason you collected it and why it might be important to your research. Good labelling and management stops you having to waste time returning to sources or trying to repeat data collection which took a long time to arrange. If you took photos of a ceremony in Tibet which was part of your fieldwork, for example, and might carry a wealth of religious, social and cultural meaning and so ownership and rights, you will have to take some time negotiating the ethics of this photo shoot and the right to use the photos in appropriate ways. You also need to get the photos right. Returning to Tibet to take them again is probably out of the question; being careful how you collected this data, like any other, and ensuring it is carefully labelled up will mean that it is ready for you to work with. No matter the size or kind of your project, this collection and management of your data will be of use to you in interpretation and during conclusions, and also in any future work. It is also a skill worth learning for transfer to a number of jobs.

Managing the data so that you can analyse it requires strict scheduling and organisation. This is a daunting task. Many people feel overwhelmed about it at some stage, but on the other hand, this is where your evidence for your claims and findings comes from. It is essential that the interpretation of the data you have gathered yourself (or have worked with others to gather) is going to contribute to the new points, new ideas, new findings that your research will make.

There are some difficult moments, however, when you have been very busy and collected a great deal, even 'shedloads' of data and you wonder what to do with all of it. If you are floundering in large amounts of data and unsure of how to handle it:

Go back to your research questions or hypotheses.

Remember, you are only looking at some of the issues which have emerged – directly in relation to your research questions – but do not be entirely shut off from challenges, from serendipity – accidental discoveries, revelations and errors which can lead to new thoughts.

You need to make the most of those marvellous, utterly surprising, original finds which emerge sometimes, especially when we are reading in a careful, focused way through our data or when combining across data sources, such as seeing how answers to questions in a questionnaire relate to those later pursued in an interview.

Preparing and entering your data

Data needs to be tided up before being entered into any manual or mechanical technical-coding activity and analysis package. Tidying up means, for instance, removing the questionnaires which were not completed (unless you are only actually looking for a section of responses), were damaged, or falsely completed (some people just put their answers straight down the middle or a single column of choices – to cut the time), labelling and numbering the transcripts or the questionnaires, colour coding sections, logging them.

If you are using questionnaires

- Pre-code or categorise closed questionnaire questions (for example, yes/no answers, 1–5 Lickert scale choices) for ease of analysis.
- Code any names for data protection.
- Read carefully and code up less structured, more open-ended questions (such as 'Please tell us what your views about . . . are . . . ; Why do you like visiting . . . ?) after completion.
- Analyse questionnaires in batches (chunking).
- How are you analysing? By hand?
- Are you using SPSS? Or another statistical package?
- Are you using factor analysis? Or mean average scores on several sub-scales?
- Are you looking at simple responses or comparing across responses for patterns of relationship?

As mentioned previously, for the really complex comparative work, you will find the more specialised books helpful (see below). This is a brief introduction and does not touch complex statistics and their analysis at all.

For interview data

Have your tapes transcribed or transcribe them yourself. If you can do it yourself you can hear the patterns of response to certain questions emerging, make annotations in the corners of transcription, make notes as you listen to whole tapes. If you are transcribing yourself or if you have a machine or package which indicates the time and numbers on the tape, you can listen, select appropriate parts and transcribe only those in relation to the emerging themes and patterns, thus saving many hours. Do beware of feeling that being busy is all the research is about. Managing the data and then analysing and interpreting it is essential. Without interpretation there is no contribution, only description.

- Type up or transcribe tapes as you go, then you will not be overwhelmed with too much data to sort into the kind of shape that will let you prepare it for analysis.
- Read it all through, yourself; transcribe it yourself if you can – so that you are hearing it and can start to spot themes, trends, categories, new ideas and surprises.
- Keep copies/back up on disk/memory stick, and label.
- Remember your conceptual framework and your boundaries as well as working with an open mind: open to the surprises when starting to analyse data.
- Consider all your data. What themes and issues emerge? What is unexpected? What is as you expected? What else?
- Select what relates to your questions – there will be masses of data which is fascinating but irrelevant to *this* piece of research – your 'slice of the cake'.

How are you analysing? NUDIST/NVivo enables thematic analysis once you have identified themes. You will always have to sit and read through the interviews etc. to identify the themes and differences, and new information so that you can inform the data management package what themes and key words to look for. There will be data it will miss, and that you might spot, since sometimes the same meaning is conveyed in an interview without using the key words.

Questionnaire and interview analysis

- In the margins, annotate your transcriptions from interviews thematically.
- Summarise and generalise trends, patterns, emerging categories and themes of response.

Do this initial annotating, and thematic commentary and coding, immediately you find the themes and categories. Don't wait until it is all analysed using IT or manually. Respond to your spontaneous hunches and reflections. They are often very sound and, if not, will at least give you a sense of the variety of ways of interpreting what you are finding. But do use specific examples and selections from data presented visually and discussed. Ask your data fundamental analytical questions related to your research questions and the emerging themes. Follow up hints/hunches – tracking them through careful scrutiny of data to prove/disprove them. Track arguments and themes as threads through a variety of data from different sources. Double check (or more) before coming to any conclusion. Be absolutely certain you can back up what you argue/claim with specific data.

You need to consider:

- the significance of your findings;
- generalisability;
- reliability;
- validity.

Look below at an example of a short data analysis exercise and consider how you would work with the data, and so what you could do with the data your research produces, for instance from your:

- questionnaires;
- interviews;
- sketchbooks;
- notes from novels.

What might these research methods and vehicles produce for you and how you would look for themes, patterns, categories, surprises, then how might you present this as part of an argument related to your conceptual framework, underpinned by theories and addressing your question?

Data analysis exercise: What do I do with all this data?

Below there is data from two sets of social science research. The first asked a closed question about the dissemination of project findings in a variety of opportunities within a university. The data was produced as (a) questionnaire responses, and then added to later as (b) part of an interview. What you have below is the question and the analysis of the questionnaire responses to that question. The researcher straightforwardly counted numbers of responses in the different sections on offer for the answer, and has shown these as a table.

Layout of data as analysed

The researcher has produced a visual chart to show the number of responses in each category – where respondents can choose as many categories as are true for them (the overall number of responses is not divided up according to the number of respondees).

Questions
How have you disseminated your findings from the fellowship? A number of options are given here. Please answer Yes or No to each option.
Symposium
Workshops
Publications
Consultancy
Internally
Externally

Figure 14.1 is a graph indicating the results from a survey carried out asking exactly these questions. The numbers of respondents answering 'Yes' to each is indicated in the analysis through the bar chart size, where numbers are on the left-hand vertical column and the choices are on the horizontal line beneath the chart. Respondents could say 'yes' to the questions if they wanted to, so we are not trying to divide a total number up into sub-sections here.

The second set used an open-ended question in an interview about the use of a CD-Rom package which takes doctoral students through a mock viva.

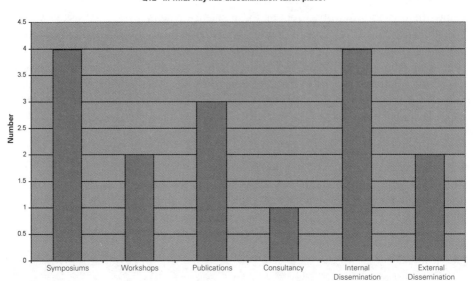

Figure 14.1

Interview data

Question (using an interview model based on appreciative enquiry, which asks for the positive responses in relation to something)

How useful was the CD-Rom in helping you to prepare for your viva? and in what ways was it useful?

Student A

You can simulate a viva completely, you know. You have actually got faces in front of you which are, which are mobile and this kind of thing.

[Going through the Interviewer CD-Rom] was a good thing to do because it made me think hard about particular generic questions that might turn up . . . and I was able to formulate a . . . well thought out answer to each one.

Student B

What was most useful to me is the opportunity to speak. I have a problem with my level of speaking the English. So, for 5 days I didn't stop to speak English and now I know that it has helped me a lot to speak fluently enough. First of all, I tried to answer exactly to the, to the, to the questions and even I wrote my, my answers and, and tried to remember them by heart. And after 1 or 2 days I felt that there is no chance that I can remember it and I started to speak with the computer fluently with mistakes, with the gap between, you know, sentences. And that, was the main, you know, helpful points in this CD-Rom. The opportunity to speak like you speak with people in front of you. I think that what is more useful is the tips that they give in the CD-Rom. Because the tips are put more widely, put in focus more widely than the, than the question. So some of the tips are so, know like a distance from the questions. All the area, many, many small questions that prepared you to answer not only one question but four or five according to the number of the tips and also the remarks in the end, what examiners want from, from you is, it also helpful.

I don't think that I could answer these questions without answering before about all these tips and, and questions that the CD-Rom suggest me to answer.

Student C

The points and the tips that were given and those were very, very helpful . . . I have seen some preparation for viva notes beforehand of other people and other resources but this is unique. And the uniqueness of the Interviewer is that it really gives you the examiner's point of view and it gives you a few tips of what might the examiners look for in answering the questions. How to satisfy, how to understand the questions, what perspectives you can take the questions to and, and then, you know, hopefully your answers are much better. So, in that respect it was really helpful. Besides the sense of realness that it gives you because the examiner actually talks to you.

It is not so much the questions as the situation, you see, it really gets you into the situation, the setting, the atmosphere, the context of the viva and it really gives you a sense of realness about the viva.

Analysing this requires you to read carefully, annotate the kinds of responses students produce, then categorise and code them. They seem to be identifying as useful:

1 rehearsal
2 tips
3 ability and opportunity to speak
4 sense of authenticity
    (a) of the questions
    (b) of the context
5 explanations of what is required in typical viva questions
6 speaking English at this level and this amount (for students B and C who are international in origin).

You would need to look at all of the transcripts, identify the categories and themes, then return to them all and see if they can be analysed in relation to the categories and themes, then select extracts from the interviews (short ones) to illustrate the categories and themes and develop a narrative discussion which includes making claims about the categories and themes, and producing extracts (short – shorter than these above) to act as evidence.

Then you would need to identify findings and to draw some conclusions based on these findings.

Findings

Students argue that the rehearsal, tips, opportunity to speak English at length in a realistic context, are all very useful for their viva development.

Conclusions

The use of a mock viva, particularly with a CD, enables an authentic rehearsal and practice to help students in their confidence building for the real viva.

Activity

Now please consider:

- What could you do with this data?
- How do you feel when presented with such amounts and kinds of data?
- What questions would you like to ask of it?
- What do you need to know FIRST in order to ask any questions or interpret anything?
- Why might you want to use this particular data? What might you be seeking?
- Why use this *kind* of data?
- What else – what other information from other research vehicles and methods – might you want to use to help back up (triangulate) your findings from this data? And why?

Look at the information about categories. Can you draw any tentative conclusions, make any suggestions about interpretation or meaning from any of this? How do the categories and how does the further information help your analysis and interpretation?

- What processes would you go through to categorise?
- What questions would you need to ask?
- What answers and information would you need, to make sense of analysing all of this?
- What will you ensure you do in order to analyse and interpret your own data?
- What could go wrong?
- What kinds of precautions can you take?

Analysis of qualitative data

Whatever the amount and variety of the sources from which your qualitative data has been drawn, the main task in its analysis is to understand the themes and patterns which are emerging from it, in relation to the research questions, problems, or hypothesis and the underpinning theories which will be used to help find a route through the data. You will have collected a vast amount of rich data, only a portion of which will relate to the question you asked, and therefore can be used in your research project or dissertation.

Using variables creatively: an example of cross-relating variables in a piece of research on gender and discrimination

Some of the most interesting new ideas emerge from seeing links and contrasts, in other words the links between certain variables. Perhaps while you were looking at 'discriminatory practices', different responses might produce some interesting ideas which emerge from the ways in which cross-relating – such as comments related to gender discrimination with those related to age – could throw up a very original or unexpected sub-section of response. You might find, for instance, that it is not only older women who face discrimination, but younger just post-adolescent men. This might be discovered by seeing patterns in their responses when listening to and analysing tapes.

Something of a pattern emerges when combining variables, such as gender and age, where one pattern was expected and the other is a surprise. It's the surprises that are so exciting in research.

Gather together the data from the different sources.

Read through, annotate and see if and where patterns start to emerge.

Colour or number code the patterns and gather the data into groups in terms of the colour or number codes.

Coding is the way in which you align the data with some way of handling it, managing it and then relating it to the ideas and theories which can help you to interpret it in the course of asking and answering your question.

> Codes represent the decisive link between the original 'raw data', that is the textual material such as interview transcripts of field notes on the one hand and the researcher's theoretical concepts on the other. (Seidel and Kelle, 1995, p. 52)

The codes you might develop and use in this process could be:

- Key concepts.
- Theoretical ideas.

- Key variables identified in the literature.
- Emergent themes from the data.
- Events.
- Actors – anything or anyone who does anything to generate data.

And the codes which emerge can be composed of words, time, varieties of response or any other manner of identifying clusters of response.

Look at your questionnaire: a straightforward code example will have numbered responses or several responses divided into sections, so that a question:

| Do you own a TV? | has the single response, | Yes/No. |

While a more complex question will have several sub-categories which need coding if you are to represent the different responses produced.

Please indicate the various ways in which you used the library during 2007–8 and how often you used it.

	Never (a)	Monthly (b)	Weekly (c)	Daily (d)
(1) Borrowing books				
(2) Internet access to online holdings				
(3) Working in the archives				

This allows you to code up the answers.

What does coding do? It helps you to see the wood for the trees, find your way about the data through labelling units in terms of their differences and so on. When you stand back you can see the patterns emerging from the coded data. It is just the first step towards analysis; the standing back and reflecting, and perceiving the patterns and their importance in relation to the research question and underpinning theories, is the next step.

For example, you could find from the library usage records, examples of patterns of very frequent usage of the Internet sources and infrequent uses of the books; you would then want to understand what this meant, why it happened, how it contributed to your exploration of the changing issues of library holdings among undergraduates (if this was your topic). You code the answers, you see the proportions and you see the patterns. The seeing is the real beginning of the analysis but it is not possible, without coding, to collect and label the units for you to scrutinise.

Handling different kinds of data produces a further need for categorisation into type.

Tactics for generating meaning

From descriptive to explanatory, and concrete to conceptual

  1   Noting patterns and themes
  2   Seeing plausibility
  3   Clustering
  4   Making metaphors
  5   Counting
  6   Making contrasts/comparisons
  7   Partitioning variables/differentiation
  8   Subsuming particulars into the general
  9   Factoring
  10 Noting relations between variables
  11 Finding intervening variables
  12 Building a logical chain of evidence
  13 Making conceptual/theoretical coherence

(Miles and Huberman, 1994)

Note how, with analysis of text, using NUDIST/NVivo identifies description of categories previously discovered from reading through the text and listening, then cuts out the identified sections and pulls them all together for you to read as continuous prose, with the sections from where they came identified above each section.

Laying out the information from the data

There are many different ways to treat the data. One thing to remember is that the presentation must be appropriate, useful and accessible to a readership. It must also be translated for them so that it is interesting, not merely laid out. And do discuss what it all means – don't just leave them with a bar chart or a pie chart! Figure 14.2 is an example of a bar chart.

The results presented below relate to a questionnaire given to 500 students in 2008, asking them about their satisfaction with various services in the university. Initially the results were represented as a simple frequency table, then converted into this bar chart in order to visualise the different kinds of responses which have been produced by the different questions. The bar chart in itself is useless unless we match it with the questions so that some sense of what these choices mean can be produced.

Questions

What elements of the university's services have been most useful and satisfactory to you during your three years here?

1 Campus learning environment – buildings and grounds
2 Learning and teaching quality

3 Student services support
4 Entertainment
5 Learning development support online
6 Student Union
7 Accommodation
8 Library and IT facilities

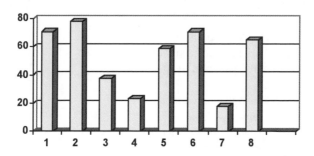

Figure 14.2

Clearly, in this example, these students did not find the entertainment very satisfactory but were pleased enough with the learning environment.

Information can be presented in a number of ways. The bar chart enables us to compare single items or clusters of items against each other, focusing on proportions or percentages of the whole responding in a certain way. It is useful if there are a couple of variables involved.

A pie chart (see Figure 14.3) shows the proportion of a whole which the item or question selected relates to. This can then be seen in relation to the whole, visually.

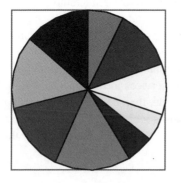 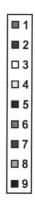

Figure 14.3   Pie chart: proportions of students studying in different subject areas in the faculty of applied science

Key:
1 = Biology 2 = Chemistry 3 = Physics 4 = Forensic Science 5 = Radiography
6 = Animal Sciences 7 = General Science 8 = Biochemistry 9 = Ophthalmics

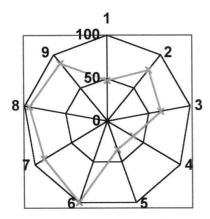

Figure 14.4

Radar charts

Radar charts (see Figure 14.4) indicate patterns of choices and behaviours for individuals or groups in relation to the categories of answers chosen.

Radar Chart with markers: Analysis of response to a questionnaire on preference for kinds of holidays – which shows the patterns of response across the preferred types of holiday.

1 = cruises in the Mediterranean
2 = beach holidays in Greece
3 = city breaks in Europe
4 = city breaks in the UK
5 = beach holidays in the Far East
6 = Australia outback trekking
7 = New Zealand snowboarding
8 = Canada snowboarding

From the choices, you can see this is an adventurous kind of holidaymaker who prefers trekking and snowboarding in faraway places.

This information might help you to decide which brochures to send them, and what to advise them to look at for their next holiday, were you a travel agent.

Choices

Each of the numbered areas relates to a specific kind of holiday choice. The individual who has been analysed has a variety of preferences and this chart enables us to see these in relation to each other. There are many different kinds of layout possible for your results and you will need to choose the most visually suitable.

Activity

Consider:

- What kind of layout would suit the kinds of research you are carrying out and the kinds of questions underpinning your work? Your sample? Your data?

- Are you looking for percentages, proportions in relation to the whole, comparative samples, variables in operation?

Summary

In this chapter we have considered:

- Ways of categorising and labelling data according to themes and patterns.
- Analysing and interpreting what you have gathered.
- Not drowning in data.
- Laying out your data.
- Interpreting your findings.

Further reading

Miles, M. and Huberman, M. (1994) *Qualitative Data Analysis* (London: Sage Publications).
Seidel, J. and Kelle, U. (1995) 'Different Functions of Coding in the Analysis of Textual Data', in U. Kelle (ed.), *Computer-aided Qualitative Data Analysis: Theory, Methods and Practice* (London: Sage).
Tufte, E. (1990) *Envisioning Information* (Cheshire, CT: Graphics Press USA).

15 Managing Your Tutor or Supervisor

This chapter looks at:

► how to work with your tutor;
► how to work with your supervisor;
► managing your expectations;
► agreeing on ways of working together;
► how much the supervisor can do and how much is your work – from benign neglect to independence and autonomy;
► overcoming differences and getting the best out of your supervisor.

Your relationship with your tutor or supervisor is the primary one on your research journey when you're undertaking a dissertation or a project. It's important to be able to get on with your tutor or supervisor in a friendly and professional manner and also to clarify right from the beginning what your expectations of each other are with regards to how you can communicate with each other, expectations of responsibilities and regularity of meetings, production of work, time management and management of the project.

When you are researching for an essay or other piece of work, your relationship with your tutor or lecturer, depending on who marks the work, is important. You need to clarify titles of work, locate any full instructions on paper or on the course website, and if possible check with them that your planned work sounds acceptable. Sometimes at this point they can help you to narrow down a topic or title which you have chosen yourself, or prompt you to ask research questions rather than setting out to describe the whole field of study. This kind of clarifying relationship is extended and deepened when you carry out longer research for a project or dissertation, so the following ideas about working with your supervisor can be scaled down if carrying out research for a shorter piece of work.

As an undergraduate you will probably be allocated a supervisor for your project or dissertation, or you might start to identify who you would like to work with, as you find out about the interests of the staff, and how they coincide with your own interests in what you would like to research and write about in your project or dissertation. Whoever your supervisor is, and however well you feel you do or do not know them when you start to work together, it is important to get clear agreement between you of how you are going to work together, what the time and responsibility expectations are from both of you, and how they would like you to communicate with them.

Managing expectations in this way and agreeing clear working practices are essential to support you in your research work through to completion whatever the size of your project. Because this is a human interaction, there is plenty of scope for building good working relationships or completely misunderstanding each other – and all points in between. If you have never worked with this supervisor before, or with any supervisor before, you might have excessive expectations of how much they are going to support you, what they can do for you according to the regulations, and how they can work with you. It is important that you can develop a balanced way of working so that the supervisor neither:

- does all the work for you – in which case you won't develop research capabilities yourself and it would not be your own work; or
- neglects you completely, perhaps arguing that this will increase your independence – it might, but you might also feel deserted and produce rather narrative or descriptive work when the interactions would raise the level of your work.

Probably the best balance would be a supportive, informative supervisor who offers examples and encourages ideas, suggests, and yet lets you get the work done yourself, providing models, and dialogue about your development, through feedback and suggestions. It is possible that supervisors need to behave slightly differently at different stages in your work, sometimes being more informative and prescriptive and sometimes promoting critical thinking and dialogue, exploration and creativity. You need to remember both your rights to their time, and their rights to their time in a busy schedule. Students' comments about how much support they have received from their supervisors range from 'they were great, they were always there for me and supported my work from start to finish', 'my supervisor lent me books, responded very quickly when I sent in questions and drafts', to 'I hardly ever saw them. I had to sort out childcare, pay for childcare and drive 100 miles round trip and the supervision always seemed to be interrupted by phone calls. I always felt I was a bit of a nuisance', or 'I could never find them.'

As the model above suggests, a good working relationship with your supervisor should lead you to gradually develop more autonomy in your own ways of working and researching, feeling supported rather than either neglected or totally disempowered and controlled – neither of which would enable you to develop the kinds of research approaches and skills you will need for the rest of your university career and in your employment afterwards. For an undergraduate dissertation or major project, you might find you are entitled to anything between four and six hours of their time. Find out what you are entitled to, and discuss with your supervisor how to work together in this time.

Supervisors agree to work with you because they want to support you in your work, but they also have limitations on their time and you need to develop your capabilities as a researcher, so it's not a good idea to depend on them at all hours of the day and night or expect them to do much of the basic research work for you. However, you can expect support, guidance, and some models of how to go about your research and how to write it up. You can also expect them to comment on your question, plans, and early writing. Do agree a manageable set of expectations and exchanges with your supervisor so that you know what you can ask for help with.

A few thoughts about choosing your supervisor

Your university will probably select a supervisor for you for your undergraduate dissertation or project. The head of subject will choose your supervisor because of their specialisms. You might decide to do a particular project because you've been working well with a tutor during the past couple of years as a student and so want to work in their area. If you are hoping to work with someone you know, it's a good idea to approach them in advance and see whether they would be willing to take you on in the area your project dissertation focuses on. This way, together you can start to think about the area, topic, and title in advance. If the system allows it, it would also be a good idea to let the head of subject know, or ask your potential supervisor to let them know that you would like to work together.

It is possible that the supervisor you would like to work with has too many students to be able to give you the time that you need, in which case, you will be allocated another supervisor. It is also possible that the most eminent person who has published the most in your area will be too distant and too busy to supervise you properly. So do check whether they can give you the time before you approach them formally. Whoever you work with, however, you need to be able to get on together well and to decide when you are going to see each other; how you are going to produce work, at what pace; what the supervisor is willing to do to the work that you send them; when is a good time to contact them; and how you can agree well spaced out supervision, so that you can keep up the pace of work through to completion.

> ### Please think:
>
> - Who do you think you can ask to be your supervisor, or who have you been allocated? And what do you know about their way of working?
> - What do you know about their specialisms, the number of students they are supervising, and their personality?
> - Have you already met, and started to plan your research?

Once you have approached a supervisor and/or they have approached/been allocated to you (whatever the process is in your case and that of your university), you need to get a clear definition of how much and how far your supervisor can and will work with you on your project, and to agree with them about responsibilities. As soon as you have cleared up who is responsible for what parts of the work, you will both get on better together.

Working with your supervisor: managing expectations, initial agreements, and ground rules; regularity and kind of supervisions, and at what stages

You need to agree with your supervisor what you each expect of each other in terms of work, communication and responsibility.

Try and agree on a clear plan of when you will see your supervisor, how much time you have been allotted with them, what stages of work are expected and when. It is important to set up regular supervisions in the early stages of your work, and these will probably become less frequent once you are fully engaged, and then increase in length and frequency towards the end of your project as you finalise and write it up. It's possible now that quite a lot of the work you do with your supervisor will be via email. Some supervisors are happy for you to send short questions to them asking about work or reading or problems that have arisen. You might well agree with each other that if you have a short question you send an email with that in the title, e.g., 'short question: problem about sample'. This lets the supervisor know that they can answer your questions quickly.

Example: email from Sophie

I thought I'd do my dissertation on African American writing, Walker's *The Color Purple*, some of the work by the men, like Ellison's *The Invisible Man*, and relate it to rappers now – what do you think?

Supervisor: Great idea! What thoughts do you have about what they are dealing with? – oppression? identity? marginalisation? Speaking out? Find the main ideas and questions you want to look at. Is there a developmental line between the three of them? What is it? Get back to me – I'm around Monday and Tuesday afternoons if that helps.

Ground rules about meetings

One of my own students has taught me how to be very organised in the way in which I worked with him and so I have developed similar systems and practices with students I've worked with after him. He had already worked with me in the past and so approached me to be his supervisor.

He said

- 'Should I let you know when I'm going to send some work to you?'
- 'Shall I contact you about 10 days before I send it?'
- 'Should I send a couple of questions or a brief agenda before we meet?'
- 'Would it be helpful if I kept the notes during supervision and wrote up what I have agreed to do and anything you've agree to do and send it to you afterwards?'

He was very organised, whereas Sophie needed some direction to help her narrow down her area of focus, the question and the texts. I needed to ask her questions to help her to focus. He knew how to time manage his work, and he worked to make sure that his face-to-face interactions with me were quality time.

What have we learned from this?

Agree with your supervisor how much work to send, when, and how. Agree on ways in which you can send them small questions when you need to. Agree the times when they are willing to respond to you online – don't expect them to respond immediately, especially if they have a heavy workload and domestic responsibilities.

Don't expect responses midnight on Sunday!

When you plan to talk about the work at the supervision, decide on a couple of questions and issues on which you need direction so that this can be a focused discussion. If you can send them to your supervisor in advance, then they will be ready to deal with them when you need to.

Do keep a note of what you have discussed and what you have agreed to do. Follow up on these agreements. Make sure you've planned the day and time for the next supervision when you leave.

Timeline of planned work with supervisor for a year-long project or dissertation

Often projects span an academic year. This means that you identify your title and a supervisor probably at the end of the second year, and hand in the project or dissertation at the end of May or earlier, in the third year. Supervisors will not be available during all of this time, and there are different planning points and supervision points you will need to take into consideration when deciding when to book in to see them and what to send them, when to send first and final drafts, and so on. You also need to find out how much of your work your supervisor is allowed to look at and comment on in relation to the regulations. This varies from university to university and can be as little as 10% of the overall project or dissertation, right the way up to the whole amount (maybe 3,000–8,000 words), and several times.

May, Year 1   Identify broad topic area and meet possible supervisor or advisor – discuss topic and title, ask for suggested reading.

June–September   No contact. You do the reading, both primary (the theorists) and secondary (people who have used the theories in research and practice in areas related to your project or dissertation).

September–October   Meet to discuss the reading you have carried out and refine your title, based on your now clearer research question, identified problem or hypothesis. Sometimes at this point you have changed your area or question and so change your proposed supervisor.

You need to develop ground rules for your meetings and work in between. For example:

1   You agree to send short questions by email with the question in the title.
2   Meet the supervisor every two weeks for half an hour/an hour (whatever is agreed).

3 Before you meet you will send them an outline of the work you have done and any drafts of writing, plus a few questions, e.g. How can I find the right reading? What about this problem that is emerging? Access to samples? Contradictions in the reading? And so on.

4 After each session, you will send them a brief set of agreed action points (half a side of A4):

- you agree to – (carry on with . . . write up . . . explore . . .)
- they have agreed to – (send on reading, read a draft . . .)

October–March Regular meetings once a fortnight or once a month – send in advance:

- Work in progress.
- A few thoughts and questions.
- What you are looking at – identifying the theories and theorists who will help you ask your questions. What are their main arguments and issues? How do these help you:
  - problematise and question what you are doing and the reading you are becoming aware of;
  - work with your problem; how do they help you to explore your hypothesis?
- Agreement on the methodology and methods and the research vehicles for asking your questions/exploring the problem and so on in the field. This will help you get the research under way.
- Comments on:
  - how the reading, then the data collection, reading and analysis of documents, fieldwork or practical art producing (whatever your processes are) are developing;
  - how the writing is progressing.
- Questions and suggestions about:
  - how to code up, analyse, and ask questions of and interpret your data (depending on your research area);
  - how to carry out the different kinds of writing – the descriptive, the critical, analytical, evaluative and conceptual writing;
  - writing the abstract and the conclusions;
  - laying out the references properly and ensuring good presentation.

You can expect your supervisor to work with you on:

Turning a question, a fascination or a general topic into a research question and title that you can realistically get on with researching.

Title and scope of the project Discuss the overall project with your supervisor and ask for their support in defining and clarifying the research title, the research questions, and getting started in terms of reading. Remember how important it is to get your title right.

University regulations   Informing you about university regulations, where you can find information about the time to completion, length of the piece of work and its expected presentation format, rules and criteria for assessment. The supervisor should be able to direct you to where you can find the information, which will probably be online as well as in hard copy. They will also know these details and be ready to remind you.

Some basic time management and action planning   Research design, development and management of the day-to-day process.

Advice and suggestions about reading   These might be quite general, such as 'you need to read something about identity', or they can be quite specific. Your supervisor might be happy to give you references, lend you books and articles, email new websites and appropriate written pieces that they find. However, you cannot expect them to do this regularly because, after all, you're the one who is carrying out the research and foraging around for the literature to underpin your research is part of the research process. So don't expect them to do all of this level of the research for you.

You can expect them to guide you about **appropriate methodology** (based on your discipline, topic, question, and the way you can go about gathering knowledge or creating it), your research design and methods (the ways you gather your research data and information, such as documentary analysis, survey method) and research vehicles (such as the surveys themselves, the actual wording of the interviews).

You can expect your supervisor to guide you about how you can go about your **data analysis** in a practical sense, if your research project will include statistical data, interview data or documentary analysis, which it might do if it is a social science or related piece of research.

You can expect your supervisor to give you regular feedback on the **appropriate and agreed amounts of written work** which you send them. See below for how to interpret such feedback.

Depending on the regulations, you might well be able to expect them to **read a first draft of your work, or select parts of your work**.

Towards the end of your work, your supervisor should be able to help you to ensure that you are producing a coherent project, or dissertation, laid out in the right format for the regulations of this award. They will remind you to check that:

- You have clearly addressed your question or tested your hypothesis.
- You have engaged with concepts and theories and that they underpin your research and your interpretation of data and your findings.
- You have interpreted your data and expressed it clearly in the text.
- You have actually engaged conceptually, i.e. at the level of meaning and ideas.
- You have determined themes throughout your work.
- Your argument runs throughout your work.

- You have up-to-date references that you have referenced appropriately in the text, and you have laid out the bibliography appropriately according to the guidelines of your discipline and of the university.

They will probably be able to help you develop an abstract – which is quite a difficult piece of writing – and to advise on the conclusions. See Chapter 21 for suggestions about these two essential pieces of writing, which begin and end your project or dissertation and show how it has explored a significant area of research and made a contribution to meaning.

They should remind you to ensure that your project or dissertation is being presented on time, to the right length, to the right place, and that it fits the rules and regulations for that project or dissertation.

After the first stages, you will need to see your supervisor regularly, as you have agreed and they are expected to help keep you focused and on course in your research, BUT the will power, the sticking power and the hard work is all yours!

You will be able to ask them questions, to hear about further sources and contacts. They will also need to be closely involved when you are developing complex concepts, to check whether your interpretation of the reading and data is appropriate and at the right level, so far.

It is important that you remember that, although you are under the direction of a supervisor, your research is your own activity. Carrying out a research project or dissertation is seen as important in itself as a way of developing research approaches and research skills that you can use later on in your employment or in future research for other qualifications. The autonomous student who also ensures that they abide by the rules, and keeps in regular communication, checking their results and writing up appropriately, is the student who is genuinely undertaking their own research.

You need to keep a balance between managing necessary autonomy and individual, independent research, without losing touch with your supervisor. You also need to make sure that your work fits the demands of the university regulations.

Understanding supervisor and tutor feedback

Supervisors and tutors tend to give feedback on your work in several different ways at several different times. What follows is a range of their kinds of comments and what they might mean, or expect you to develop, or explain:

Supportive 'Well done! I can see you've done a lot of work here.'
This is congratulating you and is recognising that you have carried out a lot of work. It might also be leading into saying that your work should be more complicated and conceptualised, i.e. based on ideas and theories rather than just facts and details.

Celebratory 'These are very impressive findings. Now you have finished all your data analysis, well done!'

This also celebrates the work you have done. It will probably lead into asking you what your interpretations of your findings are and how you are theorising them.

Informative 'You need to have a colon before a list of bullet points. Your abstract should not be more than 350 words long. Abstracts tend to be written in the third person passive, such as "it was discovered that . . .".'

This is giving you specific information about how to express and lay your work out. You are expected to follow this advice throughout your dissertation or project. Such informative comments might include models of how to express yourself and lay out your work, such as in the brief example of the language used in an abstract.

Prescriptive 'There is no need to discuss every single piece of data. Do not include all questionnaires in your actual dissertation.'

These comments let you know what the rules are about in this instance, using your data as evidence. They are probably based on the general rules of how to write up the research so that someone can read it.

Problematising and questioning 'Why do you think this is? What do you mean here by the concept "homelessness" for example?'

This kind of questioning aims to prompt you to further ideas, questions, theories, and thoughts. It intends to raise the level of your thinking, whereas the earlier comments intend to raise the level of your organisation and presentation. These questions ask you to move beyond the gathering and expressing of facts, the discussion of your reading and your data collection, to asking fundamental questions about the ideas, concepts, theories, arguments and points of view that you are dealing with, whether they are those you have read about in the work of others, or those you are developing. If you can get into the habit of always questioning and engaging with theorising and arguing in your writing, you will be really developing as a researcher rather than someone who just gathers information discovered by other people and takes this as fact.

Suggesting forms of words 'Why not change "it is in my opinion that . . ." to "it can be argued that . . ."?'

These forms of comments help you to express both what you are discovering and what you are arguing in a way which backs up your points of view, research evidence and theorising. Much of the level of your thinking as the researcher is shown in the way you express yourself, and here your tutor is suggesting that you move beyond statement of opinion to putting forward a case and arguing the claim based on underpinning what you have discovered, whether it's other people's arguments or theories, or your own coherent argument.

Modelling ways of asking and answering or expressing something 'Here is a short model of the way in which an abstract is worded. Can you rewrite yours to be in the third person, passive, and to engage at the level of design and meaning? For example:

Most research into students' success in school in relation to gender has been conducted focusing on the learning of girls aged 14 to 18. This research looks at reasons for success or failure among working-class boys of 14 to 18 and argues that there is a relationship between their engagement, their identity in their peer group and their results.'

Here your tutor or supervisor is very helpfully modelling the kind of language that you need to use in different parts of your writing. The language of an abstract is very difficult to develop because it is distanced (third person passive), suggesting an overview of the reasons for conducting research and why it was conducted in order to contribute to knowledge. If your tutor models part of the language you could use in different parts of your assignment, project, dissertation or essay, then you need to analyse this for the tense, tone, kind of words and order used, and practise writing like this yourself a few times, then apply it in a piece of written work. You are likely to be using several different sorts of writing in any one assignment, project or dissertation. If your tutor does not supply a model, have a look at the work of other students who gained high marks, or at essays and journal articles (not student essays) which are published on the Internet in your subject area, and see how they have expressed the language of argument, the management and theorising, and expression of the information and ideas.

Suggesting that you work more conceptually (that is at the level of ideas and meaning rather than factually and descriptively alone)   'What does this contribute to our understanding? If you engage the identity theory you are using earlier with these results, what kind of argument can you develop? There is a difference between identifying the ideas and concepts you are using or somebody else is using about your topic, and writing that presents information.'

Your tutor here is trying to raise the level of your thinking and expression by asking you why you are asking the questions you are, how you ask them, what they mean, and what answering them or addressing them will contribute to our understanding and the overall level of meaning in this area of knowledge. If you're not sure what the conceptualised level of writing might look like then ask them for a model. For example, writing which is just informative and descriptive might say the following:

(A)   Of the young white working-class men who enter higher education, 40% leave by the end of their first year of study. They are usually the first from their family to have studied in higher education. An analysis of the subject choices in higher education indicates that 60% of them have chosen subjects that expect a great deal of theory and the writing of long essays rather than practical application.

A more theorised, conceptual piece of work (i.e. dealing with ideas and concepts, theories developed upon research, by experts, which help you to understand, make sense of, interpret, put your findings in a frame and a dialogue with those of others) might read like this:

(B)   'Yorke (2002) has identified a link between the lack of preparation and experience in theorised study and study skills more generally among young white male working-class students entering higher education in subjects which demand a great deal of theory and very little practice. Of the young white working class men who enter higher education, 40% leave by the end of their first year of study. They are usually the first to have studied in higher education in their family. Theories of readiness, the effect of preconceptions upon behaviour (Zimitat and Horstmanshof, 2004) would lead us to suggest that they could have unrealistic expectations which are not matched by their experiences and that this affects their ability to stick, and commit to their study. An analysis of the subject choices in higher education indicates that 60% of them have chosen subjects that expect a great deal of theory and the writing of long essays rather than practical application. Theories of retention (Yorke and Knight, 2000, 2003) suggest that there is a relationship between previous study, preconceptions of the kind of studying undertaken in higher education, social class and age and gender.

The second piece of writing links the data in with theories of social class, gender and studying, and retention and their success. This theorised, conceptualised version suggests concepts such as 'retention', 'preconceptions of' and 'approaches to learning'. It offers interpretations and relationships. Such theorising helps to interpret the data and later might help to suggest what could be done about problems indicated in the data and the findings.

Making some very general suggestions   'More reading needed. Expand.'
This is not terribly helpful in many ways because they have not suggested how much more reading, what kind of expansion; however, perhaps they don't want to write too much and really just want you to say more because you have an underdeveloped argument or have not made enough of a piece of your own reading for the reader.

Making some very specific suggestions   'Your quotation should be no more than three lines long.'
This is prescriptive and that can also be quite helpful because you might not have seen many models of how to go about expressing youself.

Letting off steam in haste   'No!'
You probably need to ask them to explain what it is they expect you to write next. This is just a short emotional response and it probably does not mean that all your work is a problem, maybe just a small expression of disagreement might be meant by the word 'no'. If you're worried, ask them to clarify.

Some of these feedback responses are more useful than others. You will need to learn to respond to each of them and if you are not sure what to do, such as in the general suggestions and the letting off steam, you might need to go back to your supervisor or tutor for clarification.

At different stages in your project, you could well find that your tutor or supervisor is addressing different issues in their feedback. It could be very alarming if you find your work is given back to you covered in comments about a whole range of issues such as the presentation, the question, the level of comment and conceptualisation, the way you are arguing and expressing yourself, your referencing, and a whole host of other areas. It is possible that your tutor or supervisor will choose to feed back at different levels or at different times on different pieces or elements of your work. Just because they haven't commented about one area it does not mean that is perfect. They are being selective.

You will also probably find that they don't cover the whole of your work with red pen and comment on everything that you write. Quite often supervisors will comment on all elements of some small part of your work in great detail and then ask you to take that level of response through the rest of the piece. They might be commenting on everything from working at the conceptual, i.e. meaningful, level to expressing yourself grammatically or avoiding typos. Do be sure to read their feedback very carefully and then revise the whole of your piece of writing accordingly rather than just responding to their local comments.

What happens if things go wrong? Managing difficult and changing relationships

Your relationship with your tutor or supervisor is a human interaction. We do not always get on well with each other and sometimes we may have to clear up misunderstandings. Many of these will be everyday misunderstandings easily cleared up by discussing with the tutor or supervisor. Maybe they have asked you to do some work and you are not sure what is involved, or maybe they gave you some feedback which confused you. Start by sending an email for clarification, or a note, or popping round to see them – they will probably be unaware they have confused or upset you or not been clear in what they have said.

Sometimes – we hope this does not happen! – the relationship might seriously or irrevocably breakdown. Or seem to. Although this might seem quite difficult, the first person to discuss any problems of communication with is your tutor or supervisor. If this really does not work and you cannot work out a procedure for getting back on track in relation to working together and your own writing – then you might need to ask the Students' Union for advice, and then after that perhaps talk to the head of subject, course tutor or someone else in overall responsibility for your study. It is possible to change supervisor, or tutor supervising a project or dissertation, so don't feel trapped. But as with most communication breakdowns, it is often the case that a third person can help clear up the misunderstanding and you can then actually just get on with working together again – so don't panic, and don't take extreme steps in the beginning of any such problem in communication!

What might go wrong?

They are not in touch:　There could be many reasons why they are not in touch or don't seem to be giving you full enough responses.

Perhaps you are expecting too much. At the start of the relationship with a tutor or supervisor it is important to agree on what is appropriate communication and how frequently you can meet, and what they are allowed to comment on in your work. Perhaps this is only half an hour's tutorial for an essay, and reading 250 words. Do find out.

Perhaps they are so busy they have assumed that you're working happily on your own, but you've actually got a problem.

Perhaps the email that you sent them about such a problem was copied into their junk mail by accident and they never saw it.

Perhaps you have not been clear in letting them know that you need support, clarification, some suggestions about how to overcome problems that you are meeting. Be friendly and approach them in person, by notes, or by email, and ask to see them and ask them to look at your work. If your communication really breaks down with your supervisor, which is, hopefully, a very rare occurrence, after you've tried to communicate with them you will need to talk to the year tutor or the head of subject about your concerns. But do this only after you've discussed the problem with the supervisor because it might be easily resolved.

There is a range of literature now about the supervisory processes. Gurr's model (Figure 15.1) might help you to position where your relationship with your tutor or supervisor lies, on a continuum ranging from excess support that takes away your own freedom, autonomy and independence to develop as a researcher, to what is known as a kind of 'benign neglect' where they really are not in touch. Most supervisory relationships

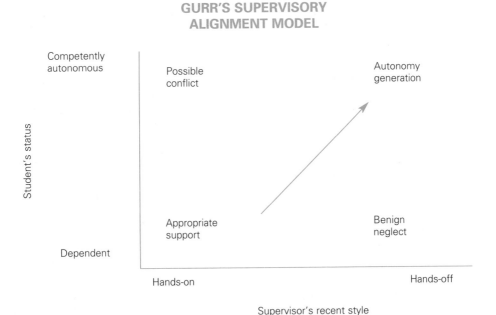

Figure 15.1   Gurr's Supervisory Alignment Model

Source Gurr (2001).

are amicable, proceed in a planned and supportive fashion, and end with a good piece of research being finished and a good sense of a sound relationship which can be drawn on in the future for further research and jobs. They will differ in length and amount of interactions, depending on the assignment. Do check.

Please consider:

- How does your supervisor or tutor supervise?
- Are you able to gradually develop autonomy?
- Do you have appropriate support? Or are you suffering from benign neglect?
- Do you think they feel they are supporting you adequately while you feel they are neglecting you or overwhelming you with instructions?
- Do you see the relationship and the support element in the same light?
- How can you help nurture your supervisory relationships so that your supervisor/tutor can support you to become an autonomous enough competent researcher while guiding and supporting your work with reading, feedback, and critical questioning?

Others can help too

You also need to remember that your supervisor is not the only person who can support you in your research.

You will find the subject librarians very helpful in guiding you towards appropriate sources if you explore with them what the area of the research is.

If you can develop a buddy system or a peer group with others who are also undertaking research, perhaps a project or a dissertation, then you can discuss how your work is developing, share frustrations, problems, excitements and discoveries together. Obviously it's not a good idea to work so closely together that your work seems to be the same! But this is unlikely and mutual support and discussion about developing research is actually building good habits for research in the future, which is rarely conducted completely on your own and does after all intend to contribute to a larger dialogue about developing an understanding and further knowledge in your field. Find a critical friend who can read some of your work, and discuss the wording with them and then improve it. If you have computer problems, see if you can get help from the IT specialist, who will normally be contactable in your department or faculty and can probably sort out your problem very quickly, thus reducing a lot of frustration and time wasting. There are other people who are experts in the field, who your supervisor or other tutors can put you in touch with and who are willing to share readings, or discuss with you some of the things you're finding, either face-to-face or over the email. They won't be doing the work for you, but they will be contributing to the dialogue, which is the development of research and its contribution to knowledge. Finally, look online. Many universities have good study support systems. The University of Brighton, for example, has an online support system for students, called BYGs, and specific FAQs sections.

You might also be building some useful contacts and some very good habits for the future.

Summary

In this chapter we have considered:

- Finding your supervisor.
- Developing good working relationships – ground rules, contact times, regular supervision, preparation and contact.
- What you can expect from your supervisor at different points in your project.
- Dealing with feedback.
- Working with other people as well as your supervisor.
- What to do if things go wrong.

Further reading

Gurr, G. (2001) *Student–Supervisor Alignment Toolkit*, available at: www.first.edu.au
Wisker, G. (2005) *The Good Supervisor* (Basingstoke: Palgrave Macmillan).

Managing Your Time, Life, Paid Work and Research

Establishing and maintaining the balance between work, research and life is important for you if you want to learn good habits to manage your time now, and for the future. This all makes good sense of course, and people have their differing ways of managing their time. This chapter helps you to think of ways of timing the stages of your research, and balancing its demands with the other demands of life, at different stages in the research and in your life. It considers a range of time-management practices to help you to balance your research work and the rest of your life and develop good habits for the future. It also helps you to consider work rhythms.

A useful tip is that on the one hand, if you work all of the time you could get a lot done, but could easily become jaded and perhaps put yourself off ever working that hard again. However, if you procrastinate, put work off and get very little done, you could well miss deadlines, underachieve and feel bad about yourself.

Somewhere in between lies a version of a manageable time-management routine, where you have good habits to get your research and other work done, and a more balanced life around that with neither excessive work nor excessive social or domestic activities. Easier said than done perhaps, but if you start somewhere with a realistic balanced plan and spot problems and adjust where necessary, you are bound to get more done in a balanced, satisfying way than if you do not plan at all.

Balancing demands on your time

You will have many demands on your time. In order to maintain your own wellbeing, you need to make sure you work out what these demands are, identify if the areas of your life and the demands on your time are becoming unbalanced, and if this is so, whether it is temporary or long term, and so work out ways of adjusting your work/life balance so that you have enough time for all aspects of your life. Everyone's demands are different and everyone's balance is different. Sometimes it is only when we try to identify how we manage and balance our time that we can see there is an imbalance and consider whether this a problem and, if so, start to work out how to adjust what we do so that there is enough time for everything we want to do.

Carrying out research as a natural part of your study should be calculated as a necessary part of all the work you do. Taking on a long-term research project such as a dissertation will demand adjustments in the way you manage your time. You might well need to look closely at your work/time-management plan for taking on a longer project in order to enable you to fit in the stages of the research, allow time enough for setting up some parts of the research in advance, such as ordering books on library interloan; finalising proposals to gain any ethics approvals; improving your computer access or facilities; updating any of your own skills; buying a good reading lamp or other items to help you study. These adjustments enable you to carry out daily parts of the research and other work alongside each other and ensure each part of the research work takes place when you need it to, but that you do not neglect paid work, domestic responsibilities or your friends, hobbies and exercise.

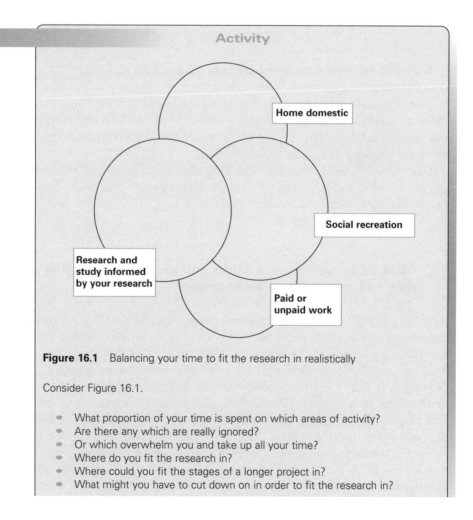

Figure 16.1   Balancing your time to fit the research in realistically

Consider Figure 16.1.

- What proportion of your time is spent on which areas of activity?
- Are there any which are really ignored?
- Or which overwhelm you and take up all your time?
- Where do you fit the research in?
- Where could you fit the stages of a longer project in?
- What might you have to cut down on in order to fit the research in?

- What skills, problems, demands and strengths, or rewards and enjoyments, appear in each of the circles?
- What overlaps are there?
- Are there any strengths and enjoyments in one area which could usefully be developed and used in your research? For example, if you carried out research on the internet to find a temporary job or a holiday, could you transfer these skills to your research activity?
- Are there any specific social, domestic or other areas of relaxation, personal development and enjoyment, which you can deliberately use to balance some of the stress, concentration and other demands of the research. For example, if you go to the gym or do community volunteering you could ensure that you carry on with all of these activities to balance the demands of research concentration. Some of your other activities, including community volunteering, will both help you to develop research skills, and can then use those skills.
- The clue is to decide what kind of part all these areas play in your life, and note in what ways unstressful, sporting or social activities, or alternative demanding roles, help you to lead a balanced life where some activities are deliberately different and others influence and help develop each other.

We are all different, so only you can carry out this audit of the way you spend your time and effort, and you might need to return to it at different points in your time as a student, and afterwards. Recognise what you thrive on, and what to avoid. I know that I thrive on variety but with some overlap. You need to decide what kind of balancing act suits you, and readjust your time and life balance if it stays out of balance, with too much effort and emphasis on one area than the others.

Sharing your research activities with close friends and family can be helpful if they support the work, but off-putting for all of you if they find it boring. So be careful! Some people and some activities are there beneficially in your life just because they have nothing to do with your research.

● Good time-management habits and timelines: Managing your time and research and other tasks

While researching for essays, presentations, group work and other assignments is part of the process which needs some timing in, undertaking longer research projects and dissertations is very time consuming. You also need to consider the importance of long-, medium- and short-term planning. Look carefully at what the assignment is, and then estimate how long it will take you to carry out this piece of research, from the ideas development, through the information acquisition, and the writing up of the research into an essay, project, dissertation or other form for assessment. You will then need to plan backwards from the finishing date, to ensure that you leave yourself enough time for each of the stages, and some slippage in case something takes longer than it should, or goes wrong, or you discover something unexpectedly interesting and your project plan needs to be adjusted.

● The bigger picture and the longer term: Overall planning and the cycle of the research

What follows is an outline of the stages of research for a longer project or dissertation. Actually, all research follows this kind of plan, although for a short presentation each stage would be completed more quickly than for a year-long, undergraduate dissertation, for example.

Stages of the research for a dissertation or long project

Research and analysis follows the kind of trajectory or journey shown in Figure 16.2.

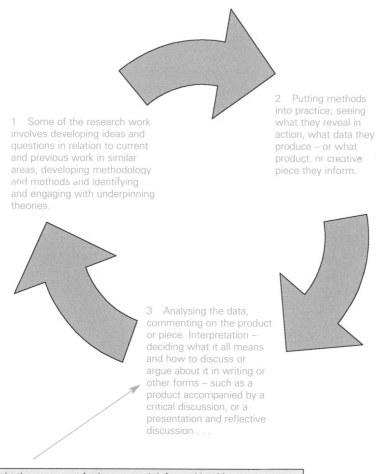

1 Some of the research work involves developing ideas and questions in relation to current and previous work in similar areas, developing methodology and methods and identifying and engaging with underpinning theories.

2 Putting methods into practice; seeing what they reveal in action, what data they produce – or what product, or creative piece they inform.

3 Analysing the data, commenting on the product or piece. Interpretation – deciding what it all means and how to discuss or argue about it in writing or other forms – such as a product accompanied by a critical discussion, or a presentation and reflective discussion . . .

You might then carry out further research informed by this; or

Write it up and move on to other research, now you are more skilled in research skills; or

You could use the skills in another context.

Figure 16.2

A few tips about managing your time

Whatever time plan you develop, your research, and so your time plan, will change. Some activities will take longer than you expect, and others will not take anything like the time you imagined. This is no excuse for not planning. It is a great deal easier to deviate from a plan than to work without one. When you develop your time plan you need to consider all the demands on your time, from the domestic through to work and social, so that the research doesn't become something that you resent because it takes you away from all the other things on which you need to spend your time. One colleague in the Open University where I used to work suggested that before students started their studies they should make sure that they painted the spare room (if it needed it), set up somewhere to work, set up a plan for taking themselves and/or their children on various outings during the time they were studying, and booked a family holiday around which they would do their work.

This sounds like a time plan which might be more suitable for mature students. But however mature you might be, you will have a variety of calls on your time. Students today have to balance paid work with their university work (THES figures, 2008, suggest that 42% of undergraduates are working in paid employment) and often domestic responsibilities as well. You will need to start juggling these three demands (at least!) on your time, and learning to juggle effectively will make you a really good time manager for the rest of your life.

You will need to plan for settling into your course, where you are living, your social group, the new kind of timetable and then the kind of work you are expected to engage in, which will include carrying out many kinds of research activity.

Whatever plans you have at the start of your research, whether it's for an early assignment or a long dissertation or project, don't try to achieve too much too fast because it is possible that you might just put yourself under too much stress due to unrealistic demands, and this could drive you to only work 'hard' rather than 'smart'. Working 'hard' means being very busy but perhaps some of this work is unnecessary or could be carried out more quickly another way, and working 'smart' means managing your time and tasks well to achieve the appropriate outcomes. This in practice means knowing what needs to be done in the research, and what (a) can be done quickly, or (b) might take a little longer because it involves persuasion, searching, comparison, theorising, thinking and writing very carefully to ensure coverage and quality thinking time. Recovering from whatever goes wrong and dealing with unexpected discoveries all need to be costed into your time plan and any re-planning necessary.

Take control of your own time, don't let it control you. Plan for yourself clear dates and clear steps in your research from coming up with the ideas, through to planning, carrying out the research, acquiring information, keeping notes, reviewing what you found, reading, writing as you go along, analysing any data, interpreting the data, developing it into findings and drawing conclusions. Developing practical projects such as artworks, engineering designs or videos from sketchbook notes and other notes might well take even longer than a largely paper or people based piece of research because you need to plan in the time to develop, produce and finalise the product as well as carrying out the accompanying research of which it is the evidence, the research process, the product, or all three.

In their book *500 Tips for Researchers* (Kogan Page, 1995), Sally Brown, Liz McDowell and Phil Race talk about 'the 10%' of time which gives you some idea of managing your time better:

> remember that in life in general many things get done in the last 10% of the available time. This means, in fact, that they can be done in much less time than might have been anticipated. This in turn means that you can get a surprising amount done in any 10% of your total time allocation – plan not to depend on that last 10%.   (Draft published by the University of Northumbria, 1994, p. 5)

You need to make sure that you allow time for problems, changes of plan, the exciting developments which are part of the research process, and the odd disaster. If you plan these in and give yourself a little leeway you will be less surprised when they happen and so can take them in your stride and learn from them.

Make sure you allow time for continuing to write about what you are doing and discovering, the difficulties and the surprises, in your journal and as part of your writing up.

Be careful that when you're collecting and analysing data you don't forget to leave sufficient time to write informatively, reflectively, think critically and analytically and in relation to your arguments, and then refine, edit and edit so that your written piece develops your argument, is presented well and does justice to the amount of hard work you have put into your research.

Make your plan visible

It's a good idea to produce a time diagram then a log or chart. The latter enables you to plan different demands on your time competing against each other, so that you can plan the domestic needs, the work needs, the study and research needs all alongside each other and see when the peaks and troughs, danger periods and relatively slack periods take place. Figure 16.3 is an example of a time chart and the suggestion that you think about and plan the time you use at different points in your research work. This one is to develop research and the work to underpin a presentation.

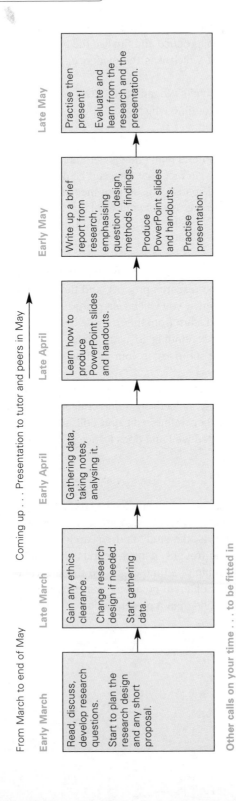

Figure 16.3   Timeline for a 20-minute presentation using your research: an example

Can you produce a timeline for a piece of assessed work using your research?

Do be sure to include:

- Other work you have to complete.
- Staged development of the research through identifying the issues; developing design and selecting methods; developing the vehicles, e.g. questionnaire, and interview schedule for the methods; reading; questioning; data collection; managing data, interpreting the data, writing and turning it into PowerPoints and handouts if needed; rehearsing the presentation and seeking support; or turning it into an essay, a report, whatever is appropriate for the task.
- And if you need to develop any new skills such as Internet searching, or to book in any AVA (audio visual aids) – help with PowerPoint® or posters etc., the actual technical support on the day – ensure that you do this well in advance.

Different time frames in carrying out research

1 Early time	2 in the middle time	3 late time	4 deadtime

It might be helpful to look at the different activities at different points in time in the research project and to consider how best to use your time.

At the beginning of a research project of any size you are spending quite a lot of time – early time – planning it and gaining permission for the ethics to be approved, if necessary, sending off library requests, building plans for interviews, starting to make jottings and sketchings, looking round at other people's artwork, or at historic buildings, listening to music – whatever are likely to be the sources of inspiration for the research, as well as later perhaps, the source of your data. This looks like potentially a very frustrating time because you're waiting for the ethics committee to get back to you, or you are not sure what your sources might be; you have to plan to make appointments; you have to collect materials and ensure you have computer access and all the necessities of everyday research work before the inspiration emerges. Don't waste it! During this time you should also be gathering journal articles and books which are available, reading them, keeping notes and references, and thinking about how they will underpin your own work, including, if you're doing a dissertation, the literature review or 'theoretical perspectives' chapter. These things you are looking at or reading are affecting the way in which you are thinking about your research, so don't underestimate the usefulness of this time of reading and thinking.

It is time also for some 'serendipitous' reading such as of magazines, and some discussions with your peers and colleagues on, and about, your topic for research. Here you can share ideas and develop them, and in the reading, ideas will start out of them if you take notes about your thoughts. You can also carry out some early research on the results of these activities. They can all feed into the research at some point and will certainly have helped develop the conceptual and critical work you are doing, not just the busy work, because they were fed into your thought processes.

The same is true of the transitional '**deadtimes**' in the **middle** of your research when you're waiting for the data to come back or to be analysed or you're waiting for people to get back to you. These are crucial parts of the research. Count these as useful periods when you can discuss the work so far with your tutor or supervisor, discuss with your colleagues, continue to read and search the Internet for topical comments on the work you've been involved in, look back over what you have written so far and start to work on it so that it better expresses what it is you want to say. Search for some up-to-date references. One of my students said to me that the best thinking time he ever had was when he was walking to the library in the morning. This is really good use of what I'd call 'deadtime', which, for example, is when you're on the train or the bus, when you're ironing, when you're mowing the lawn, or when you are walking. These are all moments when you could be thinking through a problem or an issue to do with your research. But do not start to mistake deadtime for well earned rest and leisure time, or social time. You do not have to be thinking about your research all the time. That is not necessary. Using the deadtime to good use will give you a sense of moving forward when everything else is still. I enjoy thinking about my research when I'm stuck in a traffic jam on the M25. It makes me less frustrated.

Endtime!   Do not leave your final writing and finalising of charts and references to the very last moment when you need to submit! You need to plan to finish some way before the deadline, preferably a week or two, depending on the size of your assignment/dissertation, so you can cope with unforeseen disasters, and the kind of final touches which often raise the level of your understanding, thinking, argument, and certainly the quality of your presentation.

At the end you need to make sure there is time to make final checks.

- Check your information: finalise your data, check some of those statistics and quotations.
- Check the level of the work: have you really expressed the significance, the importance, the really central message of your work in the abstract, and the conclusion? Is it conceptual, theorised, well argued enough?
- Check the expression, coherence, presentation and layout: ensure the parts of the writing are cohesive and well expressed, re-check the information about laying out statistics, charts, images, references, punctuation, and ensure that the whole is smooth – there are links between paragraphs, the headings are in the right case. This endtime needs to be focused and well used to get more marks for your work.

Longer research projects

Longer projects can be seen to involve several stages which have expectations with regard to your thinking, planning, acting, and producing research outcomes.

Stage one

- Choose ideas and topic.
- Develop research questions.
- Outline proposal development.
- Literature surveying and searching – what should you read? What has been written about this topic or similar before?
- If a piece of literature research – plan to read the primary texts.
- If social science-related research – decide on your methodology and your methods; your population and your sample.
- If practical and creative arts – decide on your methods to carry out the research in practice – outlining, sketching, building, painting, sculpting, weaving, writing.
- Write pilots, drafts and trials.

Stage two

- If this is social science-related research this stage would involve –

  - carrying out fieldwork using your chosen methods;
  - gathering your data.

- For literature/art –

  - actually writing critically or building, writing, weaving, composing, based on what you have tried out and researched;
  - writing critically and reflectively about your creative work or critical work.

- Initial data analysis – what does this all mean? What can you say about it? How can you interpret it and develop an argument or discussion about how it relates to your original question and the underpinning theories?
- Writing up drafts, both notes of what you did and why, and analysed, theorised interpretations of what it means, what you have actually found, what you can say and argue about it.
- Refining, reflecting on and reviewing findings.
- Reinterpreting re-planning.

Stage three and stage four

Move on . . .

- draft more written discussion, analysis, interpretation;
- further refine your findings so they do move your questioning on, answer your question;
- reflect and modify;

- write up and edit, edit, edit what you are writing so it reads clearly and well and makes good use of the theories and what you have read, discovered, worked on, produced;
- ensure coherence throughout the dissertation/project/assignment and between paragraphs and chapters;
- ensure threads of themes, theories, arguments run throughout the whole;
- check referencing, layout and presentation.
- Submission!
- Examination or assessment.

Activity

Draw up a draft long-term plan considering the stages of your research, what you intend to do and when.

- Plan the time realistically.
- Ensure you will have access to your subjects, sample, texts, materials, technology.
- Ensure you have the time to learn any new skills, and to persuade others to help you if this is necessary.
- Ensure you have the time to carry out analysis.
- Ensure you have the time to draft and re-draft, to improve the level of your work conceptually, critically and in terms of its presentation quality.
- Keep in contact with your tutor or supervisor, to ask questions and send them work in development.

Look through your plan and, if you can, discuss it with a friend.

- What might you have overlooked?
- Is it realistic?
- How can you fit it all in?
- Who might help you?
- What can you cut out?

Realistic time plans in the middle of the work

Whether this is a shorter or long-term research project, you need to produce some kind of plan which suggests the endpoint and works back from there. This way you can learn time planning as a useful activity and skill. Plan back from the writing up, to the data analysis, to the data acquisition, and ongoing reading, and writing.

Deadlines

If there are formal deadlines related to University hand-in dates, it's a good idea to set yourself a deadline which takes place before this so that you have some spare time in which to correct it and improve your work.

In your learning journal, you can log the amount of time spent researching, analysing the data and writing, so that you can learn how to plan research appropriately in the future from the work that you undertake.

'To do' lists and time audits

We can all benefit from producing 'To do' lists, which help us to focus on the short-term priorities and so to focus the mind and enable us to get through task after task. Those who are carrying out their research part-time and balancing domestic and work responsibilities might find it useful to produce a time audit for the average week or month.

Look at the demands on your time from your paid work, domestic responsibilities, and the research. See if you could fit these different demands into a different part of the day or the week, making sure that you have some downtime when you can rest and recuperate, or socialise.

If you construct a chart that lasts longer than a week, you will probably find periods when work, domestic life, or research are each more demanding than the others. Being aware of this, you can plan in these demands so that you don't feel guilty (about not getting each demanding element completed) all of the time and can celebrate each part of your life and get involved in it.

If you are researching alongside your work, you might well find there are some useful synergies, but also some possible clashes between the demands of your work in terms of time, and the demands of the research. You have to make sure that your employer knows what you are doing, recognises and fully supports it, and is aware of how useful it will be to have somebody who is engaged in research and able to ask questions and work conceptually, critically and creatively in their job as a result of carrying out research. Some projects that students can be involved in are directly related to their work and so can inform the development of work practices. If this is the case with your work, then make sure your employer is aware how useful your carrying out the research will be to them. This way they are more likely not to resent the time spent on the research, and to continue to support you.

However, working alongside research can be difficult in terms of the management of access to resources. Can you get access to the library? Nowadays, with many of the resources that we need online, that question can be answered with a 'yes', which means that you are able to work evenings and weekends. Do be careful not to let your research take over your entire life! However, balancing it with work demands and domestic demands in this way can be very rewarding.

Do make sure that your tutor or supervisor is aware of what you are juggling so that if you are undertaking a dissertation or a larger project, they won't expect you to produce at exactly the same rate as somebody who is doing it full time.

Demands and plans

Consider:

- Others to depend on – and others' needs. Who can help you? Who needs your support? How to plan this all in.
- Time demands and the demands of part of the year such as the school year.
- Plan for work each day – peaks and troughs – allocate a day a week to the research, or an afternoon, or an hour a day, or . . . Create spaces round the week/month/year.
- No time!
- Where do you work? Library? Home? Balance where you can work, set it up, keep the space and time free to work.
- Commitment to the research is important – ensure good organisation – be aware of and manage your learning styles.
- Serendipity – ideas come at odd times, so do keep reading – and think through new ideas and problems in deadtime, solve problems when driving/ironing/ (but keep safe).

Look at the example of a critical path analysis (Figure 16.3 on p. 192) then:

- Draw up a critical path analysis which considers mapping the stages of *your* research until, for example, the end of the year, setting stages of the research against -
  - work demands;
  - family demands;
  - the unknown!
- Share this with your tutor or your friends – is it realistic? What problem periods might occur? What can you do to minimise possible clashes and time-related problems?

'To do' lists

Make sure that you develop 'To do' lists and check off what you've managed to do, and ensure you are repeating those things that you haven't quite yet managed to do. Include everything, from the small tasks easily sorted out, to probably the longer-term ones which depend on other people.

A 'To do' list (mine for tomorrow)

- finish the draft of the chapter on time management and research
- browse the Internet (Google Scholar) for some critical response to Ishiguro's *Remains of the Day* for another piece of work
- comment on [someone else]'s writing and send that feedback back
- look through the transcriptions of the interviews on the doctoral learning journeys research and see if I can spot any early themes emerging
- re-adjust chair at desk to make less uncomfortable when typing
- cook chicken
- ring Mum

I find that I need a list so that I can plan accordingly and then I can check off what I have accomplished and can plan the time for each task. Some of these are everyday activities and domestic. Some are directly for other elements of research and work tasks.

Some of these are longer-term research project tasks and some relate directly to the main project I am involved with. Others are personal or domestic, but all relate to my ability to get on with my work and my life. I am also over-ambitious about what I can get done, but at least it makes me do more!

Task

Can you produce a 'To do' list for the next week of your work and life? Ensure you plan in the range of activities you must be involved with.

To do list

1

2

3

4

5

6

When you have completed what you can . . .

Then celebrate! When you've managed to do something which you had on your list – if you can't celebrate yourself, do something to give yourself a break – go out into the garden, go for a walk – whatever it is that you do in order to recognise your own achievement and reflect for a moment.

When things are going really well, don't rest on your laurels – there will be more work to be done in the future, and you need both to be thorough in completing and making notes about what you've done and also to plan for the next phase of your work. There are always more mountains to climb.

You do not have to work at the same pace all the time!

Some of the quiet times in research are the ones which are actually most productive in the end (remember 'deadtimes'). Some of the time, you might be manic and gathering data, analysing it and writing about it. Some of the time, you are actually thinking and being creative. This might look only like deadtime. In fact, you might seem to be half asleep or in some kind of a trance when you are actually thinking creatively, and the most developmental thoughts, which help you cross conceptual thresholds, i.e. start to work at a higher critical and conceptual level in your work, might be produced during this time.

Breaking down research and writing tasks into manageable chunks

Work rhythms in research

Research and writing have many work rhythms and some are more suited to your work rhythm than others but perhaps you are unaware of your work rhythm?

Do you:

- Plan the week's and day's activities, time them and systematically work through the work allotted to completion?
- Have a vague idea of what needs to be done and an even vaguer idea of how much, by when and what it might look like? Get started on a variety of small tasks, give some up and forget about them, while others loom over you and make you constantly worried that you are not getting on with your work? But you don't worry about it because it will all come right in the end?
- Put off large, complex, conceptual tasks and focus instead on the small, do-able ones – the taking of notes and writing them up, the annotating of research data? This is fine, but you will need to do both, in the end: the busy work and the more complex lengthy work.
- Brainstorm and visualise in a diagram the elements of the ideas in a questionnaire or identify the parts of a large problem, break this down into areas of action with which to approach the problem or question and systematically work through each of these areas, returning and refining?

Planning

Do not write up everything at the end of your research; instead:

- Keep careful notes all the way through and start writing descriptively, then thoughtfully, conceptually, with arguments and examples, from early on.
- Start some large tasks and keep them running, while undertaking some small tasks whenever you lose energy over the large ones or the results are not emerging, or the sample, population, books etc. are not available.
- Whenever anything goes wrong, do not despair and do nothing; instead, despair briefly if you must, then go and do something else which will contribute to the work (or something completely different, to have a break).
- Plan a variety of different activities to take your mind off the research when you seem to just go round in circles on one small point. Take yourself away from the work when immersed in an insuperable problem and then return refreshed.
- The only really dangerous approaches in this list are the ones where you avoid the work altogether, and those where you end up exhausted through excessively detailed work with no breaks, and no time to consider the overall patterns, the overall conceptual ideas and the bigger picture. This is not a positive way to approach your work if you want it to rise above detailed fact collecting.

Doing several things at once

It is often argued that women are better at multi-tasking than men, but whether that is the case or not, let's look at multi-tasking as a way of breaking some bad habits in research, such as the way you can run out of energy and enthusiasm when data is not appearing, the books and primary sources are missing, the piece of writing you are doing is stuck, you feel you really can't think out a particularly large-scale complex idea and are going round in circles, or you are waiting for feedback from a tutor or supervisor and meanwhile doing nothing.

- Think of the research or the writing as a patchwork quilt.
- There are many patterns of work in here and yet the whole quilt needs to be finished before it can go on your bed.
- You can actually plan out the shape of the whole quilt, and then work on some deeply researched squares which take a lot of complex stitching, some obvious ones you can make quickly, some fillers, some which repeat, some which are essential and fit centrally, when some of the rest of the quilt's in place. Consider these as different parts of your work.

You can:

- Continue to send off for articles; Internet search for, read and annotate journal articles while you are also waiting for people to fill in your online survey, or for NVivo to turn out the chunked responses from the transcribed interviews.
- Transcribe the interviews and think and make notes as well on another sheet of paper to help you focus on the emerging themes at the same time.
- Plan and set up interviews while you are waiting for the library inter-loan to get the essential books. Parts of writing can be tackled in the same way.
- Take time out for a particular, dense, thoughtful, complex piece of argument which involves engagement with complex critics and theorists and is fundamental to underpinning your own work, and ultimately will help you make meaning out of your work – and just read something short which might suddenly unlock the whole set of ideas, or at least contributes to the gathering of necessary other notes.

The argument about suggesting multi-tasking in a managed way is that you are less likely to become stuck, and instead know that you are moving on. If you feel you are indeed getting somewhere, then you will get several tasks completed and so actually move on. You won't be stuck and will be less likely to get depressed about that as a result. You are keeping busy when you cannot be conceptual and complex, and you are using time wisely, and so you develop a sense of self-satisfaction.

> Don't worry if you find keeping more than one task on the go really distracting and disturbing – this is not for everyone!

● Just hanging about or actually thinking it through? Wellbeing

When you are studying and researching, you're involved in a whole variety of learning activities and some of them are intense while others appear to be completely self-indulgent and irrelevant. Release from the intense focus of working in the library, and choosing to write up one's work later on in the day, can really enable creative thoughts – ways of dealing with problematic situations, ways of thinking more conceptually, more deeply – to take over from the equally necessary activities of focusing on gathering data, reading, taking notes, analysing, writing and so on. It might look like a waste of time, but it uses the opening in the space and places the shift in location and action in such a way as to free up different kinds of thinking through different elements of the management of research and work processes.

If you are stuck, think about going for a walk. The Countryside Commission in the UK is now really arguing for what the Romantic poet Wordsworth knew all along, i.e. that a breath of fresh air does you good and that there are physical and mental benefits to getting out in nature, the countryside, or walking between locations in a more natural environment, taking a moment to sit on a beach or to look at a lake, or the sea, watching the birds, walking your dog, planting something in the garden. All of this provides time out, which your body needs, and space to think differently, which your brain needs.

Those who research creativity also recognise that many of the really creative thoughts and breakthroughs occur because we stop focusing forcedly for a moment and allow the confusions to dissipate and the new ideas to come in. Neuro-linguistic programming suggests that thoughts start to appear on the left-hand side of our brain. Our minds come into focus gradually and then there are new ways through, new perceptions, and creative thoughts. This is a point of engagement with those troublesome, difficult moments which will allow you to make the transition to a new 'learning leap' and move on in your thinking and work, and so make the kind of breakthrough of understanding which is necessary in all enquiry and problem solving, fundamentally at the base of research. Much of the recent research on students acquiring threshold concepts, those essential ideas differing in each subject area, recognises that the development and acquisition of such concepts often feel troublesome, a disturbing of one's habits of thinking and seeing the world, and that the development appears as a kind of revelation at any moment, a shining understanding and a new way of perceiving which begins. And while some of these might appear if you force your thoughts, read and read and work and work, mostly they will come to you while you are allowing yourself to think freely and creatively.

Try it!

Managing stress

Many of the activities suggested for such a creative release are also excellent for relieving stress. While sometimes it is necessary to focus and push yourself until you understand and move on in your thinking or your analysis, for others, it is good to let go and move into another state, listen to music, read for pleasure, walk in the garden, watch a movie, play with the dog.

Often, knowing you have the essay or dissertation there to do can take your mind off other problems. Do try not to let it be the problem. If it makes you too stressed, take a break, even to the point of taking time out and intermitting, returning with renewed energies.

Summary

In this chapter we have considered:

- A variety of ways of managing your time on the whole project.
- Using 'To do' lists, balancing work/life demands, and making the most of time opportunities.

Good luck with your time management.

Further reading

Brown, S., McDowell, L. and Race, P. (1995) *500 Tips for Researchers* (London: Kogan Page).

17 Putting Ethics into Practice

This chapter considers:

▶ scrutinising your ethics issues in practice;
▶ typical procedures and their history – Declaration of Helsinki;
▶ codes of practice, ethics committees, checklists and forms;
▶ informed consent – why?
▶ participant consent forms;
▶ access;
▶ power;
▶ ownership;
▶ harm and no harm.

Ethics are important in research at whatever level with which your work is engaged, although you will probably only need to seek your university's ethical approval for your research if you are carrying out experimental work on animals or people in the sciences and gathering information from human subjects in the social sciences for a project, a dissertation or another long piece of work.

The main aim of ethics in research is to ensure that research is not undertaken for harmful or evil purposes and that no harm comes to anyone or any living thing while research is carried out. Confidentiality and consent are also important. Anyone who acts as a participant in the research needs to be asked to give their approval, and all details of who is involved and what they provide as evidence are kept confidentially. This is so that no one else except you as researcher can access the information unless it is agreed, and that the data is only used for the purposes the research intended, rather than being handed on casually to other people after the research is complete. Ethical considerations are about safety, protection and rights.

In all research, you should act in consideration of safety, and the rights of those who provide you with information, i.e. your participants, your sources. However, if you are doing library research, if you are not working with human subjects, if you are carrying out education research which is approved by the school in which it takes places, or if you are only doing a very short piece of research, you are unlikely to have to seek formal university ethical approval for your work. Later on, however, you might have to consider ethics for a longer project or dissertation, so do read on.

Activity:

An ethics chart for social science, education, humanities, arts, business, management, non-clinical health research

Please look at the chart on page 211. What kind of research is yours? Might it need ethics scrutiny by a supervisor/ethics committee member? A full committee? Is it likely to need to be re-designed? What developments are likely? Might you have to re-submit? Fuller information on each element of the process follows in the rest of the chapter.

Kind of research	You and supervisor consider ethics issues	Ethics sub-committee considers	A full committee considers	Make any changes to proposal	Agreed – carry on with the research	Not agreed/turned down – develop another proposal
(a) Library only	X				X	
(b) No people or animals involved						
(c) Non-clinical, involves participants, no harm, no confidentiality issues	X	X Research approved – some or no design improvements needed		X Deal with any small research design changes, develop participant information and consent		
				confidentiality		
(d) Non-clinical, involves participants, possible upset/harm, power or confidentiality issues	X	X Generally approved and referred to full committee	X Research approved – some or no design improvements needed	X Deal with any larger research design changes, develop participant information and consent	X	
				Confidentiality		
				Returns to committee for re-scrutiny and approval		
				Or – still major problems		

Scrutinising your ethics issues in practice

Looking carefully through the issues of ethics and confidentiality actually helps you to review your methodology, methods and design of the study. For example, if you are doing social science research in which you need to ask people questions about something, you will need to review your research design to explain who you will be sampling, and why, in what way, how you will gain access to them and consent from them, and how you will ask your questions, collect the responses and analyse and interpret them. These question all help you to see if the research you have planned is realistic, practicable and fits together. Reviewing your research design, while thinking about the ethical considerations, ensures that you consider access, data acquisition, your subjects, and potential harm. It also makes a better, more robust research project.

Those carrying out research using people or animals, and involving, for instance, clinical trials or experimentation, have always needed to seek ethical approval for their work as standard procedure. Those studying health where it relates to social issues, social scientists, those involved in community research, in business and management, anything which involves people but is not intrusive, experimental or criminal, might well not have needed to seek any ethical approval in the past. It is possible your university do not expect you to be concerned with ethics procedures at all because the procedures do not affect undergraduates, or because of the kind of non-intrusive secondary research you are carrying out. However, it is best to be safe and to find out. You could find out at the end of your research that you cannot use the data should you discover that you ought to have sought consent and approval, and did not do so.

It is most likely that you will have to seek ethical approval if you are undertaking a project or dissertation. Usually, smaller pieces of research will not need ethical approval and neither will those where you are re-using someone else's primary source information on human subjects.

If you are carrying out research that focuses on literature or art, you are likely to need to consider ethics *only* when writing your proposal or carrying out your research if it deals with people directly, such as in interviewing your author or artist, or using bodies in the art work.

Typical procedures and their history – Declaration of Helsinki

Concern with ethics developed after the unethical experimentation on human subjects during the Second World War, which resulted in the Declaration of Helsinki, dealing mainly with clinical research, and aiming to protect research participants. It has gathered momentum since the late 1990s to consider non-clinical research using human subjects. There are many issues concerned with gaining ethical approval:

- gaining access to particular subjects;
- ensuring the information they give you is safeguarded and not spread to others beyond the research, and ensuring that they are treated with respect, as is the information they provide;

- ensuring the information they provide is only that which is needed in your research, not just gathering information for the sake of it;
- ensuring that there are no risks in the gathering of information, either to your participants (reputation, health, security and so on) or to you (emotional upset, danger to your person).

Methodology and methods are important in your research and scrutinising your research for ethical issues, safety and risk can often lead to you realising that there are problems with the design or the access. You might realise that you are not using the appropriate methodology and methods in the appropriate research design, or with the appropriate sample of the population to whom you actually ask your research questions in the first place. Sometimes the scrutiny of your research design for ethical approval forces you to be aware of the risks in carrying out your study, risks that could include a disappearing population, inappropriate or wrong data, untruths, limited data, irrelevant or inappropriate analysis methods, or risks to the whole project from flawed information gathering, its storage or management.

Activity

Please consider:

- What ethics issues and practices might be relevant in your research design?
- What, if any, have emerged for you in your work so far?
- Is your research practicable? Can you carry it out? Might you have to change the methods or design of the study to comply with ethics procedures?

Processes

Find out about your university or college ethics processes, and procedures for approval of your research and for protection of your research population and the data they produce. Usually your research will need to be scrutinised first by your supervisor or tutor, and if it presents any potential sensitivities or problems it will then probably be scrutinised by a committee, who might make some recommendations for changes (and in extreme cases advise you against carrying out that research if it is badly designed, poses a threat or could lead to a breach of ethics or of confidentiality).

Codes and committees

Because ethical issues can and do arise so frequently in research of any kind that involves human (or indeed any living) subjects, a number of general and specific codes of practice now exist.

After the Second World War, the Nuremburg Code of 1947 spelt out the principle of informed consent (Robinson, 1992, p. v).

The Declaration of Helsinki identifies the following requirements.

- Clinical research should be based on adequate scientific principles and research design.
- The individual conducting research should be scientifically qualified.
- The inherent risk to subjects should be in proportion to the importance of the research objective.

Therapeutic research (which benefits the research subject) and non-therapeutic research (which has no obvious benefit to the subject) are distinguished, and stringent constraints are placed on researchers undertaking the latter.

Ethics issues also include access and truth, so, in some instances, students might find they (a) cannot get access to the people or information they need, or (b) meet a white-washed situation, missing the real issues they set out to research.

Ethics and confidentiality involve the following:

- Ethics checklists.
- Information about the research and the use of data, for your participants.
- Participation agreement, or consent form.
- No harm.
- Confidentiality of all names and data.
- Protection of information and its use.

Other potential issues in the ethics and confidentiality of your research:

- Confidentiality and access.
- Are people being open?
- Your intrusiveness, position and power.
- The very phenomenon you research changes as you involve it/them in your research.
- There will need to be more than one cycle if it is action research – will it take too long? Will your participants still be available?
- Can you do anything about what you find out if it is dangerous or criminal? Or should you? Should someone else? How can results and findings lead to action?

> ## Activity
>
> In relation to carrying out your research, please consider:
>
> - Will participants agree to take part?
> - How can you ask them?
> - Can you share information and results with them?
> - How can you protect their interests?
> - How can you protect yourself?
> - Are there or could there be any issues of access, interpretation, etc. which could be affected by you or affect you personally?
> - How can you manage these?
> - How are you managing the information and data?
> - How are you storing data? Is it safe?
> - Analysing data and drawing conclusions – how are ethics issues involved here?
> - What happens to your research afterwards? Are there any ethics issues here?

University procedures

Typically, universities usually produce an ethics checklist for those research projects which are:

(1)   Not merely library or documentary/literature-based.

(2)   Not being carried out in schools as part of a Higher Education teaching course where the project is to be approved by the appropriate school/college authorities.

The checklist completed, it would then go to someone related to a University Research Ethics Committee, who might be your supervisor, or someone appointed to look at checklists and decide if they need to take the ethics approval any further. If they decide that they do not agree with you about the lack of need for clearance and that they need fuller information, then a longer form would need to be completed in consultation with the Ethics Guidelines, which most universities publish on their Graduate School or Research websites. These longer forms ask you to scrutinise your research proposal and see where the ethical issues lie – such as access to participants, gaining their consent, confidentiality of participants, keeping the data secure. You explain what you are going to do to deal with these issues and practices and if the committee members who look at the form need further information or are worried about what you hope to do, they will ask you to reconsider those parts of the research design which they feel have ethical problems.

Usually you will be asked to complete a questionnaire or checklist and then decide. Here is a checklist from a university, which is fairly typical:

CHECKLIST	YES	NO
1. Does your research involve human participants? (including observation only)		
2. Does your research involve accessing personal, sensitive or confidential data?		
3. Does your research involve 'relevant material' as defined by the Human Tissue Act (2004)?		
4. Does your research involve participants who are 16 years and over who lack capacity to consent and therefore fall under the Mental Capacity Act (2005)?		
5. Will the study involve NHS patients, staff or premises *or* Social Services users, staff or premises?		

If you have answered NO to *all* the above questions, you do not need formal ethics approval. You do, however, need to submit this checklist signed and dated to the relevant Faculty Research Ethics Panel (FREP) Administrator prior to starting your research.

If you have answered YES to *either* or *both* Questions 1 and 2, you need to submit an application, including this checklist, to your FREP.

If you have answered YES to Question 3, you need to submit your application to either your FREP or an NHS Research Ethics Committee (REC), even if the study does not involve the NHS. Please seek further advice if you are unsure about which committee it needs to be submitted to.

If you have answered YES to Question 4, you need to seek approval from an NHS REC, even if your study does not involve the NHS.

If you have answered YES to Question 5, you will need to obtain approval from:

a. Both an NHS REC and the NHS Trust(s) where you are carrying out the research (R&D Management Approval) *or*
b. The Local Research Governance Group (Social Services).

Please note that you must send a copy of the final approval letter(s) to: RESC Secretary, Research, Development and Commercial Services.

Additional information

Participant consent

- Participants need to be fully informed verbally and by way of an information sheet – they need to be told the purpose of the research and how the data will be used.
- They need to know that participation is voluntary and that they can withdraw at any time.
- They need to give their consent to taking part by signing a consent form.
- They need to know that the data will be held securely and confidentially and that their names and locations will also be kept confidential and not revealed in the findings.

Ethical guidelines are also developed by research associations such as the British Educational Research Association (BERA). The following might be of use to anyone undertaking educational research, but there are similar issues, questions and considerations for those researching in social health practice, or organisational contexts, for example:

> Researching your own practice as a teacher (whether for a Special Study or any other purpose) raises particular ethical issues, especially where your colleagues or students are also your research participants. In any conflict of interest, your duty of care to your students should always take priority.   (Based on British Educational Research Association (BERA) Research Ethics Guidelines)

The form and the scrutiny are important, but the main issue is still the robustness of the research.

Why is this all so important?

Informed consent

> To consent to something just means that you *agree* to it. But to give *informed* consent implies that you have sufficient information to make a valid judgement. (*Nursing Times,* 1992, p. iii)

Participants in research need to know:

- The purpose of the research.
- The exact procedures in which you would be involved.
- The qualifications of the researchers.
- The funders of the research.
- The way in which findings will be used.
- What will happen if you *don't* take part in the research.
- The amount of time involved for participants.
- What will happen to participants who do take part – will there be loss of dignity, side effects?

Those who *cannot* give 'informed consent' include:

- People who do not speak fluent English and who do not have access to an interpreter.
- Children under the age of consent.
- People who are either mentally handicapped or mentally ill.
- People who are acutely ill, terminally ill or dying, and those who are very old, frail and infirm.

Embryos, foetuses and the deceased cannot give consent on their own behalf, either. Sometimes if people cannot give consent it can be obtained from their next of kin.

Ethics issues are broader than dealing with just obvious harm, however:

> Other issues of ethical concern are those of eroding dignity or causing injury. Students need to ensure their procedures (in health, science) or questions (social science, etc.) neither erode dignity nor cause injury or harm – which includes psychological and emotional harm.   (Robinson, 1992, p. iv)

An information sheet and a participation consent form

Your university will probably have examples of these on the website. Here are typical examples for a writing project.

PARTICIPANT INFORMATION SHEET

'Improving undergraduate students' writing for academic purposes'

The purpose of this project is to explore and discover ways of supporting the writing process for undergraduates. The project will use interview-based methods of narrative inquiry to explore students' writing processes and how they deal with 'writers' block'. We have located concepts and practice which we believe may help and hinder the writing processes of undergraduates.

The research is led by *Sue Smith*, B.Ed student at Fenland University. The results of the study will be written up for the B.Ed dissertation and could be used for future publication.
If you have any queries, please do not hesitate to contact:

Sue Smith
School of Education
Fenland University
Canal Lane
Fentown
F45 2CL
s.smith@fenland.ac.uk

You have been invited to take part in this project as you are an undergraduate writer. Participation is entirely voluntary and you are not obliged to participate. Should you initially decide to take part and then later change your mind, you are free to withdraw from the project at any time.

If you agree to participate, you will be invited to describe your experiences as a writer. This activity is not likely to lead to any risks to your health and safety. Agreement to participate in this research will not compromise your legal rights should something go wrong. You do not need to take any special precautions before, during or after taking part in the study. Information that is collected from you will be anonymised and stored on password-protected computers and, in the case of paper-based information, in locked filing cabinets. No reference, either direct or indirect, will be made to you as an individual in any publications of any kind.

You will be given a copy of this information sheet to keep along with your consent form.

Participant Consent form

I agree to take part in this research **'Improving undergraduate students' writing for academic purposes'**.

The purpose of this project is to explore and discover ways of supporting the writing process for undergraduates. The project will use interview-based methods of narrative inquiry to explore students' writing processes and how they deal with 'writers' block'. We have located concepts and practice which we believe may help and hinder the writing processes of undergraduates.

The research is led by *Sue Smith*, B.Ed student at Fenland University.

I have had the principles and the procedure explained to me and I have also read the information sheet. I understand the principles and procedures fully.

I am aware that I will be required to answer questions about my experience of the writing process.

I understand that any confidential information will be seen only by the researchers and will not be revealed to anyone else.

I understand that the results of this project will be written up for the B.Ed dissertation and could be used for future publication although all data provided by myself and other participants will be anonymised as much as possible.

The researcher has explained to my satisfaction the purpose of the study and the possible risks involved.

I understand that I am free to withdraw from the investigation at any time.*

* However, in the event that I withdraw from the investigation, I give permission for data to continue to be used in an anonymous form.

Name (please print): ....

Signed:...

Date:..

If you have any queries, please do not hesitate to contact: Sue Smith
School of Education
Fenland University
Canal Lane
Fentown
F45 2CL
s.smith@fenland.ac.uk

Confidentiality can be a real issue in health-related and some other social science research. The researcher is obliged to respect confidentiality, but he or she is also obliged to disseminate the results of the research, including an account of what happened.

Power can also be an issue. As a student you might find that people do not want to reveal information to you, or on the other hand that they trust you more because you are carrying out research and do not have direct power over them. If you are an insider to the organisation or group from whom you are seeking your information they might feel obliged to reveal things to you, and either this could be helpful or it may be an abuse of your position. Ethical clashes can result between the professionalism of gathering the research and your own personal involvement, so you must be careful how far you influence your own research, the research sample, and the interpretation of the data. It is possible that you might be gaining research data from individuals or groups with whom you do not agree, and this can affect your interpretation of that data.

> There are moral ambiguities involved in role playing, especially with problematic groups whose values might be at odds with those of the researcher.   (Fielding and Lee, 1991)

> Lee calls such compromises 'guilty knowledge'.   (Lee, 1993, p. 139)

Reflection and self-awareness can enable you to understand the processes of research and produce more credible results. If you feel that you are being affected by your sample, the subject, or your position, acknowledge this as a 'limitation' in the study and minimise it by being straightforward, honest and objective in what you record and what you analyse and interpret from it.

Developing the appropriate methodology, methods and research design as well as ensuring ethical clearance, consent and confidentiality are all sensitive issues crucial to your own sense of involvement in and responsibility with the research, the field/sample/group and data. Sensitive negotiation of ethical issues is necessary to enable you to carry out useful (and safe) research.

If you have to seek ethical approval for your dissertation or project or even if you *do not* have to seek ethical approval for your smaller, shorter-term research for an essay or similar assignment now, *but* know you might have to later on for a dissertation or project, do take part in the next activity.

Activity

Please consider these ethics cases:

What should these students do to ensure they comply with ethics procedures, gain access to their subjects, cause no harm, protect their subjects and keep their data secure:

(1) Ruth has discovered her questioning of her population is causing them distress.
(2) Mira has so far been refused access to her sample because she is an outsider to that group.
(3) If Jamal uses extensive quotations or provides any full information about his sample it will be obvious to a reader who they are.
(4) Ben has found out some information important to his research that it could be dangerous to reveal.

What would you advise them to do to ensure sound ethical practice?
   Are there any implications for your own practice arising from ethics for YOUR work?

Summary

In this chapter we have considered a variety of issues to do with ethics in practice, including:

- Ensuring that your participants are well informed about the research and able to give their informed consent.
- Ensuring confidentiality about participants and any sensitive issues, names and other information.
- Behaving ethically and not causing any harm.
- Keeping all the data in a confidential and safe manner and only using it for the purposes for which it was collected.

Further reading

Buchanan, D., Boddy, D. and McCalman, J. (1988) 'Getting In, Getting On, Getting Out and Getting Back', in A. Bryman (ed.), *Doing Research in Organisations* (London: Routledge).

Fielding, Nigel G. and Lee, Raymond M. (1991) *Using Computers in Qualitative Research* (London: Sage).

Horn, R. (1996) 'Negotiating Research Access to Organisations', *The Psychologist*, pp. 551–4.

Lee, R. M. (1993) *Doing Research on Sensitive Topics* (London: Sage).

Robinson, Kate (1992) 'R4: The Real World of Research', *Nursing Times*, 88(44): suppl. i–viii.

Useful website

Anglia Ruskin University (nd) *Guidance Notes for Faculty Delegated Approval*, available at: www.anglia.ac.uk/ruskin/en/home/central/rds/services/research_office/research_degrees/ethics/application.Maincontent.0012.file.tmp/Guidance%20Notes%20for%20Faculty%20Delegated%20Approval.doc (accessed 21 August 2008).

Part 3

Difference, Writing and Moving On

18 International Students

This chapter considers:

▶ starting to research as an international student;
▶ similarities and differences between your learning background and the research practices that are expected of you;
▶ making 'learning leaps';
▶ carrying out useful research projects that benefit from your international background.

Students are increasingly mobile and many students reading this book could well be defined as international, i.e. studying in a country from which their family does not originate.

Of course, the whole of this book is for international students as much as for students whose families originate in the country in which you are studying, students of immigrated families, and, in Australasia and elsewhere, indigenous students who might be the first of their family to study at university. Any advice about the practice in undertaking research which is aimed at you as an international student will also be useful for all students, and vice versa. There are, however, some useful points which can help you in your research as part of your learning at university, particularly for some international students who have been learning in a non-Western/European context. For those of you, there are often a few issues about differences in previous learning expectations and practices which make moving into the problematising, critical thinking and questioning, and independent work required of research more unusual and even confusing.

As an international student studying in the UK or Australasian context, you might need to become used to Western or European ways of learning, teaching and assessment right from the start of your study. The same is true for research or enquiry expectation and practices. It is possible that in your studying at home what has been rewarded is:

- Repeating and directly using material and notes provided by the tutor, or copied out of a textbook.
- Tutor-guided questions, workbooks, completion exercises.

Your study, so far, might well have been based upon a deference to authorities, and in respect for the knowledge and wisdom of others as experts in their field. Such respect in some cultures means it is not expected of you to question, query, critique, debate with, or argue with the information and interpretations provided by authority figures and the statements made by experts including your tutors.

As we explored earlier in Chapter 2, in starting your study at university, you will be expected to work quite independently, managing your own time, often developing your own essay, assignment, project or dissertation questions, and finding out new ways to acquire and manage ideas and information, and to use them appropriately in your own work. You will be encouraged to see that all knowledge is constructed and so constantly the focus of debate, and that knowledge can be differently constructed and differently understood and used in different contexts for different work tasks. Debate is understood in a historical and cultural context. Because of this, you will need to read about balance and debate between (or argue between) differing interpretations and views. Lively debate among the established experts in your field, and the critics or practitioners who have been using their work, is one of the sources of such debate – so you need to read carefully and see how they develop ideas and argue from different perspectives, how they use the evidence and theory, and then show you understand, can synthesise, analyse and use their evidence and theory to underpin your own work. You will find that you can gain further ideas and arguments from discussing the issues with your student colleagues in seminars and out of class, and can gain other views from the staff. Discussing and adding to knowledge and interpretation of information, development of arguments based on reading and the management of different views, are all part of the learning experience at university and help feed into your study and research. At first, this could be a little alarming, but don't worry, it's normal and expected of you to join in the discussions both orally and in writing just as soon as you have done enough reading and thinking and have started to develop your own views based on evidence and reading.

We will be looking, below, at ways of going about your research to ensure that you engage in thinking and debating the ideas, interpretations and arguments that you read about and meet. Chapter 21 deals with this at length.

When you are set your first pieces of work, you might well be asked to go and find out about, discuss or evaluate, analyse or critique some reading. This does not mean that your main job is only to note and then repeat the information that you find from reading the textbooks or other critical sources. Of course, you need to read these, but what you will also need to do is to treat your reading as a source of ideas, information and arguments, not of the whole undisputed, indisputable truth. You need to read critically and select from your reading, reflect, think, consider –

- Why are they saying that?
- What are they arguing?
- How is what they're saying based upon examples, on evidence?
- What version of and interpretation of the evidence are they giving me in each of my readings?

You need to enquire about the content, and the argument and the evidence for whatever someone is saying in a book, whatever discipline you are studying. Question everything, so that you can start to understand it more. You can ask questions about everything that is written, whether this be about the practices of keeping order in the classroom on an education degree, comments on stage directions and their effect when studying a play, instructions on putting rules into action, such as leaving a burning building, when studying practices of Fire Services on a public services degree, ways in which to make decisions about patient care in a nursing degree, or views about the competing theories of philosophers Merleau-Ponty and Sartre, on a philosophy degree. All disciplines will require you to:

read;
focus on the main issues;
take notes of the main points, the key themes;
identify the topic sentences in the work you are reading;
summarise the arguments and the main points; then
evaluate what is being said in relation to other people's views and the evidence given;
analyse the arguments;
discuss what is said, and disputed views, in relation to the question, to other work you are reading, and to any direct experience you have of the issues.

You will be expected to engage your reading with the question that you have developed yourself or which has been asked by your tutor, whether this is a topic to research ready for the next seminar or workshop, an essay question, or a longer piece of work such as a project or dissertation. You are researching even when preparing ahead of time for lectures and seminars. You will need to carry out exploratory reading for those lectures or seminars in order to identify the main issues and points in the topic to be taught and discussed, so that you can think about the lecture while you listen to it and take notes, and contribute to the seminar and take notes of the ideas and information that you engage with.

Notes from lectures and seminars

Notes are more than writing down every word that the lecturer says; instead they involve thinking and reading in advance and noting the main ideas and evidence. This is easier to identify when you have done preparatory reading and understand the themes of and differing views on the topic as expressed in that preparatory reading.

Lectures   After a lecture you will need to tidy up your notes, ensuring that main points are underlined and noted again in a list at the bottom; the references are fully noted; and debates between views and interpretations are expressed.

Seminars   You also carry out preparatory reading and research for seminars, where you will be expected to become involved in exploratory talks and conversation, which leads to learning by sharing ideas, reading, and interpretations with your fellow students. The more prepared you are for such discussions, the more you can engage, contribute, and understand. Engagement is not merely by reading books, but also by thinking about the issues and debates on the subject, identifying what your views are about them and the evidence for these. The more you prepare, research and think, the more you will get out of these interactive sessions with your colleagues.

The more you think reflectively before you go to a lecture, or undertake a learning task, the deeper and richer your learning will be. You will find that you need to consider the contribution the research you are doing is making to your learning. Consider the searching for the reading, the analysis and note taking from the texts, the preliminary questioning and looking at some primary sources yourself if possible, all as ways both to gather information and to help you to critically engage with the course. The more you critically engage, the better your marks should be, because these are exactly the skills and practices you need to develop to get the best out of the course. You need to concentrate on all aspects of the course, asking questions, gathering material, data, ideas, and developing arguments as both evidence and debate to help interpretation and argument. In this way you will be able to build up your own views and arguments based on the work done by others, and the work you are involved in, whether practical or theorised analysis and discussion. This is all contributed to by the activities of discussion in a seminar or lecture, note taking, synthesising, interpreting, analysing your notes in relation to other reading in order to address or answer the question.

● What do they really mean? Making sense of the questions set

Whenever you change levels of learning, such as going from school, college or work to university, or between the years at university, and whenever you change your cultural context by moving to another country or into another work culture, there is much to learn about the ways in which people ask questions, explore knowledge, develop knowledge, question what seems to be given, interpret meaning from information or from gathered data, draw conclusions, write and act. Because you have moved from another culture, another country, and are also now working at another level, i.e. undergraduate level, you will be doubly aware of making the 'learning leaps' – the transitions to different kinds of learning in a different learning context. It will be extremely useful for you in the future once you've mastered ways of working out the different messages, modes and expectations in a different cultural context at a different level. The next time you change context, culture, or level, you will know exactly what to do in order to ease that change to your benefit and everyone else's.

However, in the first instance, it's probably going to be a little confusing to work out exactly what is expected of you in some of the first assignments you are given. Here is an example of an assignment question which expects you to carry out some basic research. What do you think the tutors are looking for here?

Please use research and other skills to answer the following:

'What do you know about Beethoven and his works? And what do you feel and think about his music?'

What do you think this question wants you to do?

Actually, it's a badly phrased question, but some of the home-based students knew exactly what was wanted just because they had met questions phrased like this before.

They researched not merely what Beethoven produced by way of music, but also critical responses to that music, and so put together a very short debate about his production and reception. They then engaged in a short critique of different views, to which they added their own. However, some of the international students (quite reasonably in my view, given the phrasing of the question) thought the question was about (1) repeating Encyclopedia type of information about Beethoven, which they duly researched and wrote up, and then (2) saying why they liked him and what they liked.

Of course, this is what the question was asking, rather than what it wanted you to do – but the home-based students knew how to interpret it and so the research which they did enabled them to *identify different views and develop a debate*.

If you are unsure of exactly what the tutors are asking you to do, ask them for clarification. Everyone else in the class, whatever their origins, will be grateful for this clarification too. You are not losing face by asking, you are simply asking them to explain just what the question is and what the kind of learning behaviour, what kind of research strategies and practices, are expected in order to answer.

Expanding your experience of different research methods

You often need to use different research methods for different projects or assignments. It is really useful to have experience with a range of research methods, which is one of the reasons we have been looking at a wide range in this book. With different questions or contexts you might need different methods to get close to your field, your sample, and address your question. You might have research methods with which you feel more secure and familiar, and which have been used in your previous learning. These might not be the right ones for the next piece of research you are undertaking, however, whether this is in a different discipline, or interdisciplinary, relates theory and practice, or is a different kind of question or research task from anything you have carried out before, and so would need a different research design. You might well be more comfortable with quantitative research methods such as surveys and questionnaires, the gathering of data, which you analyse and process into statistics. You might be more used to gathering facts and repeating them rather than debating them from the different perspectives of different theorists.

In any university in a UK and Australasian context, you will be expected to be able to develop a range of research methods in order to approach each new research-related task with such a range from which you can select appropriate methods to enable you to ask your research question. You will need to be able to use quantitative methods and/or qualitative methods where they can best help you ask your research question. You might be more used to undertaking research in order to find out facts and the truth, based on the belief that these can be discovered. This is a more positivistic view which, while appropriate in the sciences, and popular in some cultures when undertaking social science research, is often contested in UK and Australasian universities and research, where knowledge is seen as both constructed and interpreted, and neither as value-free truth or fixed, discoverable reality. In the social sciences and other subject areas such as non-clinical health professions, education and management, which use social science methodology and methods, the methodology underpinning the methods is largely based on the belief that knowledge is constructed. You might well find that you are expected to use qualitative methods with which you are not very comfortable or familiar. However, it will be useful to know and use a range of methods and to ask fundamental questions about how we find out about and construct knowledge so that in your future research you can develop a more problematising approach, can question given truths and interpretations, and make decisions about the appropriate research methods for each piece of research.

For longer research activities for individual projects, dissertations or for group work projects, your tutor might well put you in touch with other students who are working in similar areas. You can discuss together the appropriate methods for asking your question or addressing your problem. You can support each other in self-help or support groups looking at questions, theories, conceptual work, methodology and methods (look at Chapter 8 on methodology and Chapters 11 and 12 on quantitative and qualitative methods). Debating the research design with others will enable you to develop, hear and share different arguments and to clarify the pros and cons of each suggestion and to what extent, in what way, different approches can enable you to address your research question or problem.

Building on and developing your previous experience

If you have learned how to undertake research which asks and answers factual questions, and if you have been studying in an educational or other context where you are expected to gather and manage facts, you will have a number of skills which are very useful to the research process.

What you will probably be very good at from your previous learning experiences includes:

- taking good, detailed notes from your sources;
- taking detailed notes on your data as it emerges;
- categorising and labelling facts, and data;
- summarising points made in your reading;
- drawing factual conclusions;
- making recommendations based on asking and answering a research question which has a fact-based answer.

What you might find less familiar is:

- engaging in the debate between experts in the subject;
- synthesising, analysing, contrasting, critically evaluating, and enabling your own grasp of what the experts or critics are saying;
- confidently exploring what you have to contribute to the developing debates.

It is also possible that you have learned how to undertake certain research activities such as data collection and analysis, or the critique of journal articles and other people's views, but have not actually devised research questions or put research methods into practice yourself yet. This could be because you have possibly, as Janette Ryan comments, 'previously learned in a text-based way, rather than through activity-based learning' (*Teaching International Students*, edited by Jude Carroll and Jeanette Ryan, p. 104). You might find you need support in putting theory into practice, testing theories in practice, reading technical instructions, working on practical tasks in small groups. These are all important opportunities to develop, share and articulate the ideas you have which result from your experience and research and then feed into your ongoing research. In this way, the work you finally produce can make a contribution to knowledge and debate in the field. If you need any clarification or support with new ways of learning and research, do discuss this with your tutor and your colleagues, who will be happy to help you out. Don't forget that discussing shared learning with your peers will help you develop your English as well as your research skills.

Your writing

As Jeanette Ryan points out, in some cultures, such as Asian and African cultures, writing is more commonly used to make statements which show the authority of the speaker, and persuade the reader: 'to demonstrate one's educational level of accom plishment, and to win the reader over to the author's point of view'. Some culturally affected writing tends to make statements of fact rather than develop argument. Some might use philosophical, classical or poetic phrasing to assert authority, credibility and empathy. The actual shape of a research essay or journal article may differ depending on the cultural background of the writer and the ways in which you have been taught and directed to write and rewarded for writing. This can lead in some instances to a short piece which states the question, the research methods, and the data and findings, as in a scientific report, and in other cases it can lead to a discursive piece which takes the reader on a long journey but might not come to conclusions. Ryan comments, 'The writing process takes a more circuitous approach, where the reader is gradually taken along the journey in the argument, the main thesis only appears at the very end' (Carroll and Ryan, 2005, p. 105).

Western culturally influenced expression tends to be less circular, less based on the rhetoric of argument. It is more common to establish the main aim, the question and then the main issues and argument, which run logically throughout the work, using evidence and excerpts from your reading (as I have done above with the examples from Ryan) in order to introduce and then to back up the developing common thread of your argument.

If in doubt about what might be a new way of writing for you, contact your tutor early and try out a small part of the written work to see whether you are expressing yourself appropriately for this assignment and in this cultural context. Look at other people's work from previous years, or at a journal article, or analyse the shape of a lecture, not just its content. You might find it useful to keep a small learning log or journal to which to add new technical words, new words used in argument and expression in assessments, and phrases which link together your argument, or your arguments and those of others whom you have read.

Do find out how to use appropriate referencing practices for the assignment in this subject. Many research cultures reward the use of authorities where they help theorise, underpin, or back up your arguments, but in Western research cultures they must be fully referenced. If you use other people's words in your own written work, you will need to indicate clearly where they are taken from, and explain why the quotation helps to further your own argument, or to put it in context, or argue against it. You might find that a practice which has been rewarded back home such as that of repeating the words of the experts is seen as plagiarism, a form of cheating. The way through this potential problem is to ensure that whenever you need to quote the exact words of an expert, you indicate exactly where you got them from. Your learning is shown in your own discussion of the ideas and arguments expressed by the experts, your developing of a debate between the different views they have, and adding your own arguments into that debate. To do this, you will need to very carefully select short quotations from the extracts of their work, note where they come from, ensure they are properly referenced after the quotation, and again at the end of your essay or project. You will need to make sure that you use the quotations, fully contextualised and explained, to form part of a dialogue between those you have read and your own views and your own evidence, rather than substituting for a discussion itself and standing as if they were fact. I always think a page which reports reading and research data should have no more than three extracts or quotations of any length, by which I mean no more than four lines in any quotation or about an inch of statistical data. This is a rough and not absolutely fixed idea of how much to use. Sometimes it is less, sometimes more – but no huge quotations or pages of data! or you could be seen to be reproducing what people say, all of what you have read, or all the data you found, without synthesising it, analysing it, discussing it, evaluating it, critiquing it, and putting it in to your own words in your own argument, fully referenced.

Below are some good ideas about the writing process adapted from the Palgrave Macmillan skills4study website, see Palgrave Macmillian, www.skills4study.com (accessed 30 May 2008). Colleagues give advice about the writing process for international students.

For further advice, see chapter 8 of *Study Skills for Speakers of English as a Second Language*, by Marilyn Lewis and Hayo Reinders.

Talk with the lecturer about your draft copies

Some lecturers are willing to read drafts when the supervisor makes a suggestion about work to be done. Do check whether they are saying you really *should* do something or just that you might want to do something. Is it essential or just a suggestion about how to broaden your study if you have time?

Practise writing

If writing is difficult for you, it could mean that you write less and so gain less practice. Find ways of writing regularly and of working on your writing to improve it so that you get plenty of practice. Ask a friend to look at the writing and see whether you are saying things as clearly as you hope to do. If not, revise it and try again. Perhaps read it out loud to yourself or to a friend and see whether it sounds clear, logical, well expressed.

Write first, revise later

When you are writing, try to keep going with your ideas as long as you can without worrying too much about the language or expression. As one student said:

'My words don't stop my thinking.'

Use the best words you can to write your assignments, but get your extended notes, your ideas, your comments on the data and your arguments down and then return to the writing later and improve it by editing.

Learn from good writers

Students can learn if they see good examples of essays. One student notes on this website:

'I read aloud from good essays. That way I can hear good language in my head.'

When you look at an essay that has a high grade, remember to read the comments from the marker. Why did the essay have such a good mark? Has the marker made any suggestions for making it better? Even an essay with a high grade could improve. Some people say you should look too at the essays with the low grades to see the difference? What does the marker say is wrong?

You can also read aloud from published journal articles or parts of any textbook so that your ear can hear the rhythms and language of argument, and how others' words are used in quotation, how others summarise, synthesise and critique writing. Then you can model these different ways of using language in your own work.

Talk about essay writing

Try to talk with others about how you write essays. Share ideas and reflect on the processes you use to ask questions, collect and comment on notes, write the theory, the methods, and the data; and discuss parts of your written assignments including essays, reports and dissertations.

- Do you write differently in different parts of your essay, report, or dissertation?
- Do you and those to whom you read parts of your work, or who read parts of it, think you have the right tone, formality, language and construction of your argument and evidence for the piece you are writing?

Once you have discussed your writing, what can you improve and how can you try it out with your friends and fellow students?

Use the computer to improve your writing

The computer can be very helpful when you are writing essays, assignments, projects or dissertations. Word-processing software has functions that can make the writing process easier. The spellchecker can check both spelling and grammar, but do be careful to check it yourself in case it has misunderstood the word you really wanted, and replaced it with a similar one ('from is often turned into or left as 'form', for example). If you make a mistake, or the spellchecker doesn't recognise a word you wrote, then it will make suggestions. Later versions of these programmes also have a built-in thesaurus that gives you synonyms of words you have used. Some sophisticated spellcheckers get used to the mistakes *you* make and learn how to correct them. Using voice recognition.

There are several voice recognition systems, such as Dragon, which you can train to recognise your voice, and to turn it into type. However, they also tend to develop different mistakes so you will always need to check what has been written (for example, I wrote 'John Keats' and it turned it into 'junkies').

Learn from textbooks

Many students find that having a textbook is a help, even if they do not or cannot attend a class. Textbooks take you logically through the course material and you can return to them to study them several times, but you will of course need to take your own notes, comment on what you note, use the textbook as a logical guide to stimulate your thinking and wider reading and, if you use the textbook directly, quote where relevant and reference it. You may be able to find a book that can guide you through essay, project and dissertation writing in your own subject.

(Adapted and extended from www.skills4study.com, 2008.)

Learn from the course online

Many courses now have an online presence in Blackboard or another Virtual Learning Environment (VLE) or online learning management system, where the handouts, Powerpoint presentations and some of the essential readings are collated. Often there is a clear logical course guide to accompany these. This can also be very helpful to use both as a guide and as source material, properly referenced.

In some courses, the tutors provide discussion questions and chatrooms. In the first, a threaded discussion about what you are reading and studying can be developed, you can ask and answer questions and share thoughts with other students and the tutor, develop and try out arguments.

Tutors who have worked with international students online say that some students who are quiet in class because it takes them longer to form their ideas into the words (in a second or third language) that they feel genuinely reflect the quality of their thinking, respond very well online where they can take their time to compose their comments, where contributions are often quite informal, and where discussion and debate can be built up equally between those contributing, rather than seeming to be confrontational. These discussions can help your thinking and expression as you carry out your research and start to comment on what you find, problems that you have, and questions which arise.

You can also ask research questions and others will make comments and sometimes offer help, or examples, and debate your ideas. This early form of peer support and review accompanies the trying out of your expression and can lead to building up response, analysis, thought and expression and to a focused, clearly expressed piece of work which begins to share and develop your research with others.

Using your international experience

One major asset which you bring to your study as an international student is your own international experience. One of the main processes and one of the aims of research involve finding out different interpretations, different ways of exploring the world, and constructing knowledge from different perspectives. If you come from a culturally different learning background from the one in which you are now learning and researching, you will already have met and experienced that there are different ways of reading and learning, different perspectives and ways of interpreting information, data and argument. You need to build on this awareness to help you develop your insights, your problem identification and problem-solving attitudes. You can become an enquiring student who can see all issues and arguments from more than one angle and understand them in more than one way.

Internationalisation of the curriculum is attempting to engage all students with this experience of seeing things from culturally different points of view and enabling them to explore the construction of knowledge differently. You have something new to offer.

Your internationally influenced perspective might well be shown in the topic you choose for a project or dissertation. If you can choose one which builds on or brings in your own experience or context then you will be adding some new cultural context to even a relatively familiar topic.

You might also be able to contribute something new through referencing sources that you are aware of from your own context, which you can add into any debate. You can build on this awareness of difference to add originality to your work.

Earlier we thought about the more circular, philosophical, or highly scientific and logical formats used in written work by some cultures. It could be that you will have the opportunity to express your research in a form more usual in your own culture, and this could be an element of originality in your research work also. However, do check with your tutor first about the issue of layout and presentation because it is possible that the form which is common at home might not be acceptable in your new learning context, and there is no sense in losing marks because of that.

Summary

In this chapter we have considered:

- Research and learning as an international student – what to expect.
- Culturally inflected learning differences.
- Clarification: What do they really want when they set an assignment?
- Engaging in knowledge construction, and working independently or with others.
- Some issues about writing, including using online opportunities.
- Capitalising on your cultural capital as an international student.

Further reading

Carroll, J. and Ryan, J. (eds) (2005) *Teaching International Students: Improving Learning for All* (London: Routledge).

Lewis, M. and Reinders, H. (2003) *Study Skills for Speakers of English as a Second Language* (Basingstoke: Palgrave Macmillan).

Palgrave Macmillan (2007) *skills4study,* available at: www.palgrave.com/skills4study/index.asp (accessed 30 May 2008).

Reinders, H., Moore, N. and Lewis, M. (2008) *The International Student Handbook* (Basingstoke: Palgrave Macmillan).

19 Researching and Writing in Different Disciplines

This chapter considers:

▶ the different kinds of research processes;
▶ language and written or other products you might need for the humanities and the arts;
▶ creative and practical research.

All the literature on research-based and dissertation writing indicates that you need to be encouraged to research in both rigorous and sensitive ways which are generic, and recognise, observe or cross disciplinary boundaries. The generic elements include making sure you develop a research question, develop an appropriate research design, work at a conceptual level. You also need to take note of discipline-related research processes, questions, and even the format of the written product. Start writing early and learn the conventions of your disciplines in terms of how you write, what you write, the language you use and the shape of the dissertation or other assignment (see Murray, 2002; Dunleavy, 2003).

Like most books considering research projects for undergraduates, most of the research processes, language and products on which this book has focused so far are social science oriented in the broad reading of that definition, to include education, non-clinical health, business and management, much travel, tourism and hospitality, and some humanities. We have not attempted to focus on the sciences, although experimental processes have been mentioned.

All disciplines have their own language, sometimes jargon, sometimes just necessary terms which explain the discipline to insiders. In educational and social science research, you learn to use a variety of established terms by which you can identify their methodology and methods. These include the research terms: 'inductive' and 'deductive', 'triangulation', 'validity' and 'reliability'. These specific terms frame and focus your research work, yet they are not likely to be words used by either a scientist or a literature researcher.

What are the objects of study? And how might the research be carried out?

We discussed primary sources in Chapter 9 and have thought about varieties of research approach throughout this book.

Arts and humanities researchers focus on a range of products and issues, their production, the ways in which they construct and represent the world, and their reception. Historical, art history and some literary researchers might use documentary or archival research.

Documentary analysis

Analysis of documents, both as primary and secondary sources, looking at their origins, contexts, how they are constructed and expressed, who produced them, when and why, and the effect they have had.

Archival research and the sources themselves

Researchers might need to explore archival material, which is original material stored, and catalogued. They could be asking questions about and looking at work produced at the time of study, tracking down and classifying these primary sources, to develop an argument about their original meaning, intention, how they grew from the artist/writer's time or background.

They might look at an author's or artist's papers to identify how and in what ways they were influenced, used the materials in their own work, contributed to ongoing dialogues, kept up correspondence.

They might be looking at the production and publication of or the reception of primary sources or products, focusing on the cultural reception of films or texts, looking at audiences and audience response in order to identify who responded to what, and in what ways and why.

A humanities researcher might look at books as primary sources, their production, use and intention. If they are a librarian historian, they could be identifying instances of armorial stamps (usually gold family arms resembling heraldic crests placed on the front cover of a book to indicate who owns the book – many of which date from medieval and Renaissance times) and so exploring the provenance of books, who produced them, published them, owned them, and passed or gave them to whom (or had them stolen by whom), and what that says about habits of book ownership and reading through the ages. This is both archival research, looking through old collections and lists, through databases, and also very 'hands on', involving visiting book collections in the more ancient parts of ancient libraries, or public schools, or ancient universities round the world.

Another researcher, one focusing on literature for example, might be looking at how primary sources on scientific disasters and genetic modification influenced an author, Margaret Atwood for instance, in her writing of a work of fiction such as *Oryx and Crake*. They would consider the effects of the sources on the development of an argument within the book, and the critical reception of these ideas by readers.

Literature research – other variants

For literature researchers, the actual process of research, the critical practice and the framing of questions, methods, decisions made about approaches, are quite likely to be assumed, taken for granted. In literature, other humanities, performance and creative arts, students sometimes claim they have no need to be as 'jargon ridden' as their social science colleagues and often they might even argue that explaining the process of the research kills the creativity. But actually, they are overlooking the research processes they are using. All students ask research questions, develop theoretical perspectives, research design and methods, conceptual frameworks, and produce results, although they are in different forms and use different expressions from those produced by students using social science designs and methods. You need to be able to communicate your intentions, design, processes, and what is achieved to aid both your own under-standing and that of others.

Whatever arts or humanities research you are carrying out, whether it is culturally engaged, creative, personally engaged, it needs to have a research question, a concep-tual framework, to use theories, develop a research design of stages and methodology and methods, and carry out the research. If it is a research piece based around or oper-ating through a creative piece, the two processes will need to be carefully timed to relate to each other. You will need to document, chart and record the information, data, any responses, decisions made, and analyse the data produced whether it is information about cultural response, provenance, personal decisions, published critical reception, or something you have created as part of the research process, whatever is appropriate to your research question.

Some arts and humanities research uses social science strategies, particularly in subjects close to the social sciences, such as history, and cultural studies. However, much of the research in the arts and humanities uses quite different strategies. You will need to interpret any product or data and turn this into findings and some conclu-sions which are themselves underpinned by the theories and the research question. The whole research piece is then written up and presented in an appropriate form. This can be conventional in shape, such as a dissertation in literature which focuses on asking a research question about the work of an author or group of authors. Or if appropriate it can be creative in shape. Answering questions about response to texts in context, engaging with personal response to cultural difference, exploring self-development, family history, the creative responses of others to events, have produced creative work accompanied by critical, discursive, analytical work. These include quilts, videos, song cycles, multilayered texts, poetry sequences, and photo sequences.

Some arts and humanities research can seem to the reader, the non-artist or the researcher themselves, to be amorphous, highly subjective. It needs to be conceptually, clearly organised and managed just like any other research but if there are any creative elements, or personal involvement and expression, this must have space to develop too.

Arts and humanities students undertake a range of research projects. They will all have elements of the:

- conceptual
- critical
- creative

in them, but in different places and at different times, in different ways from social science research.

A student might be looking at how an artist or author goes about their own artistic and creative work. They might need to interview the artist, match what they say critically about their own work to what the work presents, and how others view it, in context.

They might want to know about the explicit creative processes the artist uses to creatively change and develop their sketches, thoughts, influences, into their own work.

They might be looking at the work itself and exploring themes and issues, cultural engagement, innovation, and so they would need to critically engage with the work, use the thoughts of theorists and the work of other critics and commentators, and look at it in context – cultural, social – in terms of critical trends (modernism, writing the body . . .), cultural trends (socially relevant art, the adult education movement and its work with adults as artists in the community) and so on.

Or they might be researching to carry out their own piece of creative work.

There can be a focus on the discovery, collection, analysis and critical commentary upon data, which would be gathered from different sources including documents, collections, images, literary and other texts. They might have interview data from authors or artists who are interviewed, and they might combine critical responses to the artist's work with the comments they make in interview, and some personal, critical and/or creative responses themselves. All of this needs to be in a framework which is explained, defended, and which helps to address the research question. If the aim of the piece of research is towards a creative product rather than the critical analysis of others' work it could be accompanied by a reflective and analytical piece looking at decisions made about research processes and the development of the work, the creative piece.

Sometimes the research process itself enables the creative process, or indeed the creative process *is* the research process. You might decide to explore your own responses to a cultural or historical issue (for example) by producing a series of poems and pictures. You would need to use theory about creative writing and art as expression and comment, keep a journal or log about the decisions made in the creative process in response to stimuli and critical reading, problems, discoveries, thoughts. You would need to analyse and explain the ways in which the creative work addresses your question.

In *The Postgraduate Research Handbook* (Palgrave Macmillan, 2008) I developed the idea of the documenting, critiquing and creative continuum. This is elaborated below.

Creativity and research

Sometimes you could be researching your own creative processes and sometimes you are carrying out research FOR your own creative processes. You need to acknowledge your involvement in the work.

Arts and humanities research can be seen as lying on a continuum related to:

- information gathering, questioning and documenting
- critique, analysis, explanation
- conceptual work, theorising the work in relation to theories, to help interpret and understand it
- creative work, whether this is what is being studied, or being produced (and then studied)
- personal involvement – subjectivity and rigour

A literature or fine art researcher might be dealing with their own critical responses and those of other critics to a group of writers, a writer, a group of texts, or a phenomenon, theme or issue in texts, to the work of an artist or group of artists. They might be making something new out of this mixture of the personal and the established critical responses.

The researcher might be writing a creative piece, a novel or poem sequence, and accompanying that with analytical, critical and reflective versions, and with commentary. A creative artist might be carrying out visual research using sketchbooks, to build up a creative response, keep notes, work at ways of creating something out of a situation or feeling, and/or they could produce an installation, a set of paintings, sculptures, or chairs or other functional objects designed by them.

Their research:

- informs their creative thinking and production – collection, identification, selection, analysis, then the spin-off creative thinking and ideas, plans, practice, refining, product of the piece whether written or artistic (fashion, design, glass, a poem, both mixed together, a film piece . . .);
- informs their reflective and analytical processes – helps them work out what influenced this, what happened to create a response, what it might mean to them and others, how it can be interpreted in a critical and conceptual framework so that the ideas within it are bought out, and so that the thoughts, theories, work and ideas of others are brought to bear on exploring, even explaining it.

Researching your own creative work/using the creative in your research work

Many students engage in literary, artistic, musical or performance work directly, rather than through the lens of a critic. So, your research is not merely in the arts and humanities but in relating your own performance and production, your own creative practices, to these areas, seeing creative work as a product of the theories and critical contexts and being fed by them. Technically, you are therefore exploring your *own* work as if it were a large-scale case study in the social science sense, analysed critically and contextualised. You could study your own experience, as well as the product itself. If you have already been involved in creative work – art, creative writing, and video production and so on, you will be familiar with the issues of relating the actual texts, artworks or creative products and activities to an analytical framework. Stand back and apply it to your own work, theorise and analyse it. You can also keep a reflective journal for the more personal, reflective responses. One student involved in a piece of performance art developed her performance work out of her own theories – about the relationships between the virtual (technology, media representations) and the visceral (the real person, the body in the space). She then acted out the performance, which she had videoed and included on CD-Rom, as well as videoing each element in the appropriate technological format. She also accompanied the work with a standard dissertation, exploring decisions made about and the theoretical underpinnings to the performance, and the ways in which it acted as a vehicle for explorations and discussions about the critical theories between them. She comments on the way it contributes to her work, using personal comment, and critical comment on personal performance work – which has been made objective because it has been shared with an audience – and theorising.

Another student chose to explore her own relationship with her own history of artistic and personal response to her memory of life in South Africa as a woman in her family, now that she has moved to live in the UK. As a visual artist working in installations, she videoed and produced several linked pieces:

- A dissertation which set out the direction, the theoretical framework, and explored and explained the video and all her critical points about self, memory, place and artistic response.
- A journal of her developing personal explorations and critical choices about the writing. This included issues to do with the difficulty of capturing feelings and experiences, and decisions concerning visual representation, everything from the actual videoing, and the visit back home to South Africa, the shooting and the ways of presenting the video, alongside the dissertation.
- The video itself had accompanying notes, explaining and exploring links with the arguments and how it developed shape and form.

Students working with research which involves their creative expression, might also be investigating their own creative responses, and their work can include a range of different creative expressions such as sculptures, a dress, objects in installation, and creative writing. All are accompanied by critical and theoretical engagement, comment, and analysis of themes and issues of the work itself and of the creative processes.

Choose one or more of the humanities or arts titles (below) which could underpin a piece of research leading to a dissertation or other product, and consider the following.

- What mini-questions and subsidiary questions are involved in approaching this question and title?
- What theoretical frameworks and theories could you use to help you to approach the asking of these questions?
- What material could you use to help ask the questions? For example, what literary texts, artistic products, mixture of documents from different sources – historical, diary, and so on – could you use? Could you use media texts? Would you need to use social, cultural and historical information, and where might you get this from?
- Which theories are you using to develop and underpin your own? What critical, contextual, interactive and personal elements are involved in your research, and how do these all fit together in your work? How can you argue that the mixture of theories and other elements fit into a cohesive, directed, *whole* piece of research?
- Why do your questions matter, and are you sure – or how could you argue – that your explorations and theories underpinning and driving these can really help you answer your questions? What are the tasks involved here?
- What mixture of the critical, conceptual and creative will be involved in undertaking this research? How can you plan the stages of this?
- How can you shape and express your research? In what mixture of creative, documented, analysed, and argued process and product?
- Why does your research matter? Will it affect others? Cause change? Contribute to knowledge and argument? What will it do?

These are probably the main questions you will need to ask and answer of your own arts or humanities research.

Examples of titles:

1 How do students of design use museum collections to inspire their own creative work?
2 Returning to a loved place: personal, creative and analytic exploration
3 Buried selves: explorations of self and the body in Michèle Roberts' prose and poetry
4 *Dr Who*, here today and gone yesterday: how TV science fiction negotiates and represents versions of time travel
5 Journeying in creative expression

Let us look in depth at no 5.
   What follow are some of the questions to ask in order to start to research, and to answer the research questions.

Questions:

- Are you exploring the representations of journeying in someone else's work? Or in your own?

- Are you producing new work to express this? Or analysing and reflecting on your previous work, or both?
- What are the theories and concepts underlying the idea of journeying which you could use – personal journeys of self-development; physical journeying to foreign places and new encounters; preconceptions and realities of journeying; journeying as a metaphor for the growth of self, relationships, families, communities; growth and change; strangeness; 'othering', being different and perceiving difference?

Stages

Narrow the field to a question and a form – in answering this question I am going to look at journeys I have taken both physical and emotional, and explore these through poetry of my own, which I will then use critical approaches to analyse, and which I will accompany with a reflective log about development and process and decisions.

Narrow to a more manageable focus and frame – I have been travelling since I was 4 and I have also changed a lot – so think I had better either take a longitudinal approach and look at some key points or some patterns; or should I just look at a particular moment in time?

Focus – looking back? Creating something new? I think I will look for a few critical, memorable rites of passage. Significant moments, and some familiar patterns to identify the thematic familiarity – coherence through this long period. I think it might be a good idea to find some old poems, and to produce some new ones on the theme and using these theories I have just been thinking about – i.e. newness, physical journeys matching internal ones, strangeness and otherising, development and change – there are patterns in here – emerging even as I write it through.

How can I start? I can either start at the beginning of my life or at least early on. For example, I might say . . . 'when I was 4, I went to Egypt . . .'. Or I might hope that through some interesting points I could find a significant moment in now and structure the recollections and patterns through the focal point of looking back and seeing them in perspective as a life narrative with some highlights.

Because I have started to flesh this process out, even here I can see which is the more likely of the two (or more) ways to begin to write. If I have doubts about which questions or routes to pick, I usually try and jot them down in short, and visualise them on a piece of paper side by side. Divide a sheet of paper into four, put a heading or question in each quarter, then think through how you could develop the ideas, and where to find the information. Doing this, I soon run out of interest and energy on one of the topics because it is overwhelming or dull or merely descriptive. However, the meatier one gets my mind flowing and – although it is messy – I can then start to plan the activity.

Research – find out about the places, the times I want to write about – get some outside information so I don't make mistakes of detail.

Research family photos and memories and my own – sources – people and conversations, photo albums and videos, mementoes – any old diaries or photos around?

Produce – new poems, collection of older ones, reflective commentary about choice, construction, expression.

Analytical response about

- ways in which I went about this and why;
- why these choices and developments;
- what they suggest in terms of the theorising about journeys, travel, strangeness, perception, persona, reflection, development, and the creative process.

Impact – why would anyone else be interested? Well – not in me and my journey surely but in seeing it as a model for exploring their own, and ways of seeing and expressing it, self-discovering, embodiment, exploration, articulation and analysis which does not kill the creativity – I think this has some mileage.

Activity

- Think of a text or texts, and/or a personal experience, which you would like to explore using artistic forms.
- Which forms will suit your exploration and research? Could it become a video? Are some forms art or media products? Creative writing? Technology? Sculpture?
- How can you use this creative piece to explore the arguments and issues rather than merely to reflect or be a creative piece?
- What kinds of underpinning theories and critical approaches inform your work?
- What forms can you use to record the reflective critical, personal process? Why?
- How might you also produce an analytical and critical connecting commentary between the creative, personal, critical works and the thesis itself?

Summary

In this chapter we have considered:

- Arts and humanities research integrating the critical and the creative, interdisciplinary approaches.
- Creative performance and critical work using the creative and the personal.
- The specific form and shape appropriate for arts and humanities research and the dissertation or other piece itself.

Further reading

Atkinson, P. and Delamont, S. (2004) Editorial, *Qualitative Research*, 4(3), pp. 283–4.

Creswell, J. D. (2002) *Research Design: Qualitative, Quantitative and Mixed Method Approaches*, 2nd edition (Thousand Oaks, CA: Sage).

Denzin, N. K. and Lincoln, Y. S. (1998) *The Landscape of Qualitative Research, Theories and Issues* (Thousand Oaks, CA: Sage)

Dunleavy, P. (2003) *Authoring a PhD: How to Plan, Draft, Write and Finish a Doctoral Dissertation or Thesis* (Basingstoke: Palgrave Macmillan).

Murray, R. (2002) *How to Write a Thesis* (Maidenhead: Open University Press).

Wisker, Gina (2008) *The Postgraduate Research Handbook: Succeed with your MA, MPhil, EdD and PhD* (Basingstoke: Palgrave Macmillan).

Useful websites

Forum: Qualitative Social Research, available at: www.qualitative-research. net/ (accessed 19 August 2008).

Qual Page: Resources for Qualitative Research, available at: http:// qualitativeresearch.uga.edu/QualPage (accessed 19 August 2008).

Ryder, M. (2008) Qualitative Research: University of Colorado at Denver School of Education, available at: http://carbon.cudenver.edu/~mryder/itc/pract_res.html (accessed 19 August 2008).

20 Developing Good Writing Habits

This chapter considers:

▶ reasons for writing;
▶ you are your first reader;
▶ writing your ideas out and articulating your arguments;
▶ getting into good habits;
▶ taking good notes and turning them into text;
▶ finding a voice;
▶ writing journals;
▶ breaking writing blocks.

Enquiring minds are constantly asking questions. This kind of enquiring leads to research, which leads to new findings and inter-pretations. What you have found, interpreted, and can discuss and argue with others needs to be expressed in an accessible form. Learning to write 'well enough' to communicate your ideas and research findings for yourself and to other people, and learning to use writing to help you to articulate your thoughts, are essential for good research. Unless you have the ability to communicate well or the practice of communicating through presenting or writing, no one hears about what you have discovered and what you can argue. Writing helps you shape and communicate your ideas and the results of your research.

However, many people find writing daunting, believing that they can only write when they have a perfectly proven and finished thing to say, which must be said in the most elegant manner possible. Sometimes it is better to write through your ideas and return to your writing to improve its quality later on. But this is only one of the techniques you can use to help you to develop good writing habits.

This chapter helps you to consider and develop the habits of writing regularly and well enough to develop your ideas and to articulate what you have found and can argue. It should be useful beyond the research process itself, in all forms of your work and even your personal life. There are a number of good books on the writing process that you might like to consider, and these are mentioned at the end of the chapter.

This chapter looks at various issues to do with supporting and developing your writing. It is useful when thinking of writing up your research, writing essays and other forms of assessment during and beyond your degree.

Why write?

Your research needs to be articulated, discussed clearly and shared with others. There are many different forms of writing you need to develop in order to explore your ideas and enter into the discussions and debates that are going on in your subject area. There are also several different readers involved in reading any piece of writing resulting from your research work. You will need to clarify and express the question with which you are dealing in your research, to develop your argument and convey to readers your ideas, the theories you are using and the interpretations and findings from your data. None of the writing you do on your research journey is wasted, even if it is just taking notes or making notes to yourself about what to do next and why something has or has not worked out in the way you expected.

You are your first reader

One of the main readers is you. Can you express your ideas and arguments clearly to yourself? Can you make the annotations on the notes you take and the data you collect clear and engaged with the research question, so that you can turn these into analytical comments as time goes on? Can you carefully focus on getting exactly the right words and phrases to comment on what you have found and what it means, how it contributes to your knowledge and understanding of the field? Can you write clearly, straightforwardly, using everyday language, the language of the subject area and the language of argument, where appropriate? You will need to learn how to write in all these ways. It is important to be able to write clearly for yourself, your main readership who are your peers, your supervisor or tutor, and any examiner. Later, it could be equally important to write in different ways for different audiences should you publish, or should you present a report to a supervisor or an organisation for whom you have carried out a community research project.

Taking notes and turning them into text

This is not a book about note taking and study habits, and you might like to look at Stella Cottrell's *Critical Thinking Skills* (2005) or *The Study Skills Handbook* (2008) for this, but you do need to think about how you take good notes in your research, so that you can use them as you write about it. We use our reading in our writing, relating the work of others to what we think, have found, and can argue. We also use what we hear and see, in the same way, in our writing. It is important to identify the sources from which you need to take notes, whether those notes are field notes made while you are out taking part in an activity, notes from what you have been reading from a primary or a secondary source, notes which form your response to something you see, for example, accompanying sketching in a sketchbook, commenting on a play or a visit, an observation, an activity, or what you hear from a lecture or a TV broadcast, or what you read. Collecting, working on, analysing, and keeping good notes is an important step in good writing. Referencing your notes well saves time puzzling over where they came from and searching when you want to use them in your writing.

Good notes should be made in relation to your research question, not just full notes of everything you see, hear or read. You are not summarising all you see, hear or read but selecting to focus on your question. They should be focused on the subject, the topic.

You will also need to add other notes, reflective comments and descriptive detail about methods and methodology, contextual underpinning: where, when, why you did something, what it was, what you read, saw and did, and so on. You will then be able to explore and explain why and how you went about your research. If you have *not* kept notes of the 'nuts and bolts' of research, reflection and evaluation could be more difficult. The twistings and turnings of the research need recording in a log or journal and then these feed into parts of paragraphs or chapters exploring, describing and explaining why and how you did what you did, when and where, i.e. how research decisions are made. The activity of taking these descriptive and reflective kinds of notes can also prove useful if you lose your way in your research, or have a writing block. Writing notes about thoughts, problems and decisions can generate writing energy.

Note taking can be of several kinds, sometimes just informative notes about the main points, the main words and ideas, then the concepts, and the contribution to the ongoing argument.

I keep notes when listening to a lecture or talk, to use later for my research and writing. I try and take notes both of what the presenter says, and of the thoughts and responses I have to what he or she says. To do this I draw a line down the right-hand side of the page and add my own thoughts and comments about the presenter's words, or about how they contribute to my work, on the right-hand side, or in bubbles, or little blocks of comment, singling out these thinking processes while I am also taking down the facts and some quotes. I operate the same way with marginal comments about my reflective and argumentative responses when taking notes from a book or other written source. This form of note taking helps to engage a conceptual, critical, reflective and argumentative discussion alongside the information gathering, and so starts to use the information you are noting, in your own argument, for your own research and writing.

You are never just gathering information to work on it later. With research, you are always required to think about your research question and ways in which the information and ideas you are gathering relate to that question, your argument, and the theories and theorists whose work you are using to underpin and inform your own.

Always annotate data and notes you take with meta-writing, the writing that starts to synthesise and discuss what you have written, pointing out the main points and commenting on what seem like contradictions or confusions. Take notes, underline items, and write on the notes some thoughts at the side or bottom of the page, saying how they contribute to what you are exploring and working out.

If you are collecting social science data and have carried out interviews, transcribing them yourself might be a huge time-consuming activity that prevents you from engaging with the rest of your writing and work, but it might also be a really good way to hear the development of the themes, issues and patterns as they emerge. You will be able to jot the odd note down alongside what people say and start to analyse and comment on it. This is the same for the interpretive activity that goes along with gathering and collating the data from critical sources in notes, and from surveys. Write notes on these sources of data immediately, as some of the thoughts, patterns, contradictions and discussions that you see straight away can be worked on later with fuller comments. Although you will want to express yourself more clearly and elegantly in terms of the ideas, it will not all be collecting in a huge heap in a corner, a drawer, a bookcase, or your computer to be mined at some later date. Such a shedload of information untouched by your comments and thoughts could seem latterly a terrifying prospect, as if it were entirely new. It is good research practice to get in touch with your data early and it is also a good writing practice. You might find that your initial notes, if a little simplistic and inelegant, can be further clarified as you find exactly the right words and introduce the language of theory and the discourse of the subject itself.

Writing reflectively

You will also find it useful to write reflectively, keeping a note of decisions made, problems faced, thoughts about what you are discovering, and about your research journey more generally. This kind of reflection is useful for considered thought and for writing and discussing both about choices made and about interpretations and findings. Reflective writing helps you to become aware of your thinking processes, and to be more critical and articulate. Reflective writing is also good for the process of keeping up the momentum, especially if your work is stuck or confusing or slowing down. Reflect on what you are doing and learning, what is clear, what is confusing, and what to do next. Reflect during and after activities, asking yourself of each problem, question, activity or finding:

- What does it mean?
- What does it contribute to my argument?
- What should I do next?

An example of reflective writing – my own:

> I was rather stuck and bored with my writing for a couple of days – there seemed too much to do so I decided to focus on one piece at a time. I have just been correcting a chapter for two hours. I think it reads more clearly because: I moved the text around to make it more logical and to develop ideas; I decided it did not need to sound as intellectual and complicated as a published journal article so I toned some of the language down and concentrated on being clear; now it is more finished I can move on! Good!

Discussion

I expressed feelings, summed up a problem, stated what I did, analysed it and reflected on how effective it was and why I thought it was effective, and then congratulated myself a bit. This piece of reflective writing was descriptive, personal, analytical and reflective and producing it was actually helpful to my own writing processes. I can look back on it later when I get bored or stuck again, and I can ensure I am never complacent about writing, even when I produce something which is finished and acceptable.

Activity

Try the following activity. This encourages short pieces of reflective writing to engage your thoughts at different stages in your work, and also asks you to think back over your reading of this book.

1   What were the most important points in what you have just read? How can these feed into your own research and writing so far?
2   Have you met any blocks to your writing yet? What did you do to overcome them?
3   Did thinking about these help you to:
    - clarify your own reading?
    - clarify your ideas?
    - take stock of your writing processes and practices, the problems and successful strategies?
4   Can you use what you have just written in moving forward in your own writing and if so, how?

NB   You might find writing answers to these questions also raises the level of your thinking critically and conceptually, as well as reflectively. Reflective writing aids what is known as metacognition, your awareness of your learning and thinking processes, which helps you to work at a higher level and then to write at that level.

Tricks and strategies

When you are carrying out research there are many false starts and surprises, surprise issues and complicated moments, which all can ultimately help you in your thinking so you can work out the ideas, the meaning, the argument, the usefulness of what you are finding out, and then write about it and refine what you say. It is useful if you can develop a repertoire of tricks and successful strategies to support your writing as you produce drafts of your essays, presentation, report or dissertation.

Writing your ideas out

Students often feel they have nothing to write about until they have finished their reading or research. This is dangerous nonsense! You might not be contributing stunningly original ideas yet, but the sooner you begin to write, the more you will be able to reflect, alter, develop, jettison, add to and hone what you have. Getting your ideas and arguments on paper helps *form* those ideas and arguments.

Writing out your ideas and arguments is one of the best ways of clarifying those ideas and arguments to yourself as your first reader. This happens before you even try them out on a colleague, friend or family member, then on your supervisor or tutor, beyond that, the examiner, then perhaps whoever belongs to the wider audience of those who read your reports, your future journal articles and your books(!).

Writing out ideas and arguments often helps to crystallise them – so don't leave all your writing up until the end of the research – and do not worry if your first attempts at writing are messy, unclear and inelegant. The clue is to write, reflect, work it out on paper, and then polish it up later so it really expresses what you want to say, clearly.

Seizing the moment, and working hard on the writing

Occasionally, all the words I need to express myself come to me clearly, elegantly and in the right order and I rush to write them down. Sometimes this happens before I go to sleep and if I don't write them down I can't sleep. Sometimes it happens while I am driving, in a meeting or reading something else. This also happens to me with solutions to problems. The safe thing to do is to stop, make a note and return to it later.

> Whether the language is clear or not, my advice is:
>
> Capture it, store it, work on it later.

However, this super elegant expression is so rare that it is worth mentioning. Usually, the ideas come in messy forms and I clarify what I want to say by:

- starting to write, even just notes or bullets, or the odd poorly expressed phrase with mostly the wrong words;
- writing it out, however inelegant, imprecise and lumpy the wording is, and then looking back over it very carefully and trying to make what I say:
  - clearer
  - more elegantly and appropriately expressed
  - better punctuated and spelled
  - referenced to and referencing the work of others whose ideas and arguments have underpinned my own.

Overcoming writing blocks

But often we get stuck when trying to write.

One of the ways of making writing a habit that you enjoy, even if it is quite hard work, occasionally frustrating, and ultimately rewarding, is to get into the habit of writing in different ways regularly. If you do this, when you hit a block you can remember the different ways you became unblocked and try each of these out.

Some suggestions:

- Pick something you have to write. Start writing in the middle of a paragraph, a chapter, an argument. Just begin where you feel comfortable to write.
- Then step back, look at what you have written and produce a brief diagram of where it could all fit in your own piece of writing: as a paragraph, a few

sentences or a chapter, so you can add it in when you have written other parts. This is a way of working which is like a patchwork, a piece at a time.

- Remember to tell yourself it is only a draft so it can be improved! Write fast as it comes to you, and then return to edit for:
  - Conceptual level – ideas, theories, themes, as well as concepts.
  - Expression – does it say what you want it to? Clarify your expression, deal with grammar and punctuation, unclear words and expressions.

Practise forms of writing which free you up to move off into the more serious, focused writing, for example:

- 'Free-writing' – (Elbow, 1973) to loosen up your thought processes and creativity. This involves writing for five minutes without stopping, on any topic. Once you have been freed up you can turn to other writing.
- 'Splurge' – I write on and around the topic fast (and inaccurately). Then I go back over it and form it, find the right words, turn the sentences the right way round.

With these practices, you are not forcing yourself to be totally clear about what you want to say before you start writing. Clarity comes though the writing process itself. If you find it difficult to change these first efforts to something focused and well written, then maybe this is not the right loosening up technique for you! But it can be both therapeutic, because you have broken that block and are on your way again, and a way of finding the right words. If it helps, remove yourself from the writing process for a while then return to edit first drafts as if they were written by someone else.

You can also try to:

- Brainstorm initial ideas without having to express them perfectly.
- Get out of a writer's block by doing some writing – the physical act.
- Work through psychological, intellectual or emotional responses by writing about them.
- Open up ideas by writing them down and then trying to get the words right.
- Put the ideas and expressions circulating in your head down on paper so that you can move on to other thoughts and return to these later to express them more clearly.
- Gain confidence by writing – producing an *amount*, to be edited later, by articulating ideas and arguments in your head, however (initially) poorly.
- Avoid using halting, formalised phrases and getting tied up in them, so *saying* nothing.

Visualise

Using diagrams and visualisation is another way of starting to write freely. You could try:

- Expressing contradictions through writing about both, or more, sides of an issue, separating, then linking them.

Visualising complex or contradictory ideas can help to build up elements of an argument, underpinned and informed by primary sources, theorists and critics. Like free writing, visualisation helps express the kinds of complications and paradoxes inherent in research.

I use a visual image to define the research area chosen from the whole potential field of study – defining this as your 'slice of the cake', where the whole field is the whole cake. This visualisation (see Chapter 4) adds some elaboration, imagination, and development to the original idea. Sometimes visualising can really show contradictions, the rich variety of ideas, and the gaps you need to fill in an area of study.

Research as a journey and the writing as a building – a visualisation (to help you think about your own writing)

I use another diagram (see below, Figure 20.1) to compare research to a journey and the completed dissertation or project to a well-built building. You might like to think about this parallel activity of doing the research, and writing about it, in relation to this diagram. Consider the well mapped but actually quite meandering research journey and the final, neatly built building with the themes, theories and arguments running throughout the whole, and the neat transitions from chapters to chapters, paragraphs to paragraphs. It could also help you to think about translating the research, which is about

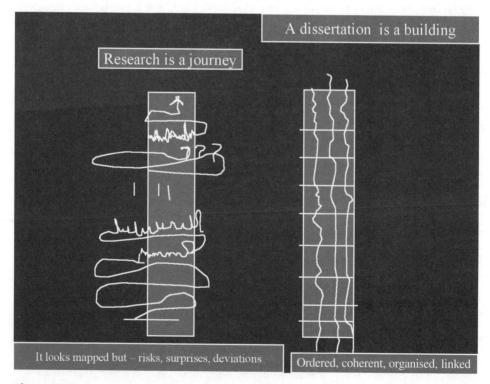

Figure 20.1

discovery, challenge, dedicated work, note taking and detailing, into a careful piece of writing, which is:

- well planned;
- coherent;
- with themes and theories running throughout it;
- with an argument running through it;
- with claims backed by evidence and evidence forming the basis of claims;
- and all the parts in their logical place in the whole.

You can also visualise using mind mapping tools – which let you explore ideas in a visual shape, a map of your thoughts and findings and questions – which then help not only to shape what you are thinking and writing, but also to show weak areas that need further work.

Figure 20.2 is a very basic mind map with some thoughts added. The question the researcher is exploring is in healthcare and is about social and cultural attitudes to hygiene among nurses, where the problem identified is that some nurses are not taking appropriate precautions to stop cross-infection. They are not washing their hands, for instance, and the issue seems to concern compliance, possibly cultural difference or identity, or something else not yet discovered. So, the main theoretical areas start to be decided by opening up the research question at the heart of the research. With the mind map it is possible to add questions and make notes, add references – and then write out from it.

Once you have identified the research question and the underpinning theories which can help you to ask and answer your question, you can read and start to write about them, can identify areas where you know little and need to read further, and can take selective, focused notes from your lectures and your reading. Visualising helps you to identify what you already know, what ideas and theories link with parts of the question, and what gaps you have in your knowledge which need filling through reading, carrying out research, and then writing.

Other kinds of writing to break blocks

You can also try generative writing, which involves the following:

- write for five minutes;
- without stopping;
- then go back and re-shape it.

Reflect back on the writing, using it as a prompt for discussion and future writing. Take a different coloured pen, annotate, correct it, cut it into bullet points, expand some elements, remove repetition, and clarify some elements. The computer helps you to do this painlessly, but you might prefer writing on the computer, printing it off and working on it manually, then transferring to the computer again. Find a variety of practices which work for you and use them when you need to.

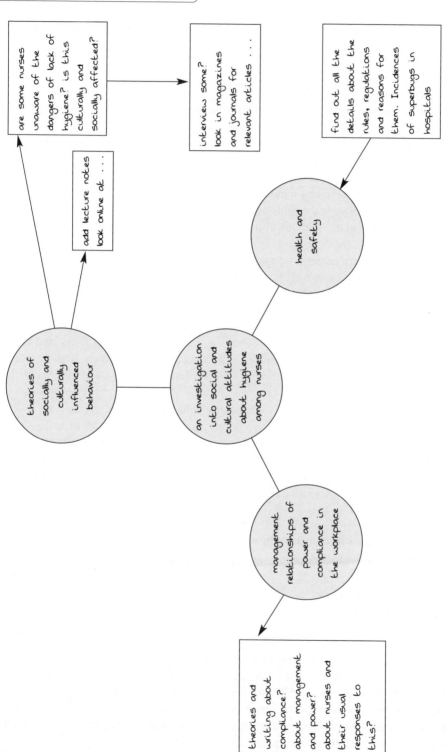

Figure 20.2

Rowena Murray's 'binge' and 'snack' writing (Murray, 2002) recognises that sometimes we don't have long to write but can write something quick, focused and useful in a small 'snack' to be followed later with some long hours of writing or a 'binge'. Write when you can, what you can, and ensure you take time later to shape, cut, edit and make it flow well, and say what you need it to say. Try it out on 'critical friends' whose judgement you trust and who can advise on whether it does your research justice and is clear enough.

Tutors can be very helpful in their comments on your writing but sometimes they say too much, or it is not clear what they want and you need to work it out. Ask them to clarify; try out some responses and see if they are what is needed to improve the writing.

Rowena Murray has a helpful typology of comments from tutors at both the conceptual, critical level and that of presentation, i.e:

- Argument
- Clarity
- 'Develop'
- 'Discuss'
- 'Distinguish'
- 'Expand'
- The mechanics, i.e.
    - punctuation, etc.
    - praise
    - probe
    - prompt
    - role switch
    - style

Sometimes, tutors comment on just one area of your writing so that you can improve it stage by stage. Sometimes, they make comments only about the level of ideas and argument, the theorisation and conceptualisation, and sometimes they seem to focus on the mechanics, for example, of punctuation. Be careful to work on both areas of writing, the conceptual and the presentation, to ensure that in the end your writing says exactly what you want it to as clearly as possible, that your ideas are theorised and conceptualised enough and well-enough argued, that you reference clearly and well, and that you make no claims without evidence and include no evidence without linking it to a claim or your argument. (Some of the above appeared in another form in G. Wisker, *The Good Supervisor*, Palgrave Macmillan, 2005.)

If in doubt about what your tutor feels will improve your writing, email them or ask them. You do not want to waste time and become anxious when clarity can help you get on.

There are also times when it is just difficult to keep the momentum up. Journalling, blogging, reflective writing and using the ways of overcoming writing blocks can all help you to maintain momentum and get through the writing process so that you end up with a well-enough written piece for your assessment and your own satisfaction.

Journalling, blogging and writing habits

As with the reflective writing activities (above), journalling helps to break writing blocks, causes reflection and articulation, and helps you make progress with your expression and your sense of your own developing research. It also helps you find out what works for you in the research process and the writing process, for future use. Try journalling, keeping notes and comments, working out thoughts, noting decisions and problematic events, and achievements and remarkable moments of revelation, reflections on discovery, and frustration. Comment on working out some of the difficult ideas and the contradictions in others' arguments or in the theory relating to what you are reading and finding yourself. Journalling or blogging help release both the physical energy of writing and the creative energy that can get stuck if we do not articulate.

If you keep a regular journal or a blog (an online record of your work and thoughts about it) of your writing and research, then you can track the journey of the research, so that later you can explain how you have changed your mind and selected what you are doing to define methodology and methods and the interpretation of your data. It can also help you to keep going.

A word of caution

Be careful not to get seduced by the journalling and blogging. They help you to sort out your ideas through expressing yourself, but they can also be a substitute for doing anything else and particularly any other form of writing. Limit yourself, do only a paragraph a day, make it count for exploration, emotional expression or admitting frustration, working things out and celebrating – don't let it take you over. You might share your blogging with a friend and so support each other through the writing process – think about this when you look at peer support, below.

You might like to look at Chapter 21, which is the companion piece to this chapter and which deals with ways of writing at different levels, and forms of presentation, particularly to complete a dissertation.

Summary

In this chapter we have considered ways of writing which enable you to:

- Develop good writing habits.
- Write notes, and use journalling and blogging to help you write.
- Break writing blocks and keep up the momentum.
- Write differently in different contexts and different parts of a longer project.
- Deal with your data in order to write about it, moving from notes through to developing arguments and making claims based on evidence from the data.

Further reading

Boice, R. (1990) *Professors as Writers: A Self-Help Guide to Productive Writing* (Stillwater, OK: New Forums).

Cottrell, S. (2008) *The Study Skills Handbook*, 3rd edition (Basingstoke: Palgrave Macmillan).

Cottrell, S. (2005) *Critical Thinking Skills* (Basingstoke: Palgrave Macmillan).

Dunleavy, P. (2003) *Authoring a PhD: How to Plan, Draft, Write and Finish a Doctoral Dissertation or Thesis* (Basingstoke: Palgrave Macmillan).

Elbow, P. (1973) *Writing Without Teachers* (Oxford: Oxford University Press).

Fowler, H. W. (1994) *A Dictionary of Modern English Usage* (Ware: Wordsworth Editions).

Gower, E. (1986) *The Complete Plain Words*, revised edition prepared by S. Greenbaum and J. Whitcut (London: HMSO).

Murray, R. (2002) *How to Write a Thesis* (Maidenhead: Open University Press).

Wisker, G. (2005) *The Good Supervisor* (Basingstoke: Palgrave Macmillan).

21 Writing Well, in the Right Shapes and Forms: the Authority of Your Research and Your Writing

This chapter considers:

▶ writing in standard dissertation form;
▶ what you are writing about and how;
▶ writing critically, conceptually and creatively;
▶ writing in the appropriate shape and language for the reader and examiner.

Your research is interesting, it has taken you a lot of work, it could be really fascinating and even groundbreaking, so it is important that it is communicated well to others. Your writing needs to show critical and conceptual engagement and be coherently organised and clearly expressed.

Much of this chapter is concerned with your writing in the shape of a standard dissertation, although it also suggests some alternative ways of expressing your research which involve writing in less standard formats.

It is actually such a long slog doing a dissertation or project that the accumulation of information, quoting, and detailing of what has been found can take all your energies. However, your research needs to be communicated to and shared with others. To this end, what you have set out to explore or discover, how you carried out your research, what you have found and the importance of what you have found all need expressing as accessibly and as clearly as possible for your readers. They are yourself, your tutor or supervisor, your peers, your examiner and, beyond that, a wider readership, should your work be part of a community project, a project for your employer, or be published. It is important to get it all clearly expressed, and underpinned by the kind of authority that good research offers us when we make arguments, suggest change in practice, comment, add to and develop knowledge.

Writing in standard dissertation form

We are going to look at using theory, developing themes, ensuring coherence and readability. First, let us consider the standard shape of a dissertation and the kind of content, focus and writing expected in its different sections.

Standard dissertation

Title

On a separate title page, one or two lines, clear, a statement suggesting the enquiry, and assertions made.

Abstract

Usually about 300 words. This answers the questions: 'What is this dissertation about? What does it argue, prove, contend?' 'What has it achieved of impor- tance?' Use the third person and passive, that is, 'It is argued that . . . in discussing . . . using . . . evidence is presented which suggests that . . .'.

The abstract is what is read *first* by a reader and so must be written clearly and straightforwardly in a manner so interesting that the reader wishes to read on. It states the aims, outcomes and achievements of the dissertation or thesis, the theories used, the arguments, and the importance of its contribution to knowledge.

You will probably write the abstract right at the end of your work and after you have written everything else, when you can stand back and get a clear picture of your achievement.

Preface and acknowledgements

Who do you want to acknowledge and to thank? Who helped? Leave no one out!

Introduction

This introduces the context for the research and how this piece of research fits into, grows out of, extends other work in the field. It establishes the gap in knowl- edge, the boundaries to the research, the researcher's own position and why he or she undertook the research. It indicates how different elements of (a) the research design have been carried out so they are seen, detailed, actioned, evalu- ated, and discussed in (b) specific chapters. The design of the research and the dissertation or thesis are introduced and explained briefly here. Introductions also explain the researcher's passion and enthusiasm for the research *journey*.

Review of the literature/theoretical perspectives

This should contain carefully explored, referenced work with the underpinning *theories* and the work of the essential *theorists* in a dialogue between the theo- rists' and the researcher's own work. It is crucial to ensure that the main under- pinning concepts, histories and theories are explored here, as are key terms. They will then be referred to and woven throughout the rest of the dissertation.

Methodology, design of the study, and methods

All researchers need to explore, explain and defend the methodology, e.g. inductive? deductive? naturalistic? The methods, e.g. documentary analysis? interviews? case studies? And the design of the study – sample population? Which part of the research was undertaken in which order and why?

Some literature and humanities students find this chapter difficult and relatively pointless because they are using critical practice, but this is the place to explore, define, explain and defend why you have, for instance, decided on a Marxist historicist reading practice involving interweaving historical and political debates and documents, with their expression, reflection and symbolic representation in texts – and how you intend to work with the primary and secondary sources of several kinds – documents, novels, interviews and so on.

Presentation of results

This is a clear, *annotated* and discussed record of what has been discovered in science, and sometimes in health. You won't usually be including this section if you are writing a social science, humanities or arts dissertation because you will include your data or information and your discussion together.

Discussion

For science dissertations there is a *separate* discussion chapter, while for social science, health or education there is integration between results and discussion. Tables, statistics, bar charts, quotations and so on, appear in *extract*, discussed fully in the main text, with narrative exploring and bringing in different results and interpreted data to develop arguments, presenting coherent points and findings. The original data or results are only extracted, or, in some cases if absolutely necessary (unusual), they might appear in full, in the appendices.

For a humanities or literature-based thesis and also often for a social science, health or education-based thesis, there are often *several chapters* exploring different themes and issues in a linked discussion.

Conclusions

Dissertations have a conclusions chapter which serves two purposes – (a) to briefly summarise what was researched and discovered, challenged, proved, disproved, how it was done, the main arguments; (b) to indicate both factual conclusions (what new knowledge or information has been discovered) and conceptual conclusions (how arguments, reconceptualisations have been able to alter understanding, enabling us to see knowledge and interpretation of the world differently, perceive new perspectives and meanings). The conclusion establishes

the importance of the work, and, finally, indicates further work (recommendations perhaps, other research, suggestions for change). You might well find that
writing the conclusions chapter is a clear, logical exercise. However, many people
find it as difficult, at least, as the abstract, and in the event, many conclusions to
dissertations, theses, essays and books are:

- rushed: 'I've run out of time'; 'there's nothing else to say';
- dull and empty: 'I said it all in the text';
- filled with ideas and things you haven't already said: 'there must be space
  to put all of this somewhere, the conclusions will do';
- filled with recommendations: 'I've done all of this work, now I must
  suggest what others should go and do as a result'.

In practice, examiners and readers often tend to read the abstract, contents page,
conclusions, references and then get into the body of the text, rather as we might
scan a book. As such then, the conclusions chapter, like the abstract, needs to be
produced with very great care indeed. And, of course, it's the key chapter to show
your contribution to knowledge. After a brief reminder about the research topic
and research designs, your findings, both factual and conceptual, should be the
body of the conclusion.

Indicate in summary what your research has produced by way of *evidence* in
terms of:

- addressing your research question/hypothesis;
- relating in a dialogue with the work of others:
  - how it has been/is informed, formed and interpreted by the under-
    pinnng and informing use of the theories, theorists and critics;
  - what contribution it makes to knowledge and understanding.

Appendices, statistical tables, illustrations and so on

Tables, quotations and illustrations need to appear in extract, with discussion and
analysis in the main text, and usually as examples, e.g. an indicative questionnaire, the participant consent form; or in full if necessary in the appendices, along
with, for example, interview transcripts, products made in the process of the
research.

References

You might not need to use footnotes or endnotes even with a dissertation.
Indeed, most essays and dissertations rely on including references in the text, in
short, after the work cited, e.g. 'Briggs (1999) suggested that . . .'.

If you need to use them, you are advised to reference footnotes systematically
and carefully throughout the text at the foot of each page or in endnotes at the

end of each chapter. References can be signalled in the text by a number [1] which leads to the endnote and reference, or by a shortened form of the actual reference, for example: 'Phillips, Estelle M. and Pugh. D. S. (1994) *How to Get a PhD: A Handbook for Students and their Supervisors* (Milton Keynes: Open University Press)' placed at the end in the references, can be signalled in the actual text as '(Phillips and Pugh, 1994)'.

Bibliography

This is usually an alphabetical list of books, journals, films and Internet sites. It is a handy reference for any reader, and if you are *not* using endnotes or footnotes you only produce an alphabetical bibliography. Each university has its regulations and consistency is crucial.

Presentation

Ensure you have read any university guidelines about layout, typeface, presentation format, references, and that your work conforms to all of these. Many dissertations meet difficulties in examination just because of presentation. (See pages 265–8.) (A longer more complex version of this advice regarding layout appeared in *The Good Supervisor*, Wisker, 2005.)

What you are writing about and how

Theories and themes

Initially, you should establish your underpinning theories, then use them to help you relate your analyses of what you have read to your data and interpret the importance of the findings in relation to, and through, the insights offered by these theories. Ensure the ideas of the theorists whose work underpins your own are interwoven with your own work, that the theorists' understanding and explanations which help your own understanding and interpretations are used throughout. You then relate your data analysis and interpretation to the same theories which underpin your whole piece of research. These are rounded off in the conclusions.

You need to ensure that themes run throughout whatever you discuss and argue and how you use your reading and data. These themes will have developed as you read other people's work, thought about it, carried out your own research and thought about it, analysed your data and identified what kind of themes emerge through the data, the reading, the theorising, your own reflection (see Chapter 14 on analysis and Chapter 7 on dealing with the literature). Look back at the diagram earlier in this book (p. 250) and consider how to construct 'the building' of the dissertation or project, to link the different sections, paragraphs and chapters together, and to ensure that your themes and arguments are clear throughout the whole piece of writing.

As you write through the whole project, long essay or dissertation, you need to ensure that you are referring backwards and forwards to the argument, the theories, the themes, to make it a coherent whole, using phrases to carry the argument on and link theory to argument to evidence, such as: 'in this respect', 'additionally', 'while it has been argued that . . . this evidence/work suggests . . .'.

Do ensure that you have developed and can use both of these kinds of writing, the conceptual and critically engaged, and the coherently expressed. It could be particularly challenging if you come from a different language culture and might be able to express yourself elegantly in your own language but less so, you might feel, and in a rather stilted fashion, in English. It is particularly difficult, also, if you are working with your tutor with drafts sent through the post or email, because sometimes there needs to be more clarification about the main ideas and arguments. Sometimes there can be difficulties about understanding the kind of feedback your tutor might give you, especially, perhaps, if you or he/she falls into the trap of only correcting all the errors of expression and syntax (important because they enable or obstruct the argument being expressed) at the expense of encouraging critical thinking, and a critical, conceptual, analytical approach. You need both in your work.

It could be useful for you to work with your tutor, supervisor or other students and identify both problems with others' writing, and successful strategies for writing:

1   conceptually, critically; and
2   eloquently, coherently.

This can be done through close analysis and critique of any journal article, book, chapter or dissertation (libraries often hold copies of previous dissertations – don't get caught up with the content, look at how it is written about and argued).

Looking analytically, critically and reflectively at successful pieces of published work is helpful in developing your own research and writing.

Activity:
Critical writing

Select two articles in your own field.

Consider:

- How well is the research question expressed? Is it clear? Or is the writer only *stating or describing* an area of work, a situation, rather than problematising and exploring the area and developing a question?
- Has the author summarised background and contextual work, work by experts and theorists? Has she referred to it? Is she showing contrasts in work and arguments developed by others? Is she analysing the work and drawing out some main points of difference, in terms not just of facts that differ but of conceptualisation, interpretation? Or does she just seem to have noted a list of other experts, produced a summary of the experts' work?

> - Is it clear what methodology or methodologies and what methods she has used in her work? Does she explore how these help her ask her question? Does she mention them in passing, then move on to what has been found, all in a bit of a muddle in the middle of the paragraphs? (Not good!) Does she defend why she chose her methods?
> - When the data is presented, is it a mass of quotations or tables with little commentary? Or are there themes and arguments being drawn out of the data and explored through selective extracts? In quotations from books or interviews, do we see themes and patterns developing, making a contribution to arguments? Do any comments really grow from the data? Or is there a mismatch?
> - In the conclusion, is the whole piece just summed up with a list of what happens in each chapter? Or does the writer draw themes and questions together, explaining how some facts have been discovered, and how the work has contributed to conceptual development – areas of thinking, meaning and argument about the subject?

Writing critically, conceptually and creatively

Reading, thinking and asking questions

One way of encouraging critical and conceptual work, which is analytical rather than merely descriptive and factual, is to set up good reading practices and supervisor/student or tutor/student interactions, which draw on these to develop thinking and writing. Delamont et al. (1997) mention three kinds of reading needed for carrying out research. We can develop their suggestions, indicating levels of response and conceptualisation which you can employ in your work. They say that 'For arts and social science students there are three types of reading to be done: reading on the topic, contrastive reading and analytical reading' (p. 57). They offer worked examples of three kinds of reading:

- Reading into the field is only one of the tasks.
- If you are unaware of debates in the field, you might merely recreate them.
- You need to work out where your research engages with the debates and what it can add.

Reading, arguing and writing is carried out in different ways for different purposes.

- *Reading on the topic* – accumulating information, establishing the field – provides facts and basic underpinning ideas you use in your work and for writing arguments.
- *Contrastive reading* – identifying discussions, debates, disagreements, different positions – helps you to critique and ask questions, then argue in a dialogue–between experts/others/your work.
- *Analytical reading and writing* – How does this work? What is it made of? What lies behind it? How does it fit in or not? Is it coherent? Why does it matter? Take it to pieces, find conflicts and arguments.

Please consider:

- How are YOUR reading, research and writing informative, contrastive, and analytical? If ONLY informative, it won't be at degree level.
- Where do you engage in dialogue? With what main theories and arguments? What are *your* points and arguments? How and where have you been analytical of theorists, research data, your own findings?

Your *thinking* and your *writing* also need to be at different levels, all of which are present in a piece of written up and analysed research. These are:

- Description.
- Narrative.
- Summary.
- Synthesis.
- Analysis.
- Evaluation and reflection.
- Engagement in critique.
- Conceptual thought – involving ideas, theories.
- Argument and dialogue with your own work.
- Contribution to meaning – creative – something new which is your own.

You will go through all of these kinds and levels of writing at different points in your work and all are useful, but if you stay at the level of *describing* how something has happened, what is the case, what are the facts only; *telling the story (narrative)*, without commenting on it or analysing it; and *summarising* other people's or your own points, you will not be working at a conceptual, creative and sufficiently critical level for a dissertation or project.

You need to move beyond and start to *synthesise*, i.e. pull the main points out of a range of writing, stand back and categorise these, find their themes, and pull them together. Then you need to be able to identify the main issues and meanings, in other words to *analyse* what you have read or written, or others have written, and work out what the important elements are in relation to your own question and argument. You need to *evaluate and reflect* on what has been read, done and written, judge it, identify strengths and weaknesses, and work at the level of the ideas and theories, *conceptual* levels. You need to relate what has been read, done and written in the work of others, engage in a discussion with others' comments, ideas and theories, and then to add a well thought out argument of your own, make *a contribution to the discussion and to your understanding, to meaning*.

Examples

1 Working at a merely descriptive and factual level, a student might produce the following:

Advantages and disadvantages of email

Email has boosted the Travel and Tourism industry because it brings more sources to use, send and work with information in a completely different and quick and easy way. Email is not just used in the Travel and Tourism industry, it is also used in all sorts of other businesses all over the world and is a simple form of communicating with other people, and is essential for particular businesses from all over the world.

Advantages:

- Free or inexpensive
- Easy to use
- A wide population uses email
- Quicker to send an email than it is to write a letter and post it
- Instantaneous
- Easy to read and quick when replying
- You're able to send big files and large documents as attachments easily

Disadvantages:

- Computers can receive viruses that can cause all sorts of problems, including loss of data
- Also, hackers can easily access your information
- You can easily by accident send an email to the wrong person
- Computers also crash a lot

---

2 Working at a more conceptual, analytical, critical level a student might produce the following:

The introduction of email into the Travel and Tourism business has revolutionised the business and has brought with it a range of advantages and disadvantages. Email enables customers and colleagues to send information fast and easily, instantaneously, to each other. Customers can book online and email about needs, changes, evaluations, problems and questions, and the travel and tourism representative or the customer service representative or business manager can stay in touch during the exchange, find out answers, engage in a discussion which helps to identify and solve problems and address needs. Email is nearly free, only depending on the start-up cost of the computer and broadband or wifi, and the regular costs for maintaining the service. Many people can be copied into a discussion, and the discussion can be stored for future use. Large documents and files, including colour photos, can be sent quickly and safely, although the possibility of hackers gaining access to the system is always a problem.

Drayton (2008) argues that no business can manage to stay in touch with customer and service changes fast enough in today's world without email, while Angus and Robertson (2008) suggest that the strength of this communication is in its rapid resolution of problems.

Some of the possible problems have now been dealt with and there are solutions. Firewalls and virus scanners help to deal with viruses and hackers, minimising the problems caused by loss of data and infection of the systems. When colleagues are appropriately trained they can minimise the possibility of sending the wrong files to the wrong people. In all, email is here to stay, and as problems develop so solutions are also found. It is fast, easy and efficient as a means of communication and essential in a business which deals with customers, services and the world today.

Both pieces are based on the same information. One is descriptive and uses bullet points, so that there is no room to develop an argument and match point against point. However, it might be useful as a summary to provoke discussion, or as notes for a presentation. The second one develops an argument, and so can finally make the point that, on balance, email is necessary, safe, here to stay and suits the industry.

It is possible to be more theorised and engaged in argument on the second piece; and notice it uses references to authoritative sources (totally fictitious as it happens – but in reality you would need to use real ones!) to back up its arguments.

Presentation

However important your research is, and however critical and conceptual, nonetheless, presentation also matters, and examiners tend to notice presentation errors.

Ensure:

- page numbers are in order,
- good visual layout of pages – so headings don't appear at the bottom,
- careful checking of all referencing,
- consistency!

> **TIP** *Ask a trusted colleague or friend to proofread the whole work. We often do not see our own mistakes when we are too close to the writing.*

Shapes and forms of presentation

When you are writing a dissertation or project, it is safer to stick to the standard thesis/dissertation or report shape. The work will benefit from coherence and links between chapters (in a dissertation or project) or paragraphs (in a shorter piece such as an essay) in terms of themes, theories and your argument. Reading is aided by link paragraphs and sentences, which indicate how each part of the work relates to and builds on the other parts. Expression is important – ensuring the right words are in the right place, linked into a coherent whole. You need to be aware of how to develop links between:

- sentences and paragraphs;
- chapters and the parts of the work as a whole.

You will find it useful to be able to use linking phrases such as 'however', 'it can be argued that', 'some theorists suggest', 'while there are differences of opinion about . . . this research suggests that . . .'. In linking between chapters or paragraphs you could ensure you remind the reader about previous chapters, your own work, and the way in which the dissertation is moving through the standard writing journey from question and introduction of context, to theory, to methodology and methods, and on to discussing the data, interpreting it and drawing conclusions from findings. Here is an example of a link between the 'theoretical perspectives'/'literature review' section or chapter, and the section or chapter on methodology, research design and methods.

> The previous chapter explored Marxist political and economic theories of the relationship between the mode of production and employees' sense of self-worth and empowerment (or lack of it), which inform this research on the role played by men and women in the 1980s' miners' strike. This chapter explains the reason for the choice of qualitative inductive research methodology within an interpretivist paradigm, using interviews with miners and their wives to gain in-depth responses about the experiences and feelings of some of those involved in the strike.

You can see how this piece attempts to round off some arguments from the previous part, and refers back and forwards to help readers navigate around the argument, and eventually, the evidence, claim and importance of the work.

You could also swap some writing with a critical friend and audit each other's work, making suggestions for improvement.

New forms

If you decide to change the shape of your written piece from a standard dissertation or project because it is more appropriate to express your work in a less conventional shape, then negotiate it with a tutor first and explain why the new shape better suits your work. If you are writing to accompany a creative piece, then you are going to be producing both a creative piece and an analytical, critical and reflective commentary on how this addresses your research question.

In a video project on the Women's Studies BA at Anglia Ruskin University, for example, two students produced a short video of their response to Caribbean poetry and accompanied it with both a reflective piece about its development, their feelings of engaging with products from another culture, and a critical, analytical, theorised piece about how it engaged with the theory and practice of performance poetry, and how it put forward an argument.

In response to a piece of research carried out into Toni Morrison's novel *Beloved* about living with the legacy of slavery one student was very creative. From her I was given:

1. A quilt which was hand and machine sewn, based upon original research undertaken into the quilting patterns used in the African American slave crossings, and some new patterns developed by the student. This was accompanied by a reflective log detailing her decisions about her research and her written piece, and an analytic commentary explaining how the quilt engaged with women's creative production and responses to slavery. (This was a long essay for year 2, BA Women's Studies.)

2. A video of short snatches of film taken when the student returned to visit her family in South Africa. It focuses mainly on the outside of the house, and overheard voices, and never shows the family. This was accompanied by a written piece – actually a folder with three forms of writing interspersed and colour coded, so a critical and analytical piece was one form of writing, a reflective another, and the third a creative response. You could read your way through each separately or one section of each after another, following the colour coding. The three forms of writing

expressed the different ways she was thinking and articulating her thoughts, underpinned by theory and her own research, in different forms. (This was a dissertation at Master's level.)

What would suit your own research and expression?

Finally – a few tips

- Look for good models of writing and learn from how they are expressed, structured, argued, referenced.
- Read and mark other people's work and get them to read and mark yours – share drafts and discuss:
  - how good the argument is;
  - how clearly expressed the work is;
  - how well it uses sources and references, what use it makes of the data.
- Read journal articles and the beginning of chapters and work out how they have established an argument, used their sources, and written coherently and accessibly – try and model a small piece of your own work on these choices and expressions used (this is not copying, it is learning by using a model).

For many of us, even if we write a lot, it is actually quite a difficult task to write well. We need to turn the gradually clearing ideas into questions, take good notes and use them well, engage in a dialogue with those experts whose work seems to have said it all, when it would appear more deferential to that work to summarise it and move on. It is a challenging task to identify the arguments between experts and theorists, to analyse, contrast, debate and *add* to what they say in terms of your own work. It is also challenging to finish off and present a well rounded, well argued and referenced piece of work, which uses your research appropriately and does what we want with research in the end – communicates it well to other people. These have been a few ideas and tips. There are many other good books you can read about developing your writing well.

Summary

This chapter has considered a variety of issues and practices about writing, in particular:

- Varieties of writing and a variety of forms including the standard dissertation form, reflective writing, and analytical, critical comments accompanying more creative work.
- Focusing on your topic, and developing your writing coherently in a well argued way.

- Writing critically, conceptually and creatively, as well as descriptively or in a narrative – whatever is the right way for your context and topic, your reader and your examiner.

Further reading

Boice, R. (1990) *Professors as Writers: A Self-Help Guide to Productive Writing* (Stillwater, OK: New Forums).

Delamont, S., Atkinson, P. and Parry, O. (1997) *Supervising the PhD: A Guide to Success* (Buckingham: Open University Press).

Dunleavy, P. (2003) *Authoring a PhD: How to Plan, Draft, Write and Finish a Doctoral Dissertation or Thesis* (Basingstoke: Palgrave Macmillan).

Elbow, P. (1973) *Writing Without Teachers* (Oxford: Oxford University Press).

Fowler, H. W. (1994) *A Dictionary of Modern English Usage* (Ware: Wordsworth Editions).

Gower, E. (1986) *The Complete Plain Words*, revised edition prepared by S. Greenbaum and J. Whitcut (London: HMSO).

Murray, R. (2002) *How to Write a Thesis* (Maidenhead: Open University Press).

Wisker, G. (2005) *The Good Supervisor* (Basingstoke: Palgrave Macmillan).

22 Maintaining Momentum: Overcoming Difficulties with Time, Writing, the Project and the Research Processes

Typically, in the middle of a research project or as you approach the end, there could be a number of concerns about ways in which you can overcome various difficulties with what you are discovering in the research, how to interpret it, what you can say about your findings, what it all means, and whether you can write it all sufficiently elegantly in the time available. There are also difficulties of maintaining momentum, just keeping going through all the hard work to produce a rewarding, well finished piece of research, which is well written and making a contribution to knowledge.

We are going to look at your work during and towards the end of a longer piece of work, which might be a large term essay, a project or a dissertation. A few thoughts: you need:

- to be able to write at an elegant level, ensuring that argument, theory, critical thinking, ideas and meaning, i.e. the conceptual level of work, is clear and maintained, and to write in an organised, coherent, elegant fashion, so that a reader can understand that you are able to pull together what you have thought, found, read, and developed into a readable and well presented piece;
- to think about how you will manage your time so that you don't become overwhelmed with all the work you have to complete;
- to be able to deal with the many possible issues which could emerge, and to maintain your momentum in your work.

In the middle and towards the end of your research and writing, there can sometimes seem like a mountainous amount of work to complete. The key is time management, planning parts of the work so that each can be completed, written about and edited.

Activity:
Audit 1

The aim of this audit is to enable you to think about your work to date and ask and answer these questions:

- How is the research going so far? (*critical review*)
- What is/are your research question(s)? (*remind yourself*)
- Why is your research important? (*argue*)
- How does it intend to contribute to knowledge and meaning? (*argue*)
- What reading have you done so far? Do you need to update? (*take stock and plan*)
- What kinds of themes are emerging? (*analyse*)
- What arguments are emerging? (*analyse and argue*)

You also need to ensure that you are not becoming so pressurised with the compulsion to get things done and written that you forget to step back and ask those critical and conceptual questions about what you are finding and why it makes a contribution to knowledge. You should relate theory to your own work, and develop an argument throughout your writing. As you come towards the end of your work, you need to make sure that it is theorised, and has a coherent argument throughout. You could audit your work now at the conceptual and the theoretical levels, asking:

- How is my work becoming theorised? In other words, I am not just making statements. Instead, where am I using the theories and referencing the theorists to help ask my questions, back up my statements, arguments and claims and interpret what I am finding? Where is this clear?
- How is my work relating to the work of others, whose theories, critical achievements and writing underpin and inform it?

This should all be evident throughout your work, and particularly in the 'theoretical perspective'/'literature review' parts, informing and helping to theorise the discussion and interpretation of the findings, and then in the conclusion, which contextualises your achievement in terms of the underpinning theories, and the critical work of others.
Also consider:

- What does it all mean? And why does it matter?
- Is there anything new here?

Activity:
Review a piece of critical writing as a model

Look at a key piece of writing that has informed and underpinned your own and see how it is written and how it engages ideas, arguments and evidence to further knowledge and understanding.

How do the theorists who develop a dialogue/arguments/debates underpin this research and help the writer ask question(s)?

Now look back at your own work and see if you are similarly engaged and clear in your writing.

The role of theorists in your ongoing work

It is really important that your research is theorised. This means it moves on beyond being descriptive or merely making claims that what you have read or found means that something is significant. Theory helps us to interpret the world, and that includes your research evidence.

Theorists are those whose ideas and theories underpin the research we do, and the ways in which we understand the work of others, because their ideas help to focus and contextualise, shape and make sense of, and provide a perspective on events, facts, discoveries, and relationships between things and events. They are interpreted and their work is used by others who have worked and are still working in the field.

You might well have used some key theorists whose work underpins the questions you are asking and helps these to be more than factual 'what?' questions and instead to ask 'how?', ' 'why?', 'in what ways?', 'why not?', 'what if?', 'what are the various versions and choices?', 'what might this mean?', and 'how does this relate to that?' These are questions which theorists and those who have used their work, the critics or active researchers in the field, would ask, and which you ask about your own work. You need to identify how your work is growing, develops from the work in the field, and contributes to both *what we know* (facts, information) and *what we understand* and can theorise, argue and claim about the meaning and contribution of the work (the conceptual). Your work needs to show how you can enter the dialogue and debate between the theorists and critics, with some level of assurance that what you have to offer is new enough, well enough argued, underpinned and informed by theory. It should show that you know how your work relates to other work, both previous, contemporary or current in the field today.

You will learn to speak with a voice of confidence against a background of understanding and make a statement about your own work and contribution. To do this, you need to show how your work fits with, grows from and contributes to the major dialogues in the field, and how the chosen, specific, absolutely relevant themes of your findings are interpreted from your data and can contribute to your argument.

Often it is necessary to make some change midway into the research. Research is like that, messy, and now is the time to look at whether the design is enabling you to ask your question. You might need to look back at your research design and ask some questions about its appropriateness for answering your research question, or whether there are any necessary changes.

- You might have discovered some interesting findings which you could theorise better once you have engaged with theories you did not originally plan to work with.
- Really finding out answers to your research question might mean you have to add another element to your research design such as an exploration of an author's biographical details because their work reveals an interesting relationship between their life and the writing, which you will need to find factual details about and then theorise.

- Locating the work might demand more historical context.
- Enriching and deepening it might involve a narrowing down from interviews and focus groups to developing case studies since respondents seem to fall into noticeable categories and you know rich data will provide a better quality story.

All of this you can discuss with your tutor as you work on it, and finally in your dissertation or project when you report on how the research developed.

Activity:
Audit 2   Design

- Have there been or should there now be any changes in your research design and planning?
- Do you need to reorganise your research design?
- Have you changed your methodology and/or your methods? And if so, why are they more likely to enable you to ask your research question(s)?
- What have you found out so far which is significant in terms of your questions and the developments in the field?
- Do you need to reconceptualise, i.e. to use some other ideas or concepts to underpin your enquiry (for example, in a study of homelessness, no longer looking at just homelessness but, having discovered that homelessness is an issue of identity, considering theories of identity to help ask and address your question)?
- Do you need to find another/different sample?

What are you finding? Data and interpreting findings

The middle part of your research is also a moment when you look at the kind of data you are producing and decide how it contributes to the asking and answering of your research questions.

Data is raw information, statistics, quotations, facts, numbers and words.

Analysed data – facts that have been interrogated and facts that have been related to questions focused on some controlling principles, and collated and understood in themes and categories and patterns and differences that are emerging in relation to the question you are asking.

Interpreted data – you have considered what these patterns and themes, these controlled and managed elements of your data might say in relation to your question and the ideas and arguments emerging from your research and work. Here you might ask yourself, what is emerging? What might it all mean? How can you draw some meaning and arguments out from these patterns and themes? How can you interpret them?

Findings are the interpreted meanings which, you can argue, make a contribution to knowledge and to the field where you have found them, and mean something. They are not just masses of selected statistics or quotations, they are selected items, a pattern, directed at and interpreted by the theories you are using and the questions you are asking. If you are finding that they are making a contribution to knowledge, to meaning, and the ongoing debates in the field, you have found something significant that can help others think further about the issue.

Maintaining momentum, some common issues with working with the data, the writing process, and keeping going

Chapter 14 discusses ways of analysing your data and writing about it while Chapters 20 and 21 look at the writing process very thoroughly, and this chapter also has sections on writing, and on time management. In the middle of your work, sometimes it is hard to manage some of the problems. We are going to look at identifying and possibly dealing with some of the most common problems that might emerge in the process of continuing with your work, analysing your data, and making sense of it.

Activity

Consider some of these problems faced by other students – how could you avoid or overcome them?

1 Luis finds that he has been very busy with his research but cannot quite align what he is finding with the question he asked.
2 Andrew has collected too much information and is not sure how to decide what to use in his essay.
3 Susan has had problems with gaining access to her research subjects or sample – who can help her? What should she do?
4 Yang's research question has produced some unexpected results and understanding them will require much more reading in theory and in the work of critics as well as a great deal of analysis and thought.
5 Angela has produced an artwork as a result of her engagement with museum collections in the Victoria and Albert museum but is finding it difficult to theorise or explain how this was produced, and what she has added with her own creative practice.
6 Every time John sits down to write up his work he gets stuck in the introduction and rewrites. Meanwhile the rest of the essay seems disorganised and lumpy.
7 Prashant has written the whole of his dissertation but it still seems to have neither an argument nor coherent links between the chapters, the abstract and conclusion are merely descriptive.

Some thoughts

These students have a variety of difficulties which could be present in anyone's work (not all of them, one hopes!). Here are a few thoughts towards resolutions.

(1) and (2)   Remind yourself of the question and keep focused on your 'slice of the cake' so you ensure the data, findings and arguments do address your question and you don't use everything you have found without any organised focus.

(3)   Can Susan gain the support of someone who will allow her access? Or should she change the research design, to only contact those subjects to whom she can gain access more easily? This depends on her question, and if she can gain support. She might also need to consider ethics and confidentiality.

(4)   Although this means more work, this is very exciting! Research often yields unexpected results and understanding them in order to share them with others means theorising and engaging with the work of those who have considered similar areas or issues previously. This will ultimately make the research more interesting and significant. If it is an enormous amount of work, too large for the current assignment, then the new discoveries could form the basis of larger and deeper research on a later assignment such as for a Master's award.

(5)   Careful differentiation is needed here between the sources of inspiration, which should be noted and discussed, and the creative product. The two and the links between the two need documenting and discussing even if the ways in which the sources stimulate the creativity are not fully understood. She might find it useful to read about how others who use such sources discuss their theorised link with their own work and use this as a model.

(6)   John needs to draw up a work plan in which he tackles other parts of the writing stage by stage, and then bring the whole thing together and write it through coherently.

(7)   Prashant's problem is not dissimilar from John's. Careful editing, reminding of the overall argument and the themes which have emerged, then ensuring (a) that there are links between each element, paragraph, chapter of the piece, and (b) that the theories and arguments appear throughout. This can be tested by sharing with a critical friend.

Writing and editing

You are your first reader, and your first editor. You can edit your own work. Think about presentation.

- Remember as you start to write up some parts that the project or dissertation must be your own work and presented in a satisfactory manner.
- Check grammar, punctuation, spelling, expression.
- Look at logic of argument.
- Ensure you have used
  - appropriate language – no fog;
  - sufficiently conceptual and critical theorised language; and
  - sound argument and clear expression.

Look back at your question and at the typical plan and shape of a good journal essay that your work should be conforming to (pp. 257–60).

Look for:

- the shape;
- the expression;
- the theorised levels;
- the control of the data into interesting and analysed findings that contribute to the development of the debates and the arguments;
- the sentences and elements of your expression that start to link up what you are saying and what you have found and make it more accessible for the reader, guiding them along.

Be a critic of your own level of work

Reviewers, teachers, critics and your colleagues can all help you look at the level of your work, achievement and expression but so can you. Step back, give your work some space and then compare what you are doing against some of the basic criteria of research work.

Criteria for a successful research project are:

- Originality and/or creativity.
- The exercise of independent critical powers.
- A contribution to subject knowledge in the research field.
- Evidence of training in research techniques and methodology.
- Being coherent and well organised.

How far does your work meet these criteria? Have you done all of this? Can you argue that you:

- have chosen an appropriate research topic of sufficient scope;
- have gained satisfactory knowledge of the background literature and work;
- have chosen and can defend your use of methodology and methods, and sampling;
- can defend your data analysis, data management and data interpretation practices?

Starting to write up

As you write up a first proper draft of a long essay, project or dissertation you need to think about shape, achievement, style and presentation, as well as the level of the research you have undertaken. Consider the architecture of a dissertation or longer essay:

- Plan stages of the writing – the paragraphs, sections, sub-sections, and whole chapters.
- Make sure you can work from your notes, first drafts, recorded references, data that you have colour-coded and analysed, files, and reflective comments on the research activities and results that will help you to develop an argument about why you did what you did the way you did it and what it means in relation to the question you asked in your work.

- Write each chapter or section carefully, ensuring you have the right contents for the section, and that there is coherence between sections and throughout the whole work.
- Ensure there is structure to your paragraphs, chapters, and the whole project, dissertation or essay.

Be sure to use the right kind of language throughout. Think about:

- introducing ideas, arguments, main theorists, and debates in the field that the theorists underpin, and that critics, other researchers, practitioners and critics have written about;
- ensuring that your language is always accessible and readable, whether it is being technical or developing an argument.

Be careful of 'fog', which is unnecessary, long words when more straightforward ones would do, or long words that are not explained. Do use technical terms where you need them, but if you are not writing for experts in the field, explain them when you first use them.

A typical plan of a dissertation

Title
Abstract
Preface/acknowledgements
Introduction
Theoretical perspectives/literature review
Methodology, methods and ethics/design of study
Presentation and discussion of results related to themes and theorists
Conclusion, including factual and conceptual conclusions
Appendices/statistical tables and illustrations
References/bibliography

When you write up and edit:

- ensure coherence throughout the dissertation and between chapters;
- ensure threads of themes, theories, arguments run throughout the whole;
- check referencing, layout and presentation;
- after submission and examination have taken place, carry out any necessary changes, clarifications or rewriting, etc.

Activity:
Audit 3   Quality and achievement of work so far

Look at the work and determine:

- How far through your original time plan have you gone?
- How much data have you collected?
- Have you analysed it? Interpreted it? Drawn findings from it?
- Have you met and overcome problems?
- Which problems? How did you overcome them?
- How much have you written? What state are the different parts of your writing in?
- Is it only notes and ideas? Is it a draft? Second draft? Nearly finished? Finished?
- Have you shared your work so far with your supervisor?
- Have you responded to their feedback comments?

I keep a chart of progress when I write, and mark off stages so I can see what to choose to do next. Sometimes the most difficult element is the theory or methodology section, which always seems to need tightening up, and clarifying in terms of expression and argument. Sometimes it is the busy, but not too intellectually taxing part such as correcting the typos, counting the responses, ensuring the references in the text match those in the bibliography and that I have found all the references and laid them out appropriately. Look at the discussion of patchwork writing in Chapter 21 for thoughts on writing differently in different parts of your work.

● Time management and planning

It is possible at this stage towards the end of your work that you could well be overwhelmed with all you have gathered, and have lost sight of 'the wood for the trees', which means you have so much information that it is difficult to work out what the patterns and important themes are. You might have your data under some control but be surprised how much needs to be sorted, analysed, discussed and put in coherent shape in the project report, dissertation or long essay. This is where you need to step back, take stock and look at your time and action plan. It is perfectly normal to take stock and redraw your time and action plan at significant moments when you have achieved something, or if you are stuck or there has been a setback. If you do it all the time you won't do anything else – fulfilling a minimal planned stage might give you a sense of achievement but it might not get the whole project completed. Trying to do everything at once will probably result in a sluggish sense of nothing being completed. These are two ends of a continuum and both your individual projects and your own ways of working will dictate what helps you to get it completed. It is useful to talk with others about how they take stock, plan their time and action activities, and then do it yourself, feel that it is an achievement, move on and mark each new step from then on as an achievement.

Activity:
Audit of time, achievement and replanning

Ask yourself:

- **Achievement** – have you achieved some planned stages?
- Can you sum up your work so far?
- How does your work now fulfil ethics requirements?

- **Focus** – is it necessary to refocus, extending or cutting back, reshaping/ further developing the topic/methods?
- Are they understood and explained?

Note what has/has not been achieved; note what has been/has not been success-ful; note what needs dropping/extending; note what needs refocusing.

- Can you focus on the rest of the project/dissertation etc.?
- Can you see your plan through to completion?
- Have you planned a suitable research programme to achieve successful conclusions?

You might find it useful to talk some of this over with a friend or peer to share ideas and progress, and/or with your tutor or supervisor for guidance.

Looking ahead

As you move through the later stages of your research project, you need to reorganise your time plan and re-plan the research itself. There might have been many or a few changes along the way.

- Produce a revised timescale/critical path analysis.
- Draw up an action plan of tasks to be:
  - started;
  - continued;
  - re-done and improved;
  - finished.

What do you need to go away and do next, immediately, in order to help you move on in your research and your writing? Remember – these two must go on at the same time. For example:

- Re-drafting some of the chapters, e.g. theoretical perspectives, methodology.
- Updating your reading (ongoing).
- Writing discursively about your findings (rather than letting data sit in a pile without comments or thoughts until the last moment, when it will overwhelm you.

Activity

You might like to fill in the final two gaps or draw up your own plan.

Activity	Issues/problems	Help	Other resources	To be done by	Action points
Check references	Cant find for ch. 4, not online	Recheck Google Scholar/Email librarian/go in	Google Scholar, librarian	Friday	Find all I can using Google Scholar
					Note the problem refs
					Email/phone librarian
Rewrite conclusions	Is it conceptual enough?	Critical friends, examples of other conclusions in key essays	Essays	Sunday	Re-read conclusions and check for the theorised and conceptual conclusions not just factual. Ask Pat (critical friend) to read it through and be honest
			Critical friends		
					Analyse the language and structure of a key essay and see if I can build up conceptual conclusions in the same way
Analyse the third interview	It is very long and I can't identify the themes		Use NVivo and the themes already entered into the analysis package	Tuesday – then add to the others	Re-read interview and identify themes
					Put it through NVivo analysis package with the themes already identified so it can select elements

Plan

On page 280 is a plan for various activities at different stages in someone's research and writing.

Please consider:

- Who or what do you need to help you in your work? What equipment? What materials?
- What extra skills?
- What do you need to change and how soon can you change this?
- Who can you share your work with as a critical friend?
- Can you now also revise your cohort support network so you can support each other's work?
- Can you plan a timeline and action points so that you get the work completed?

In re-drawing a *realistic completion* time plan please consider:

- What other pressures are there on your time?
- Have you got to change anything, e.g. your methods and sample, or not? And what are the implications for time management if you need to re-plan?
- Timing in the analysis.
- Timing in the writing, re-drafting and editing, proofing, checking, and presenting.

Activity

Draw up a revised time and action plan for:

- the next month;
- the next year to completion.

Share it and defend it, then produce an immediate 'To do' list.

Summary

In this chapter we have considered:

- Working at a conceptual, theorised level.
- Writing quality and editing.
- Maintaining momentum.
- Managing your time.
- Coping with some common problems in dealing with samples, data handling, interpretation.
- Activity audits.

Further reading

Bell, J. (1999) *Doing Your Research Project* (Buckingham: Open University Press).
Murray, R. (2002) *How to Write a Thesis* (Maidenhead: Open University Press).

23 What Do Examiners Look For? What Do Employers Look For? And How to Ensure Your Work Matches Their Expectations

This chapter considers:

► what examiners and employers are looking for; the research behaviours and skills expected in your work;
► learning behaviours and approaches;
► skills;
► CV, PDP, jobs and your research;
► further research: getting your work published and developed, and moving on into further research.

Examiners and employers expect students to be able to identify and solve problems, ask questions and work towards finding out the answers. In other words, they expect you to be able to undertake enquiry and research, through to completion. This involves a range of questioning behaviours, gathering of information, managing and analysing it, developing an argument and making a contribution to knowledge in written and other forms. This chapter will look briefly at the research behaviours and skills examiners and employers expect of you. It will then go on to suggest some ways you might further develop and recognise these practices and skills.

What are examiners and employers looking for? The research behaviours and skills expected in your work

At degree level, examiners are looking for evidence of research involvement and research skills among other skills and achievements. They aren't looking for world class, world shattering research (although they are always happy if they find it) but to recognise the ways in which you can show you have an enquiring mind, and that you know how to undertake and complete research. This involves practice, experience and skills. Perhaps you would find it useful to audit these practices, experience and skills now, using the chart on pp. 284–5, in order to identify any gaps that you might need to fill through further work before or just after graduation and to contribute to any CV or job application you develop.

When you have identified your skills, reflect in the final column and perhaps at length separately about where you have gained them and what proof you have of them so that you could say, for example, in a job application letter or at an interview, 'I am a good time manager because I have planned, managed, carried out and completed a small-scale research activity for a dissertation and written it all up in good time.'

Research-related practices & skills	A strength	Quite good/some experience	Need development	Evidence and examples
Identifying research needs and topics				
Framing and asking research questions				
Developing				
Literature reviewing				
Theorising topics and under-pinning questions with theories				
Developing a workable conceptual framework				
Developing research designs				
Time management				
Good numeracy				
Writing skills				
Problem identification and problem solving				
Self-motivation				
Working to an agreed research brief				
Communication with other people				
Selecting and using methodology				
Using quantitative research methods				

Using qualitative research methods			
Seeking out and acquiring primary sources			
Finding and using secondary sources			
Carrying out fieldwork effectively			
Gathering data effectively			
Taking notes			
Selecting, summarising, synthesising, analysing, reflecting on notes			
Managing data-catalogue, categorising, labelling, documenting			
Analysing statistical data			
Analysing text and other data, noting patterns, themes, discussion			
Developing an argument			
Writing in a coherent, readable manner			
Referencing			
Presenting an argued research case			
Finishing work off in time and to a good standard			

Employers want to know that you have an enquiring mind; you can identify and tackle problems, ask questions and help to pursue the route to answering them; you can gather information, analyse categories, themes and theories and argue about it, for instance in a report or a presentation, making a case; and you can apply those research skills selectively to tasks which emerge during your working life. They also want to be able to depend on the quality of your evidence and claims, and your presentation, since they might gain or lose contracts, gain or lose a reputation in relation to your work.

Examiners want to see that you have engaged with the course, asked questions, gained sufficient information and shown that you are able to interpret this information, and answer questions; you must show you are able to be selective with the questions you ask and the ways you explore and find out about areas of knowledge and information, and in the way you carry out different activities which enable you to investigate, enquire, find out information and try out ideas, how you explore what seems to be given as fact, investigate claims, delve deeply into taken-for-granted information and ideas and questions asked. They are looking for evidence of:

- knowledge;
- skills;
- attitudes/approaches/beliefs/values.

Broadly speaking, these are learning outcomes and knowledge outcomes which you might think that examiners are expecting from you. Evidencing their achievement might involve needing to repeat the information you have discovered or been told, so that they can see that the knowledge has been gained. But actually, they want more, and for any information or knowledge to be useful there needs to be:

- Facts.
- Information.
- Summaries of information and facts gained.
- Synthesis of different sources of such information, analysis of the information, the data in relation to the question asked. These are categories which need exploring further.
- Analysis of the facts and of information, the data gained when asking the question, exploring the area. Evaluation of the different interpretations given by different sources of this information, which themselves will have selected and interpreted and not merely recorded.
- Reflection on what has been found and a great deal of selection, and focusing on interpreting what has been found. At this point, it is important that we are reminded that there are new areas to be explored and questions asked. This is not merely an opportunity for finding out everything and anything without bounds.

Students are not merely acquirers of knowledge, but makers of knowledge, contributors to knowledge and certainly makers of meaning. Some people repeat the information they have gained and repeat the debates, but they need to go further than this and to identify, clarify, differentiate and compare and contrast the debates and the information which underpins them, selecting it to address an issue.

They are also looking for skills which could be transferred to other learning situations later.

Skills of:

- Identification of important issues, key words, the meaning behind the question, the ways you select key issues.
- Planning and identifying ways of asking questions and going about searching for information in order to address or answer them.
- Ability to understand information acquisition in a selective and sensitive, managed way from a variety of sources – spoken, written, images, archival, primary sources as appropriate, and secondary sources which are the critical and theoretical works that underpin the research and the writing and which feed into the debates into which your own arguments and management of ideas information are going to fit.
- Appropriate expression – the range of different uses of language which set up an issue, clarify a question, argue out a case.
- Ability to communicate with a broad readership or audience.
- Selection, management and organisation of the theories and arguments lying behind the research arguments that you are about to embark on.
- Engagement with concepts and ideas – with theories, in a way which shows you can synthesise, summarise, evaluate and put the case for the different views in an organised way, not merely repeating each one separately but identifying, clarifying and exploring evidence.
- Identifying the trends and patterns – selection and analysis of the information gained into categories, patterns, themes and specific areas which are there to address the question; focus on the areas under discussion.
- Ability to structure an argument in an essay or project report or whatever form the piece of writing is taking on. Being able to spot the right kind of format for your answer and produce your response in the appropriate shape is very important.
- An ability to record, shape, form and properly reference the source you have used – first using the words of your source in quotation in your own discussion, properly referenced, and then finally properly referenced in the bibliography.
- Awareness of your own research-oriented skills and where and how to select from them to deal with new needs for research and enquiry, new issues and problems.
- Flexibility.

CVs and jobs

When we began thinking about the research you might undertake, we looked at you completing a skills audit, which should have given you an idea of the variety of skills needed to undertake research and then of the skills you would probably be able to develop during the course of carrying out your research.

Undertaking research projects gives you the opportunity to work in many different ways and so helps develop a range of skills useful in life and work afterwards, forever. You will develop many of these skills further as you use them in future jobs or everyday life.

What have you proved you can do?

You have proved that you can question things and situations, events, issues, ideas which seem to be given and unquestionable, and that you have an enquiring, lively mind. You are a person of ideas who asks questions about life and everything in it and then who goes beyond this questioning and problematising to identify ways in which these questions can be answered. These areas of interest addressed, you can plan, manage time, do action plans for longer-term and shorter-term activities, and be realistic about the processes of getting from and through to completion. You know how to marshal resources to get the information you need and how to work with a large variety of people, and which sources to consult in order to ask your questions and go about forging and seeking out the information you need, the materials and the data.

One of the most important of the skills you have shown you have as a result of completing a research project, is that of completing – many people have ideas, some can be busy, but only the successful researcher can have ideas, be busy, and collect and manage information and data, question and interpret ideas, theories and concepts and also work conceptually, critically and creatively, and then bring in the project on time, write the report or dissertation, present the completed coherent whole convincingly and well – employers will want ideas, people who work with conceptual and busy levels and complete their tasks.

PDP – Personal Development Portfolios

If you have been involved in PDP, or personal development planning, with a tutor or learning development person, you will probably have been collecting evidence and reflection on the skills you have developed. If not, it is a good idea to review the following questions.

- What have you done?
- What can you do?
- What skills do you still need to develop which would be useful in a new job?
- What is transferable from the research development skills – and how?

CVs and making the most of your research

When you start to look for jobs, whether during your research or after it, make sure that you identify the skills that have been learned or furthered during your research and find ways of evidencing and discussing them with potential employers.

Look up current advice on developing a CV and ensure you develop one which reflects your research skills and achievements.

Usually CVs contain the following elements.

1   Name

2   Date of birth

3   Address

4   Educational achievements

5   Schools and college/university attended (in reverse order, most recent at the top)

This is where you expand and tell the prospective employer about what you did which singles you out from others, so – along with, for example, coaching the football team or being a mentor for new students – you can tell them about your research. Emphasise here the research you have been involved in – tell them about your achievements and special studies.

6   Employment (in reverse order, most recent at the top)

This is where you detail employment, company, full or part time, dates from when to when – and what was involved in the employment to give them ideas about what you are good at and what you want to move into. This is also an opportunity to mention any research you carried out during your employment – even if it was community work which was unpaid, or part time.

7   Personal qualities

You will have a lot to say here about good time keeping, being a team member, financial management and so on as well as skills specific to the job you are applying for – but you can also look back at the skills you developed in your research and briefly emphasise them here too – for example, research should have proved you have the following skills, and given you the chance to develop them: you are well organised with good time management, an ideas generator and problem solver, diligent and meticulous, a completer and finisher, with good writing and presentation skills. You can tell them these skills have been developed during your research for a project on . . . or your dissertation . . . Also let them know your specialist areas of interest where they relate to what the company might need.

NB   Finding out what the company might need and ensuring your CV is tailored to emphasise those elements – and that your letter of application is also tailored in this way – is a good opportunity for you to use your research skills!

● Getting your work published, developed; and moving on into further research

The whole point about doing research and coming up with interesting findings which add to our knowledge, create knowledge and expand meaning and understanding – is that it is shared with other people. You are an undergraduate. You probably cannot imagine that your work will be publishable, but it can be, and if it is not yet publishable, it might well lead you into more research, developing the work you have been doing, and then to publishing it.

Publishing

There are several possible outlets, and then several bits of advice on how to recognise, re-focus, rewrite and redirect your work towards and for the outlet you have chosen.

One big tip:

> It probably won't be straightforward to just publish in the format in which you have written your essay, dissertation or project – it will need reorganising to fit the different outlet, such as an e-zine, journal or in-house publication.

Another big tip:

> You need to be very resilient and thick skinned to get published as well as very imaginative – both help you handle rejections, rewriting, reshaping, keeping going through several possible outlets.

The web

Some web magazines or journals specifically take undergraduate work as well as, or instead of, work by academics and practitioners.

In-house publications

Are there any in-house university publications, or if you are in employment, company publications which would publish your work? This could be student run, school or department run, or university-wide such as those run by the Students' Union. At work these could be organisation or department-wide or they might be related to the professional body with whom your area of work engages. Contact them to see if they are interested in your work.

Writing for publication

Read the rules and descriptions of the online journals and e-zines, in-house publications, magazines, journals etc. which you have used yourself in your own work and see if any of them would be the right outlet to publish your work. You are looking for issues of:

- Audience – will they be interested?
- Kind of work published in here already – practical? Theorised? How long? Tone? How organised?

Match your work to this publication. This will require some rewriting. The more that what you send them looks like what they usually take, the more likely they are to look at what you have sent with a view to publishing it after the usual alterations and improvements.

Contact them to see if they are interested in your work. Give it a topical taste and spin, persuade them that it is interesting and others will want to read it; describe it in short . . .

You then either –

- contact cold – just get in touch with the right editor (or it could get lost);
- send a letter of support from your tutor or a colleague in the field along with your work;
- ring/email in advance to suggest the area of work, then call/send it in.

It could be that the dissertation or project/report you have written will need to be shortened in order to be published, or directed at a different readership, and so it will need work doing on the language, the expression and tone, the layout and even the direction as well as the length.

The more willing you are to be flexible without, of course, ruining your work – the more likely you are to be published.

Write to a schedule – get it done early, check for proofreading and referencing, and try it out with a trusted friend whose writing you admire – then see if they have some suggestions for improvement.

Whatever you send in, the editorial team/editor will send it out for review to at least one other person.

They should then return to you with some suggestions for changes.

They might reject it outright – oh well, look again at some other outlet and try and find out from the comments what they think went wrong – it could be they have published something similar already or are about to publish something similar, or it could be that your work needs some rephrasing and reorganising to get published anywhere yet.

They will probably require modifications – read this through carefully and alter your work accordingly. If you think that they do not understand something important, contact them when you re-send the work, explain this. But usually, they do not want too much correspondence. They just want you to rewrite.

When you send in the rewritten article or essay, add a short accompanying note which explains the ways in which you have changed it to fit their requirements, and indicate where they can find the changes in your text.

Many articles which could get published are stalled at this stage because the author thinks that it is not worth the rewriting or they think they have really been turned down – do what they say, let a friend re-read it and advise, and resubmit – you are much more likely to have it accepted after rewriting.

When it is published – celebrate! Tell people! Decide what to write next . . .

Further research

Many people develop their undergraduate essay topic, report or dissertation topics into:

- Master's work
- PhDs
- Projects for their employment, to bring about development at work.

Usually this requires reframing, clarifying, extending, altering, re-focusing – and certainly redeveloping. This is further research. You have the chance to look at another 'slice of that cake' of the research areas (see Chapter 4). Look back at how to develop the research proposal.

- Don't completely replicate the previous work – you could get bored.
- Do extend it or focus down carefully in an area which interests you.
- Don't underestimate how long it takes to carry out new or extended research.

Summary

In this chapter we have considered:

- Working at a conceptual, theorised level.
- Writing quality and editing.
- Maintaining momentum.
- Managing your time.
- Coping with some common problems in dealing with samples, data handling, interpretation.
- Activity audits.

Further reading

Dunleavy, P. (2003) *Authoring a PhD: How to Plan, Draft, Write and Finish a Doctoral Dissertation or Thesis* (Basingstoke: Palgrave Macmillan).

Murray, R. (2002) *How to Write a Thesis* (Maidenhead: Open University Press).

Bibliography

Atkinson, P. and Delamont, S. (2004) Editorial, *Qualitative Research*, 4(3), pp. 283–4.

Banister, P. et al. (1994) *Qualitative Methods in Psychology* (Buckingham: Open University Press).

Bell, J. (1999) *Doing Your Research Project* (Buckingham: Open University Press).

Birenbaum (1993) 'Relationships between Learning Patterns and Attitudes towards Two Assessment Formats', *Educational Research*, 40, p. 90.

Blaikie, N. (2000) *Designing Social Research* (Cambridge: Polity Press).

Blaxter, L., Hughes, C. and Tight, M. (1996) *How to Search* (Buckingham: Open University).

Bodner, G. M. (1988) 'Consumer Chemistry: Critical Thinking at the Concrete Level', *Journal of Chemistry Education*, 65(3), pp. 212–13.

Boice, R. (1990) *Professors as Writers: A Self-Help Guide to Productive Writing* (Stillwater, OK: New Forums).

Brown, S., McDowell, L. and Race, P. (1995) *500 Tips for Researchers* (London: Kogan Page).

Buchanan, D., Boddy, D. and McCalman, J. (1988) 'Getting In, Getting On, Getting Out and Getting Back'. In A. Bryman (ed.), *Doing Research in Organisations* (London: Routledge).

Burgess, H., Sieminski, S., and Arthur, L. (2006) *Achieving Your Doctorate in Education* (London: Sage).

Carroll, J. and Ryan, J. (2005) *Teaching International Students: Improving Learning for All* (London: Routledge).

Cormack, D. F. S. (1991) *The Research Process in Nursing*, 2nd edn (Oxford: Blackwell Scientific).

Cottrell, S. (2005) *Critical Thinking Skills* (Basingstoke: Palgrave Macmillan).

Cottrell, S. (2008) *The Study Skills Handbook*, 3rd edn (Basingstoke: Palgrave Macmillan).

Creswell, J. D. (2002) *Research Design: Qualitative, Quantitative and Mixed Method Approaches*, 2nd edn (Thousand Oaks, CA: Sage).

Davies, M. B. (2007) *Doing a Research Project* (Basingstoke: Palgrave Macmillan).

Delamont, S., Atkinson, P. and Parry, O. (1997) *Supervising the PhD: A Guide to Success* (Buckingham: Open University Press).

Denscombe, M. (2002) *Ground Rules for Good Research* (Buckingham: Open University Press).

Denzin, N. K. and Lincoln, Y. S. (1998) *The Landscape of Qualitative Research, Theories and Issues* (Thousand Oaks, CA: Sage).

Denzin, N. K. and Lincoln, Y. S. (2003) *Collecting and Interpreting Qualitative Materials* (New York: Sage).

Dunleavy, P. (2003) *Authoring a PhD: How to Plan, Draft, Write and Finish a Doctoral Dissertation or Thesis* (Basingstoke: Palgrave Macmillan).

Elbow, P. (1973) *Writing Without Teachers* (Oxford: Oxford University Press).

Ennis, R. H. (1987) 'A Taxonomy of Critical Thinking Dispositions and Abilities'. In J. B. Baron and J. J. Sternberg (eds), *Teaching Thinking Skills: Theory and Practice* (New York: Freeman), pp. 9–26.

Entwistle, N. J. and Ramsden, P. (1983) *Understanding Student Learning* (London: Croom Helm).

Fielding, Nigel G. and Lee, Raymond M. (1991) *Using Computers in Qualitative Research* (London: Sage).

Fowler, H. W. (1994) *A Dictionary of Modern English Usage* (Ware: Wordsworth Editions).

Fraenkel, J. R. and Wallen, N. E. (1993) *How to Design and Evaluate Research in Education*, 2nd edn (New York: McGraw Hill).

Gower, E. (1986) *The Complete Plain Words*, revised edition prepared by S. Greenbaum and J. Whitcut (London: HMSO).

Grix, J. (2004) *The Foundations of Research* (Basingstoke: Palgrave Macmillan).

Gurr, G. (2001) *Student–Supervisor Alignment Toolkit*, available at: www.first.edu.au

Hammersley, M. (1987) 'Some notes on terms "validity" and "reliability"', *British Educational Research Journal*, 13(1), pp. 73–81.

Hart, A., Maddison, E. and Wolff, D. (eds) (2007) *Community–University Partnerships in Practice* (Leicester: NIACE).

Healey, M. (see 'Useful websites', p. 296, 'Linking Research and Teaching').

Horn, R. (1996) 'Negotiating Research Access to Organisations', *The Psychologist*, pp. 551–4.

Hussey, J. and Hussey, R. (1997) *Business Research: A Practical Guide for Undergraduate and Postgraduate Students* (London: Macmillan).

Koa Wing, Sandra (2008) *Our Longest Days: A People's History of the Second World War* (London: Profile Books).

Lee, R. M. (1993) *Doing Research on Sensitive Topics* (London: Sage).

Lewis, M. and Reinders, H. (2003) *Study Skills for Speakers of English as a Second Language* (Basingstoke: Palgrave Macmillan).

McLuhan, Marshall (1962) *The Gutenberg Galaxy: The Making of Typographic Man* (Toronto: University of Toronto Press).

Meyer, E. and Land, R. (2006) *Overcoming Barriers to Student Understanding: Threshold Concepts and Troublesome Knowledge* (London: RoutledgeFalmer).

Meyer, J. H. F. and Boulton-Lewis, G. (1997) *Reflections on Learning Survey* (Brisbane: Queensland University of Technology).

Miles, M. and Huberman, M. (1994) *Qualitative Data Analysis* (London: Sage Publications).

Murray, R. (2002) *How to Write a Thesis* (Maidenhead: Open University Press).

Robinson, K. (1992) 'R4: The Real World of Research', *Nursing Times*, 88(44): suppl. i–viii.

Robson, C. (1993, 2002) *Real World Research: A Resource for Social Scientists and Practitioner-Researchers* (Oxford: Blackwell).

Roth, W. M. et al. (1997) 'The Local Production of Order in Traditional Science Laboratories: a Phenomenological Analysis', *Learning and Instruction*, 7, pp. 107–36.

Sarantakos, S. (1993) *Social Research* (South Yarra, Vic.: Macmillan Education Australia).

Seidel, J. and Kelle, U. (1995) 'Different Functions of Coding in the Analysis of Textual Data'. In U. Kelle (ed.), *Computer-aided Qualitative Data Analysis: Theory, Methods and Practice* (London: Sage).

Stierer, B. and Antoniou, M. (2004) 'Are there Distinctive Methodologies for Pedagogic Research in Higher Education?' *Teaching in Higher Education*, 9(3), July 2004, pp. 275–85.

Tufte, E. (1990) *Envisioning Information* (Cheshire, CT: Graphics Press USA).

Walliman, N. (2001) *Your Research Project* (London: Sage).

Wisker, G. (1998) *Research as Learning Questionnaire* (Anglia Ruskin University).

Wisker, G. (2005) *The Good Supervisor* (Basingstoke: Palgrave Macmillan).

Wisker, G. (2001, 2nd edn 2008) *The Postgraduate Research Handbook: Succeed with your MA, MPhil, EdD and PhD* (Basingstoke: Palgrave Macmillan).

Zuber-Skerritt, O. (1992) *Action Research in Higher Education* (London: Kogan Page).

Useful websites

Anglia Ruskin University (nd) *Guidance Notes for Faculty Delegated Approval*, available at: www.anglia.ac.uk/ruskin/en/home/central/rds/services/research_office/research_degrees/ethics/application.Maincontent.0012.file.tmp/Guidance%20Notes%20for%20Faculty%20Delegated%20Approval.doc (accessed 21 August 2008).

Forum: Qualitative Social Research, available at: www.qualitative-research.net/ (accessed 19 August 2008).

Google Scholar http://scholar.google.co.uk/

HESA, The Higher Education Statistics Agency www.hesa.ac.uk

ICQ people search http://web.icq.com/whitepages/search

JSTOR http://jstor.org/search

Linking Research and Teaching: A selected bibliography
This bibliography includes more than 600 references and is regularly updated by Prof. Mick Healey, one of the foremost writers on the topic in the country. The document is available as a pdf on the Centre for Active Learning (CEAL) website at the University of Gloucestershire: www.glos.ac.uk/ceal/resources/litreview.cfm

Literary Encyclopedia (online) www.litencyc.com/

Palgrave Macmillan (2007) *skills4study*, available at: www.palgrave.com/skills4study/index.asp (accessed 30 May 2008).

Qual Page: Resources for Qualitative Research, available at: http://qualitativeresearch.uga.edu/QualPage (accessed 19 August 2008).

Ryder, M. (2008) Qualitative Research: University of Colorado at Denver School of Education, available at: http://carbon.cudenver.edu/~mryder/itc/pract_res.html (accessed 19 August 2008).

The Web of Knowledge www.tile.net

Voice of the shuttle http://vos.ucsb.edu/

Index